Justice in
Everyday Life

Howard Zinn

Justice in Everyday Life

The Way It Really Works

Haymarket Books
Chicago, IL

© 1974 by Howard Zinn

First published in 1974 by William Morrow and Company, Inc.

This edition published in 2017 by Haymarket Books.
P.O. Box 180165
Chicago, IL 60618
773-583-7884
info@haymarketbooks.org
www.haymarketbooks.org

ISBN: 978-1-60846-302-2

Distributed to the trade in the US through Consortium Book Sales and Distribution
(www.cbsd.com) and internationally through Ingram Publisher Services International
(www.ingramcontent.com).

This book was published with the generous support of Lannan Foundation and
Wallace Action Fund.

Printed in the United States.

Entered into digital printing April 2019.

Library of Congress CIP Data is available.

To Bill Homans and Malik Hakim,
John Flym and Jimmy Barrett

Contents

Introduction:
Justice in Everyday Life

Justice is a grand word in the United States. It calls to mind enormous marble columns, the black-robed dignity of the Supreme Court, the promises of the Bill of Rights. We think of eloquent decisions interpreting the Constitution that fill weighty volumes in the library, called the *U.S. Reports*. These decisions seem to spell out a historic procession toward greater and greater freedom in America.

That is the justice we read about. But there is another kind of justice, which we *live*. We find it in the situations of every day: where we work, where we go to school, where we come home to at night. This everyday justice is determined not by the Constitution or the Supreme Court, but by the power the policeman has over us on the street, or the rule of the municipal court judge; by the authority of our foreman or supervisor or department head, if we have a job (or the tyranny of employment agencies or personnel offices or want ads or interviews, if we are jobless); by the power of the teacher, the principal, the university president, the board of trustees if we are students; by parents if we are children; by children if we are old; by the welfare bureaucracy if we are poor; by landlords if we are tenants; by prison guards if we are in jail; by the medical profession or hospital administration if we are physically or mentally ill.

Large-scale injustice has a chance of getting attention. Famous cases and trials make their way into the newspapers and the history books. Supreme Court decisions are held up for everyone to see. But millions of people—indeed, all people living in society—face the problem of injustice in their day-to-day lives. It is a glimpse of this overlooked and forgotten, and by far the most important, aspect of American justice that we offer in this book.

Such a book must be a cooperative venture, because it requires recording the ordinary experiences of people in different situations. So we depend here on many firsthand observations, using as often as possible the words of the observers themselves. We have prisoners writing from their cells, lawyers describing their cases, tenants telling their problems. A Somerville woman and an MIT student tell about their different encounters with the police. A truck driver and a factory worker talk about their jobs. A woman tells of her experience in a high-class mental institution. A black high school boy recounts his thoughts as he sat in assembly one day.

Many of the observers have been students at Boston University, in my course Law and Justice in America. We wanted the course to be more than a learning of the formalities of constitutional law or the history of important cases. And so, students explored the city. Sometimes they didn't have to go beyond their own apartment building. Jamie Wickens had only to look out of his window into the street the night he saw the police surround a man he did not know. Sometimes they sat day after day in court, watching, listening.

We draw our material from Boston and its environs. But we are sure that what we describe can be found in the other cities of this country. We pick Boston because we live here and know it best. Also, perhaps, because the demand for justice, and the workings of injustice, have so often found expression in this home of the antislavery movement, this birthplace of the American Revolution, this deathplace of Sacco and Vanzetti.

From a distance, it is hard to measure the state of justice in America accurately. On the national level, noting the Constitution, representative government, elections, we might think our country is a democracy. Only when we look at it close up do we see that there is a steady authority of power and money over our daily lives which is much more important (and much less ambiguous) than the decisions of the Supreme Court or who won the last election. On the local level, we live, at different times of the day, in different little feudal kingdoms where our subordination is clear.

Over the past four years, students of mine discovered for themselves what so many people who live in a city already know but never put on paper. They checked formal constitutional rights against the realities of everyday life in the Boston area and found these rights meaningless.

If they had just stayed in the classroom, they might have concluded that a whole string of Supreme Court decisions, from *Lovell v. Griffin* (1938) to *Flower v. U.S.* (1972) have given all of us the right to distribute literature to our fellow citizens. But they soon discovered that, on the street, where literature is actually distributed, it is the police who decide if that right exists. Or the local judge. The Supreme Court is far away and cannot help at that moment when the policeman says, "Get going!"

In Lynn, Massachusetts, a few years ago, young radicals distributing leaflets in front of a high school were arrested for "promoting anarchy" (an old, but still useful state statute). And in Harvard Square, a man named "Pepé" Jones, with one arm in a sling, selling copies of a Communist newspaper, was chased by police, beaten, and then charged with assault and battery (he spat on the policeman, the latter testified; two eyewitnesses saw no spitting). It doesn't matter that eventually those in the first case were acquitted, and the newspaper seller was found guilty; they both were deprived of freedom of expression at the time they sought it.

Money seems crucial for freedom of speech. With it, one can buy prime television time. Without it, one communicates in the streets, subject to police power. Money is also essential for the constitutional guarantee against "unreasonable search and seizure." Police ignored that guarantee when they broke into an apartment on Gainsboro Street (as a postlude to dispersing a noisy block party) and beat up Michael Mandel, a blind music student, and his wife Elizabeth. If the Mandels had lived in their own suburban house, that is not likely to have happened.

On the job, even the most progressive employer (with or without the collaboration of the union) has the final say over the most fundamental facts of our lives—the conditions of work, wages, whether indeed we will have a job. A filing clerk for an insurance company discusses later in these pages how the company controlled him and others: by a rule of silence on the job, by encouraging workers to note others' mistakes, by attributing decisions to an impersonal power ("New York wants it that way"), by transfers without explanation, by control of information through the company newspaper and wall slogans everywhere.

None of the much-hailed Supreme Court decisions on "equal protection of the laws" could reach down into the large company where Charles Ramsey, a black man from Jamaica, had a clerical job. He was tormented and humiliated for his blackness by fellow employees and was fired when he complained to the State Commission Against Discrimination, which supported him but could not enforce its decision. When someone on the job told Ramsey he would like to "kill all niggers," his employer told him he should not take that personally, whereupon Ramsey replied: "That means I am not a person!" The Constitution, it seems, cannot protect us from the greatest threat of all: being considered less than a person in our daily lives.

Young people spend a great deal of their time in school, and if the student is being prepared for the larger society, it must be that this society is closed, controlled, regimented— for that is what schools are like, in the main. The hierarchy is clear: students at the bottom, above them teachers, then deans, principals, and presidents, and above all, trustees and regents. "Tracking," whether overt or subtle, steers the kids from poor families into vocational and secretarial schools, and those from middle and upper families toward college.

Censorship is common in schools. At Wellesley High School, the showing of a LeRoi Jones play, with an interracial scene and four-letter vulgarities, led to criminal prosecutions of teachers, the on-the-spot arrest of a student who repeated the forbidden word at a public meeting ("There are students in Wellesley High School who go to church and their parents go to church, too, and they can't say a sentence without the word *fuck*," he said), and a general atmosphere of fear and punishment. Inside schools, as inside other institutions, the Constitution has no force.

The critical deprivations of liberty never get to the courts. They are settled "out of court" in the way that most such settlements are determined—by who is stronger and richer and can afford to wait. And so, for those people who can't buy a house, their day-to-day living conditions depend on the landlord: how much rent they must pay, whether repairs are made and if the house is safe (it is the poor who most often die in fires), and whether or not they need worry about eviction. The home is vital to liberty: a property owner has privacy; a tenement pushes its occupants to the streets, into the jurisdiction of the police.

Only those who rebel at the out-of-court settlements by landlord, by employer, by husband or parents, or by police, will ever get to court. And then, not the Supreme Court, but the local court. Sitting week after week in Boston Municipal Court, Roxbury District Court, Dorchester District Court, my students were horrified. Carolyn Jacoby wrote: "You do a paper on constitutional due process—great, you're happy. Then you go into court, and all that falls apart."

Carol Blackman, David Perlmut, and Nancy Watters attended a murder trial for twelve days, after which a young, freakish-looking fellow named Alan Lussier was convicted of murder. They concluded that the trial itself was "a crime," in which the looks of the defendant and the hysteria of the prosecuting attorney played upon the prejudices of the middle-aged, conservative jury. A study of the jury lists showed that young people (under thirty) were systematically underrepresented. The formal requirement of "trial by jury" had been met, but the reality of justice was absent.

The judge, student observers found, is monarch of the courtroom. If he decides, as Judge Rowe did in Suffolk Superior Court one day when he saw Julie Hankin writing, that a spectator taking notes at a public trial cannot be tolerated because "what if everybody suddenly got interested in a case?" —he can confiscate the notes. The judge decides who can testify and who cannot, who is to be believed and who is not, who should be punished and who should go free, and how many years of a person's life should be spent behind bars. He appoints attorneys for the poor (my students found the average lawyer's consulting time with defendants was seven minutes—that's how much the famous *Gideon* decision is worth in Municipal Court) and then sits in the viewing stand before a parade of human beings. He decides the fate of each in a few minutes and they stumble off, bewildered.

If the accused goes to prison (in 90 percent of the cases, he does without jury trial, a plea of guilty having been arranged by threat), he becomes a member of a totalitarian society, with daily humiliation, physical abuse, mental torture and absolute control. "If we are what we are being treated as, then we should be shot," wrote one Massachusetts inmate.

In his tenth year in Walpole Prison, Jimmy Barrett decided he wanted a kitten: "All these months and months and months locked inside a cell without love. It seemed to me to be ridiculously simple: I wanted something ALIVE in my cell, something alive and full of life, and that I could love and have crawl on me and show me affection. I jumped up and started hollering and banging." There is nothing in the Constitution to guarantee Jimmy Barrett's right to have a kitten. There is nothing to forbid it, either. But that doesn't matter. The warden and the guards decide what he can have, decide everything about his life.

These are the realities of wealth and power which determine justice, day to day. They will not be shaken by new statutes, new judges, new leaders, new court decisions. Injustice is too deeply rooted in the institutions of our society, (corporate control of great wealth; hierarchy in schools, jobs, families); in the human relationships that are distorted by these institutions; in our minds, shaped by all of this, to be displaced by the usual reforms. Rather, counterforces must appear on the very ground where liberty is taken away: on the street, at home, in schools, hospitals, courts, prisons, places of work.

Toward the end of this book, there are a few examples of such counterforces. In Dorchester, a particularly oppressive Judge (Judge Troy) was shaken loose from his throne because a group called TPF ("The People First") organized the community over a two-year period to sign petitions, hold public hearings, and create an atmosphere in which the judicial administration had to act. In East Cambridge, residents of a low-income housing project exploded in angry demonstrations when a young man named Larry Largey died after being beaten by police inside a paddy wagon—thus giving the police some pause in future actions, and implying that a forceful, permanent community presence around the police may be

the only guarantee against police abuse. At the Honeywell
Corporation, protesters picketed and gave out literature day
after day, asking that Honeywell stop making deadly antipersonnel weapons for use in Indochina; one employee resigned his job and many others expressed their support of the
demonstrators.

There are too many instances to tell about in these pages.
Tenants organize against landlords, old people march on
City Hall to reduce subway fares, women organize against
discriminatory employers. Prisoners form unions, a Mental
Patients Liberation Front emerges, and students barge into
a trustees' meeting to get a faculty member's job back.

This seems small. But it is not to be disdained. If people
can begin changing their own immediate environment, they
may create a momentum that will carry much further toward
that deep change in institutions and people that is required for
us to have a just society.

Perhaps we are beginning to learn that we cannot depend
on paternal government, its constitutional guarantees, its
statutory reforms, its judicial rhetoric—but must support one
another, in continuous assertion of our own freedom. Our
aim would be to take control individually of our own lives,
and cooperatively of the resources without which a Bill of
Rights is meaningless.

Lacking traditional forms of power and wealth, we can only
create a force out of what we do have: our assembled selves,
our ability to withhold our labor, to withdraw our compliance.
Defying authority, we can organize to take hold of what is at
hand and rightfully belongs to us—our workplaces, our schools,
our communities. And in the midst of struggle—for that is
what it will take—we can start right now to construct and
endlessly reconstruct human relationships, institutional arrangements, ways of thinking. That, done close to home, inside the small circles of our daily life, might be the beginnings of justice.

                                                    H.Z.

One: POLICE

Justifiable Homicide:
Due Process for Franklin Lynch

> No person shall . . . be deprived of life, liberty, or property, without due process of law.
> —FIFTH AMENDMENT TO THE CONSTITUTION

When Franklin Lynch, a twenty-four-year-old black musician from Roxbury, with a history of mental disturbance, was on the fourth floor of Boston City Hospital with a dislocated shoulder, he had very little liberty, and almost no property. But he did have his life, until it was taken by a Boston policeman who fired five times at him at point-blank range.

In February, 1973, a Boston University student named Paul Kaplan interviewed Chief Judge of the Municipal Court Elijah Adlow about the shooting of Franklin Lynch. He asked Adlow for a copy of the report the Chief Judge had made on an inquest in the Lynch case. The report, Adlow told him, had been impounded (when a court "impounds" a document, it becomes unavailable for public scrutiny). "The case is dead," the Chief Judge said. "In this business you don't exhume dead stuff."

Why, indeed, exhume the case of Franklin Lynch, the buried inquest report of Elijah Adlow, the bizarre events of March 7, 1970? Because while this particular combination of events was unique, there is a certain familiarity about it: an obscure man's life is held cheap by a policeman, a police com-

3

missioner, a judge, and ultimately, all of us who let it pass without comment. Its specifics are unrepeatable, but it represents the ordinary turns of justice in any American city, anytime, anywhere. In the face of this mundane and universally accepted event, it seems absurd for anyone to quote the Fifth Amendment. Especially since, as we shall see, Franklin Lynch got what the Constitution promised him: due process of law. And that should be enough, we are taught.

Franklin Lynch's blackness is important in this story. It is hard for any American even faintly perceptive of the three-hundred-and-fifty-year history of black subjugation in America, before, during, and beyond slavery, North as well as South, to believe that his blackness did not increase his chances of dying that day in Boston City Hospital. But blackness is a metaphor for invisibility, and while black-skinned people are *most* invisible (that is, as human beings: blackness makes one *more* visible to white America as something else, something threatening or upsetting), other sorts of people are also treated as if they weren't there. We shall see that when we come to the brief part in the Lynch incident played by a sixty-one-year-old white man named Edward Crowley.

It was a Saturday, March 7, 1970, in Surgical Ward Number Two of Boston City Hospital. Franklin Lynch was there, his left arm and shoulder in a cast. He was a professional vocalist, and had just made a recording called "Young Girl." He had also performed in a club in Boston. But lately he had been troublesome, according to his aunt, who had called the police several times to quiet him down. It was in a fight with his uncle that he injured his arm. And now, in the hospital ward, he was annoying other patients and the nurse.

The nurse summoned Patrolman Walter M. Duggan, who was stationed in the corridor to guard another patient in the ward. This was James Williams (Abdullah Hassen); he had been arrested the day before, charged with stabbing a Boston University security policeman, and was hospitalized with a puncture wound. When Duggan entered the ward, where Lynch and another patient were arguing, Williams got up from his bed. Duggan pulled out his gun and motioned Williams back. Williams went back. Lynch snapped a towel at Duggan's hand, whereupon Duggan fired five times. Three bullets hit Lynch, killing him.

A newspaper reporter for the Boston *Globe,* after talking to patients and the police, reported the incident as follows:

"While guarding Hassen at bedside, Duggan was attracted to an argument between Lynch and another patient, John Condon, 28, who is recuperating from multiple fractures.

"Duggan pushed the two away from each other just as they were squared off to fight, according to an eyewitness. Condon reportedly fell and broke a leg.

"Meanwhile, Hassen, the prisoner, left his bed. Duggan drew his gun and ordered him back into bed. The prisoner complied.

"Duggan, standing close to Lynch and the other patient, lowered his weapon when Lynch snapped a towel at it, police said.

"The policeman raised his gun and fired five shots and Lynch fell, the police reported."

One of those five shots hit Edward Crowley, sixty-one, who was in a nearby bed, his leg in traction. Crowley lived in Dorchester, and was the father of a policeman assigned as photographer at the police department crime laboratory. Crowley told fellow patients: "One of those bullets went right through me." The first newspaper accounts of the shooting said a bullet had passed through Crowley's abdomen, but he "is reported to be improving." Actually, the bullet had hit Crowley's kidney and lodged near his spine. Twelve days after the shooting, he died.

There were reactions. The Boston chapter of the National Association for the Advancement of Colored People said that Lynch should have been sent to a mental hospital, not kept in an ordinary hospital ward. It sent a telegram to the Department of Justice in Washington, calling for an investigation of the shooting under the civil rights laws, which make it a crime for a policeman to deprive a citizen of his constitutional rights.

Senators Edward Kennedy and Edward Brooke, responding to the NAACP, announced in Washington that they had contacted the Federal Bureau of Investigation, and it would make a "thorough investigation." Brooke said he would get preliminary results in a week to ten days, whereupon he would contact the Boston NAACP.

The NAACP also asked that the State Attorney General, Robert Quinn, investigate, as well as the Suffolk County District Attorney, Garrett Byrne. Both said they would. In addition, the police department homicide squad said it was investigating the incident.

Various black organizations in Roxbury and the adjoining South End neighborhood held a rally calling for the suspension of Patrolman Duggan. The trustees of Boston City Hospital also urged that Duggan be suspended pending completion of the investigation. Police Commissioner Edmund L. McNamara called the hospital trustees' statement "irresponsible." He said he could not suspend Duggan because of Civil Service regulations, and that critics were trying to make a scapegoat of Duggan. The policeman, he said, had "acted in the performance of his duty."

Of all the investigations presumably going on, only one was actually reported to have reached a conclusion. The Medical Examiner, George W. Curtis, asked for an inquest by the courts to determine what happened. Accordingly, about a month after the incident, on April 8, 1970, an inquest began, under Elijah Adlow, Chief Judge of the Boston Municipal Court. Adlow moved the inquest from the courthouse to Boston City Hospital, in order to hear the testimony of patients in Surgical Ward Number Two who had witnessed the incident. Three weeks later, Adlow filed his report on the inquest, and the Boston *Globe* carried the story:

"A Municipal Court inquest report which was filed yesterday absolved a Boston police officer of all blame in the fatal March 7 shooting of two City Hospital patients.

"Chief Justice Elijah Adlow ruled that Patrolman Walter M. Duggan acted properly in all circumstances and that the killings were 'the result of poor administration in the placing of a dangerous criminal and a mentally unsound man in a hospital ward. . . .'

"Adlow said that Lynch interfered with Officer Duggan's duty to guard the prisoner. If Duggan had failed to perform that duty and had lost his prisoner 'he stood to be a discredited man in the Police Department' according to Adlow."

Chief Justice Adlow's clearing of the patrolman seemed to rest heavily on Duggan's statement during the inquest that Lynch had a towel wrapped around an aluminum clipboard. This was the first time, in all the stories that had appeared, quoting policemen, eyewitnesses, and Duggan himself, that there was mention of a clipboard. In the story by Boston *Globe* reporter Robert Jordan on March 19, twelve days after the shooting, he wrote: "Duggan told superiors he drew his gun because he believed Lynch, a black, was involved in a plot to help Abdullah Hassen, a prisoner patient, also a black, escape from the ward." In the same story, Jordan reported police as having said Duggan fired when Lynch snapped a towel at his gun.

In *Globe* reporter Christopher Wallace's story on the inquest report of Chief Justice Adlow, he wrote:

"The most important fact to come out of the inquest report was that Lynch struck Officer Duggan several times with an aluminum clipboard wrapped in a towel.

"It had been previously reported that Lynch struck the policeman only with a towel. Judge Adlow said yesterday that all the witnesses to the incident concurred with this account, except for Duggan, who testified at the inquest that the towel was wrapped around a clipboard."

Thus, while every witness except Duggan told of Lynch snapping a towel at the policeman and Duggan's claim of a clipboard being inside the towel seemed to be his first such claim, one month after the event, Judge Adlow accepted Duggan's story over all the others. Apparently, *Globe* reporter Wallace, wondering about this, tried to reach Adlow, because he wrote in his story, "Adlow was unavailable for comment last night to clear up this issue."

The evening of the release of Adlow's report, Mayor Kevin White of Boston issued a statement saying that many people might disagree with Adlow's ruling, but asked, as the press reported "all segments of the community to exercise the utmost restraint in their comments and actions." Thomas Atkins, a black member of the City Council, called Adlow's decision "a great public disservice."

About ten weeks after the inquest report, on June 24, 1970, Franklin Lynch's mother, Mrs. Julia D. Mack, filed a three-million-dollar damage suit against the City of Boston, Police Commissioner McNamara, and Patrolman Walter Duggan, charging violation of Lynch's rights under the Constitution, including the Eighth Amendment's prohibition of "cruel and unusual punishment." Attorney Henry Owens, in his complaint, said that "defendant Duggan maliciously, wantonly, without provocation, and with an intent to kill, drew and fired his service revolver at Lynch five times, emptying said revolver, killing Lynch and another human being, also a patient at Boston City Hospital." The complaint said that Duggan's sole reason for killing Lynch was that he did not want his prisoner to escape from custody, so that his reputation in the police department would remain unblemished, and this conduct was unreasonable and reckless.

Three years later, in the spring of 1973, Chief Justice Adlow was retired from the bench. Police Chief McNamara was gone from the scene. There were no FBI reports, no reports from the District Attorney's office or from the Attorney General. The inquest report was still impounded and barred from public view. The suit for damages filed by Franklin Lynch's mother was buried.

It was all "dead stuff," as Judge Adlow said. The only reason for recalling it is to think seriously about the quality of justice in Boston; indeed, in any American city (and, perhaps, with changed details, in any city in the world). Surely, there is not much point in concentrating responsibility on Patrolman Walter Duggan. True, we should never stop demanding and expecting that individuals break out of customary ways. But there is a simultaneous responsibility for the rest of us to examine those ways, to hold them up to critical examination, to begin changing them, to make it easier for individuals to begin acting human. Duggan made the acceptable move in a game whose rules were set long ago and which were observed by all the other players in the game. They are the rules which determine justice in our cities. They go something like this:

A prisoner must not be allowed to escape his punishment, even at the risk of his own life or those of bystanders.

The best way to handle a problem is to summon a policeman.

The best way for a policeman to handle a problem is with a gun.

It is reasonable to be wary and frightened of a black man if you are white.

If you kill a black man, especially an obscure one, you need not worry too much about being brought to account by the law, especially if you do it while in uniform.

A policeman can do what an ordinary citizen cannot do, kill someone to hold his job or improve his job record.

If enough important people concur in a decision or remain quiet about it, there is an implication of fanaticism in anyone who pursues the issue and challenges the decision. If the district attorney, the judge, senators, the FBI, the mayor, and the general public either justify what happened or "exercise restraint" (that is, keep quiet), there is safety in doing the same. It is the Alfred Hitchcock rule, that if everyone on the train says there was no lady on the train, you are crazy to claim there was a lady and she vanished.

If, upon challenge and protest, some official goes through some procedure—an investigation, a hearing, an inquest, a trial—and everything is pronounced all right, then justice has been done, then "due process" has been granted. So it was in the case of Franklin Lynch.

H.Z.

Hemenway Street

by Howard Zinn with Mark Stern

> The right of the people to be secure in their persons, houses, papers, and effects, against unreasonable searches and seizures, shall not be violated. . . ."
> —FOURTH AMENDMENT TO THE CONSTITUTION

On the streets of the city, in the homes of the not-so-rich, the power of the police over peoples' lives is enormous. It may not be exercised most of the time, but it is there, ready. Every once in a while, this power is quickly mobilized, and when it lashes out, we then realize its dimensions, its uncontrollability. Then we know that the quiet of our everyday lives masks our ultimate helplessness, in a society where those who have uniforms and guns have the right, if they so choose, to invade our homes.

The residents of Hemenway Street in Boston learned that on a warm spring evening, May 10, 1970. It was Mother's Day. Hemenway Street is not a slum, but rather a rundown old Boston street, usually quiet, near a park, with a mixture of students from nearby Northeastern University and old people not yet pushed out by the housing shortage and the youth influx. At Northeastern University, as on campuses all over the country, there had been demonstrations against the American invasion of Cambodia and the shooting of four students at Kent State by the National Guard. Some of that excitement

11

was still in the air as the young people on Hemenway Street held block parties on Thursday, Friday, and Saturday nights. Each evening around eleven, students would gather to listen to rock music, dance, drink, smoke grass, play with Frisbees.

On Sunday night, the party was bigger, noisier, and more obstreperous. A flaming mattress was thrown off a roof. Garbage and pieces of furniture were dragged into the street and traffic was interfered with. Residents complained to the police. Just after midnight, fifty or sixty policemen from Station Four, and an equal number from the Tactical Police Force, moved into the area. They started to break up the crowd of about three hundred students gathered in the street, most of whom retreated peacefully; but a few bricks and bottles were thrown at the police. Now the police broke ranks and ran through Hemenway Street and adjoining Gainsboro Street, forcing their way into houses and Northeastern dormitories, and, according to eyewitnesses, clubbing anyone in their path.

Anthony Lukas, who wrote a story on the incident five days later for *The New York Times*, reported:

"At 110 Gainsboro Street, Michael Mandel, a blind student at the Berklee School of Music, was sitting on the steps with his wife, Elizabeth, playing the flute. He recalls:

" 'I heard people shouting, "Here they come." So I turned and walked up the steps to our first-floor apartment. I had my key out, and was trying to fit it into the lock when I heard this tremendous smash of glass and then these blows hitting my head.'

"Mrs. Mandel, who was following closely behind her husband, says that six to eight policemen broke through a glass door and began clubbing both of them. 'We kept yelling. "We live here," but they just kept flailing away. Then they just turned and ran out.'

"After lying for several hours in their darkened apartment listening to the police outside, they say, they crept out to their car and drove to Massachusetts General Hospital where Mr.

Mandel received six stitches for a wound on the top of his scalp and three more stitches over his left eye and Mrs. Mandel received two stitches to close a cut on the back of her head."

It was, according to Bob Matorin, a reporter for the Boston *Phoenix,* "a search-and-destroy mission against bodies and buildings." An elderly Austrian couple at 153 Hemenway Street were in bed when the police suddenly broke into their apartment, swept a fluorescent light off the table, smashed windows and furniture, ripped a picture off the wall, and ran out, one of them saying: "Watch it, the kids are rioting tonight."

A student named George LaPerche, who lived at 111 Gainsboro, was standing on his apartment steps with friends when the police came around the corner from Hemenway Street. They rose and ran into LaPerche's first-floor apartment, but "six or eight policemen followed, busted down the door, and beat us over and over." LaPerche suffered a broken hand, a friend four stitches in his head, another severe bruises on his arm.

A dormitory assistant of Northeastern University, Harvey Gershman, said he saw ten policemen on the roof of 103 Hemenway. They were "throwing pipes, rocks, stones, and anything else they could find onto the sidewalk, parked cars, and people." A freshman student named Tom Hofer said: "It was incredible. I saw this policeman hold a huge rock over the edge of the roof and then drop it directly on the roof of this green Plymouth."

At 153 Hemenway, Michael Ellis reported: "Three policemen raced into the middle room, striking at the students and objects in the room. I was struck five times. As they left the room I asked, 'What the hell are you doing?' One of the policeman replied, 'We're doing our job.' "

Mark Stern, a graduate of Harvard Law School, was working at the time in the Mayor's Office of Human Rights. He was asked about 1:30 A.M. to go down to Hemenway Street to help in calming down the disturbance there. A half hour later, he was lying on the floor of a Hemenway Street apartment, with six strangers, listening to someone say: "Get down on the floor, cut off all the lights, and cover your neck with your hands."

Stern wrote later:

  The last time I had been asked to take such a stance was when my elementary school principal told us to hide our heads in the halls in preparation for the day that the Russians would surely come and bomb us. But no Russians were about; just American police occupying a three-block area centering around Hemenway Street in Boston.

At this moment, he reported: "The police were racing up and down the stairways of this building in packs of ten, breaking lights, windows, door handles, railings, and maybe heads, and were kicking in the doors of some apartments."

Lying on the floor, Stern got hold of a phone, called the Mayor's chief aide, Barney Frank, and described the scene. Frank said: "The police reported to me just a few minutes ago that everything was under control and they had left the area. Are you sure?"

Mark Stern later said he was not completely surprised by what the police were doing and was not about to approach them to explain who he was and why they should consider him a friend. He recalled an earlier experience:

  I had learned four months before that one does not just go up to an angry pack of helmeted police and explain to them how you got trapped there, why they couldn't hit you, etc. At a demonstration which turned into a riot in January, I had done just that. After showing my I.D. card I was walked to the paddy-wagon by five policemen, maced, beaten, and thrown inside. They took away my camera that time, exposed two rolls of film (of my dog's puppies being born), and charged me with disorderly conduct, and assault and battery with a dangerous weapon (the camera) on an officer of the law.

After the police left, Stern got out of the building, and interviewed residents in the area. The data he collected was put into the official report of the Office of Human Rights to Mayor Kevin White. The report listed disturbances caused by the crowd before the police came:

1. A group of thirty students blocked traffic on the street.

2. A police cruiser that drove through at 10:30 had objects thrown at it.

3. A flaming mattress was hurled from the roof of Number 120.

4. A false alarm was called in and the fire trucks were also harassed.

5. Garbage was thrown on the street by some individuals, but removed by the crowd. When one hundred twenty regular and Tactical Police arrived and cleared the street, some students hurled objects at them.

But, the report said, "Their response to this problem was wholly inappropriate. . . ." Stern listed, among others, these police actions:

At 120 Hemenway Street, a Northeastern University Dorm, the police screamed obscenities to some people at the windows. One officer then yelled, "Let's get to the second floor—break those doors." Ten to twenty policemen then broke the front door down and went up to the second floor. They entered one room, smashed a typewriter, and threw a chair out of the window. They broke windows, doors, doorknobs and other objects in the hall including the fire alarm, which went off (it is not clear if this was the same alarm that was reported to have gone off earlier). They attempted to enter a second room which students had barricaded, but were unable to do so. They then threatened to shoot through the door, but did not do so. . . .

The police also entered a dorm at 153 Hemenway Street where Northeastern's Assistant Director of Housing, David Robbins, was at the time attempting to call students back into the dorms. He was beaten by police. Erick Porter, a graduate student and dorm director, was also beaten inside the dorm. . . .

John Albert Freeman, who resides at 120 Hemenway Street, went back into his apartment when the police gave the order to clear the streets. He went into his apartment along with Ruth and Larry Fehrman, friends who were visiting at the time. Mr. Freeman closed and locked the door. The door was smashed open and six to eight policemen entered the apartment and without provocation began beating the people in the apartment. Extensive property damage was done to the apartment (record players, pianos, etc.) by the police. Everyone in the apartment required hospitalization. . . .

Police were also noticed molesting individuals on the street, in the park, and in alleyways. People on the street observing were pushed into apartments or chased from the streets, rooftops, and windows. At least eight such separate incidents were reported. Only two of those incidents involved persons under twenty-eight years old. . . .

Around 2:00 A.M. the police returned to the area for the third time. They were not responding to a serious disturbance at that time. Virtually no one was on the street. Small numbers of people were on their front steps and the like. They returned without warning and cleared people off. The people from the Mayor's Office got separated. One was trapped in the hallway of 103 Hemenway by the police. When ordered to go to her apartment, she responded that she did not live there. A policeman then kicked in the door of a couple (approximately seventy to eighty years old) and told her to go in there. . . .

One of the young people on the scene was Myron Butman, a student at Northeastern's College of Criminal Justice, who had spent two months in the police department's Communications and Records Bureau. He saw a policeman on the street throwing rocks through dormitory windows. He said: "There was provocation for clearing the street, but there was absolutely no provocation for the police to enter the buildings or to do what they did after they entered the buildings. . . . They weren't police officers. They were a mob."

Even in a democratic society, violations of human rights can occur. But what makes for democracy is the ability of people to redress those rights. To do this, they must have genuine access to the organs of mass communication and information. They must be able to remove from office those who have shown themselves incapable of obeying the rules of reasonable conduct. They must be able to change the structure of a bureaucracy which seems only able to respond with major violence to situations of minor violence. The aftermath of the Hemenway incident brought none of these developments.

Mark Stern, the Harvard Law School graduate from the Mayor's Office of Human Rights, was troubled by the reactions of the press to the Hemenway Street affair. He wondered about the absence of newspapermen that night, and later discovered that the few newsmen who arrived were turned away by police just as were ambulances coming to pick up the injured.

"The part of the press's role that amazed me, however, was the fact that almost no one publicized anything about the incident in the days following that evening. The *Globe* ran a two-paragraph article Monday afternoon, but referred to it only as a clash between police and radicals that sounded about as exciting and newsworthy as a routine arrest. WEEI and one TV reporter took up the cause of the blind man and his wife who were beaten trying to get into their apartment. No one else showed any interest in the story. . . . Although a police riot had terrorized hundreds and although every major paper, radio station, and TV channel had the story from me and a dozen other sources, only the Northeastern University student paper gave it the coverage it deserved."

The story might have continued to be buried, Stern believed, were it not for the fact that a student who heard him tell about the Hemenway affair had a father on the national news desk of *The New York Times,* and telephoned him. The *Times* sent Anthony Lukas, a Pulitzer Prize-winning reporter, to Boston, and on Friday morning, five days after the event, *The New York Times* carried a front-page story, headlined, "Boston Police Foray Spurs Investigations." On Saturday, every Boston newspaper, for the first time, six days after the event, had a front-page report of the Hemenway Street incident.

Only after the news stories appeared did the Mayor ask for a report on what had happened. Mark Stern wrote the report for the Office of Human Rights within a week. But it was not released until July 30, eighty-one days after the incident. The reason given for this delay was that the Mayor wanted to wait until the police department could release its report simultaneously.

The police department went about compiling its report in a way that might seem unusual to anyone who believes that investigations should be conducted by persons not directly involved in the event to be investigated. The job was given to Lt. William MacDonald, who was transferred by the Commissioner to the Internal Affairs Division so that he could do the job. Mark Stern tells about Lieutenant MacDonald's investigation:

"I remember being interviewed by him. When I asked him where I could have people call him, he instructed me to have them ask for the Tactical Police Force Unit—not the Internal Affairs Division. He explained that he was with the latter only for this one investigation. I was curious, so I asked him, since he was usually with TPF, if he was there that night, on Hemenway Street. He said yes. I had learned that the Captain for that unit was not with it most of Sunday night, so I asked him if that meant he had been in command then. He said yes again. I didn't even bother to ask him if he thought it was strange that he was especially given the job of reporting on his own units, possibly his own personal misconduct. The whole thing was a joke. . . ."

The reports compiled by the police department added up to a thousand pages. There was also a two-hundred-page summary. But those two reports were never released to the public or allowed outside police headquarters. On July 30, the police released an eight-page press release on the incident, with the Commissioner's statement about the thousand-page report. The report suggested the possibility of police misconduct. It reported only one member of the Tactical Police Force as having been identified. This was not surprising since the police had removed their badges, their faces were covered by helmets and plastic shields, they acted in groups, there was no lineup of police officers before witnesses, and pictures of the police involved were not shown to witnesses until weeks after the incident. The one member of the TPF identified was easy to identify. He was the one black member of the TPF.

The police report was praised by the Mayor's Office, and that was the end of the affair, as far as any city official was concerned. Nothing has been heard from official sources since July of 1970.

The three "investigations" reported in *The New York Times,* in a story which might have given comfort to citizens who knew little of the history of such investigations in the United States, disappeared. Besides the police, and the Mayor's Office of Human Rights, the Attorney General's office of the State of Massachusetts was presumably making an investigation. But no factual report, no recommendations came from that office.

Only Boston's two "semiunderground" newspapers, *Boston After Dark,* and the *Phoenix,* kept the Hemenway incident alive. The *Phoenix* reporter, Bob Matorin, wrote:

"Paper is cheap and memories are short. But there are people in the Hemenway area who aren't likely to forget. 'If the police become lawbreakers,' former Attorney General Ramsey Clark said, 'who will protect us from the police?' And when they trash your neighborhood, brothers and sisters, where do you go when you're already home?"

John Noyes, a Boston University student who investigated the Hemenway incident, wrote: "In a society where the police are allowed to assault the citizens they are supposed to protect, one must examine the relationship between law and justice. Is law equal to justice?"

Beyond all these questions, there is one more, which we hope to *begin* to answer before this book closes. Its premise is that the Hemenway incident, unique as it is, represents a universal truth: that we are all subject to the overwhelming power of the police, and that our ability for redress, as well as for deterrence, is crippled by the reluctance of newspapers, radio, television, and government officials to hold up strongly before the public the kind of information which might rouse the citizenry to action. The question then is: how can the people of a community feel "secure in their persons, houses, papers, and effects, against unreasonable searches and seizures?" How can they, knowing that neither the words of the Constitution nor the institutional arrangements of the city will guarantee this security, develop the resources of information and power to protect themselves?

The Police and Johnny K.

by Johnny K.

> Congress shall make no law . . . abridging the freedom of speech, or of the press, or the right of the people peaceably to assemble. . . .
> —FIRST AMENDMENT TO THE CONSTITUTION

There are kinds of people who are especially subject to police power—to brutality, to arrest, to harassment, to punishment: drunks, "punks," kids, blacks, anyone "uppity," and political radicals. This has been true for so long, so persistently, in every part of America, rural or town or big city, that one must say it is a pattern, built into our system. In other words, it is not an "accident" when it happens. It is part of an almost biological protective mechanism for the whole society, to keep things as they are, to push down anyone who suggests by his or her actions that the system can be defied.

Jonathan K., a graduate student in biology at MIT in 1970, encountered the police when he and some friends in Cambridge decided to talk to neighborhood high school kids about the war in Indochina. It was the spring of that year, just after President Nixon had ordered the invasion of Cambodia, and exactly one day after the shooting of four students at Kent State University in Ohio by National Guardsmen during an antiwar demonstration there. Johnny was twenty-five, and he

21

wrote down what happened shortly after the incident. His story follows.

On Tuesday, May 5, about twenty of us walked to Cambridge High and Latin School from MIT about noontime to engage students during their lunch break in discussions about the war, the recent invasion of Cambodia, the national university strike, political repression in the United States, and the relevance of such to their own lives and to ours. For the most part, our group consisted of people from the biology department at MIT. Arriving at the school around 12:15 P.M., we broke into small groups to talk with students on the Ellery Street side of the building. I personally engaged various groups of boys and girls; the first thing I was confronted with was the statement by some of the boys that nobody there wanted to hear what we had to say, that we would only get beaten up if we stayed, that they liked the war, that they wanted to get over to Vietnam and kill.

Many of the boys were overtly very hostile and were into big talk, bravado about violence and physical strength and hero worship; the focus was continually on their apparent idol named Herbie, whom they tried repeatedly to encourage to hit me, using such tactics as claiming that I had said I hated Jamaicans (Herbie is black and from Jamaica). I cooled down the situations I was in repeatedly, by talking to Herbie and the loudmouths about real manhood, sexuality, and the quality of one's life, and "schticking" in a comic way about fighting, killing, and being tough. At one point I imitated Herbie's threatening gestures with his fist, which defused what was undoubtedly almost a punch in my face. I also talked about my youth in New York, gang wars, etc.

Finally asked a large group (about twenty) around me whether they wanted to have a real discussion and at least listen to why we came to the school. Lots of people (boys and girls) said they did, but a few of the boys were very hostile, so I tried to get Herbie to agree, which he did, reluctantly. I talked about high school and what it was for, about its leading to college or to the draft and Vietnam. I asked them what they thought about most of the universities being on strike, especially since they are supposedly being prepared for college. Also questioned why the U.S. has been fighting in Southeast Asia, about the history of Vietnam since 1954— made analogy of England's helping the South during the American Civil War with U.S. helping South Vietnam after we set up puppet fascist Diem.

Lots of students, and one black girl in particular, indicated to me they thought what I was saying made sense. They said, among other things, that the hostile group of boys should let me finish. I said we do not have any business in civil wars in Asia, that our army is there to control the outcome there, that we are not letting these people determine their own fate although we supposedly regard that as an American right. Then asked in whose interest the war was and said it was certainly not in ours (the students'). Some objected that if we didn't fight there, they would attack us. I just asked by what means—boats?

I tried to relate the political events with their own lives. I said that their high school looked like a prison and served for training robots to enter the army and die for other peoples' interests, not to teach people to be free and decent human beings. A majority of students I was with indicated to me by nodding, etc., that they concurred with at least some of the things I said.

I had the impression that others in our group were doing similar things along Ellery Street. Several minor scuffles occurred, and someone told me the fire alarm had been rung. Many students exited from the building in more or less orderly fashion, but broke up in the street. Several people I took to be teachers or administrators were encouraging the students to go back to class. Students were at all the windows in the building on the Ellery Street side when I looked up. Many were yelling things out to us. Several cars with students drove by stopping to talk to students who were in the street.

At that point the police arrived in force, at least two unmarked cars and one patrol car. I had observed that we had been tailed all the way from MIT by a black sedan with a phone. I was ordered across the street (Broadway) by a man in a tan sports jacket. I asked to see his identification, was shown it, and proceeded to cross the street, engaging the plainclothesman in conversation. I said I live here and I'm a member of the community. I then joined most of the others on the southeast corner of the intersection in front of the drugstore. During this time, a truck filled with students making menacing motions was stopped by the police and teachers, and the students were made to get out. We waited around for several of the others who were not seen by the police and remained to talk with students. Several of us talked with three black students about events at the school and student hostility. Then they crossed back to the school.

We finally got reassembled and left as a group, walking up Broadway, then Hancock Street, to the red truck, with the intention of going to the State House for the antiwar rally. We were followed by police in marked and unmarked cars. They observed our movements as we cleaned out the truck to make room, got oranges from Henry Smilowitz' apartment, piled into the truck and on top (four of us on top—secured by a railing) and started off for the State House rally, down Broadway, followed now by about five police cars. We were finally signaled off the road at Broadway and Elm streets, and the driver was accused of "driving to endanger." The driver was asked to produce his license, registration, and insurance. The police claimed the license was not validated by the state registrar. A policewoman consulted. They said they would have to take the driver and truck to the station to check on the documents.

They indicated that only the driver had to come, but we felt that if it wouldn't take long, we would stick together, get the charge taken care of (the driver claimed everything was in order and I for one believed him and felt the police were just hassling us because they had nothing better to do) and still make it to the rally. We all piled into the truck and drove to the Central Square Police Station, escorted by a cortege of marked and unmarked cars. We sang "Alice's Restaurant" as the people watched the procession move through Central Square.

At the police station, we all piled out and only the driver was allowed inside. The rest of us were on the sidewalk or in the street on the main entrance side of the building. About half a dozen plainclothesmen and uniformed cops stayed outside watching us, telling us such things as not to lean against the patrol cars because we would dirty them. One detective, whom I call "Blue Eyes," called us maggots. I personally engaged in conversations with several cops:

(a) with a younger cop called "Red" about truck registration and driver's license. I asked what procedures were used to check that the driver was improperly registered, whether they had called long distance to Minnesota. Chuck Cole and I both took out our drivers' licenses to see if registrars' stamps were on both. There was none on Chuck's, which is not from Massachusetts.

(b) with a dark cop, Mediterranean complexion, and the short, slight, blond-haired, ruddy-complexioned, blue-eyed detective about the war, the invasion of Cambodia, why students were out in the streets and about my joining the police force.

(c) with one cop whom I don't remember (he was in uniform) about possibilities for political change in this country—futility of writing congressmen; and about painting walls as a desperate last attempt to be heard.

Mostly the police would not talk about the war and they seemed to be irritated by our questions and by the fact that we appeared happy. Early on at the station, in fact, right after descending from the truck, Detective Blue Eyes spat at my feet and I spat back at his, both missing by a few inches and on purpose. This was accompanied by the following exchange:

HIM: Did you spit on me?

ME: You saw where I spat and why.

At one point, a uniformed cop, I think a sergeant, came out and asked to speak to our spokesman. The dark cop said I was the spokesman because I did the most talking. I said we have no spokesman. The sergeant pointed to David Baltimore and said, "You look the most intelligent," and talked to him, but loud enough for me to hear with no difficulty. He informed us that the driver had been placed under arrest for driving without proper insurance, etc., and that as soon as he was booked, we could make arrangements to get him out on bail. He specifically stated we could stay outside and wait until we could go in to make bail arrangements.

As we were standing around, I observed many cops at the window of the police station looking out at us; they seemed to be discussing us. I then noticed a man in a tan-olive suit and gray hair come out with a box camera and start photographing us. When he shoved it in my face, I raised my hand and gave him the finger. Very soon thereafter, a giant in a sports coat appeared, and said in a loud voice: "Get the fuck out of here."

I said: "You know, the police station is a public building."

He moved toward me rapidly, punched me twice very hard in the face, both times with the right fist, and then screamed, "You're under arrest."

At which point I was covered with cops, dragged into the station by my hair, kicked and punched and pulled up the stairs, through the door at the top. As I was going up the stairs, I removed my sunglasses and held them in my right hand throughout what follows. Inside the door at the top of the stairs, another redheaded cop, about forty-five or fifty years of age, flaccid and with black glasses, clapped a torture device called a claw on my left wrist. At the time I thought he was handcuffing me, and said: "That's not necessary." It was the last rational thing I said. All of a sudden I experienced unspeakable pain. I started screaming. The cop with my wrist said, but not really to me: "All right, you son of a bitch, you wanted to come in here, now you're going to find out what it's like." I was on the floor in a semiball, being pulled by the left wrist and hair and kicked from behind. I remember crying, "How can you do this to people?" Someone let go of my hair as I was dragged around the desk. As I was pulled across the threshold of the back room I felt my head being struck three or four times with a hard blunt instrument, after which I was covered with blood. My left hand was held high by the "claw" while I was half on the floor in front of the desk with the front of my body against the desk. I was continuously punched and kicked around my head and shoulders and right leg while they continued to lacerate my left wrist. As they were beating me I heard them talking to me, saying:

(a) Jew bastard
(b) Mother-fucking Commie
(c) Dirty hippy bastard
(d) Nigger lover
(e) We're going to give it to you.

The pain on my left wrist was so unbearable that my mind detached from my body so that I could ignore the pain. I tried to listen to what was going on. I stopped screaming. I felt that anything I did or said would intensify the beating. I finally decided to pretend to faint and went limp. The beating stopped shortly thereafter, the thing was removed from my wrist and I was told to stand up. I was covered with blood and there was a pool of blood on the floor next to the desk.

I was surrounded by those who had beaten me. Blue Eyes to my immediate left, cameraman to the right of him, slightly behind, the man with the claw, who was booking me, three officials and/or detectives behind him, a detective and uniformed officers behind me, Chuck Cole on the floor behind Blue Eyes with cops on him—later moved to bench behind me to the left. At this point, although I did look into their eyes, I decided not to do anything except follow their orders if possible.

They told me to empty my pockets, to take off my jacket, belt and shoes, and Bobby Seale button. One of them (man behind desk booking me) said, pointing to the picture of Seale, "Is he a Jew too?" Someone then said: "Let's get the Lieutenant in to advise him of his rights." Someone came in and I was then informed of my rights in a monotonous voice. They then booked me. At one point, a man entered the room who is familiar to me as either a police or city official from demonstrations and from TV. I looked at him and said: "Sir, is this how things happen here?"

Cameraman (to my left) said: "Don't talk to us like that."

I said: "I'm talking to *him*," and pointed with my eyes at the official. The cameraman punched me hard on the left temple and my head smashed into the iron grill which goes up from the desk on the right side.

They finished booking me. Then decided I should be taken to the hospital. Volunteers were asked for to take me. Clawman volunteered, which frightened me, and Pocked Face said he would go too. I don't know if he beat me or not but he was there. They told me to put my shoes on. Then the official whom I had addressed as Sir came up to me with a white towel and said I was bleeding (which was pretty obvious) and should hold the towel over my head wound.

Then I was locked in back of a wagon and taken to the accident ward of Cambridge City Hospital. The doctor who stitched me up and surveyed my injuries is Dr. Felicia Hanse. When asked—by her, another doctor who came in, and by the hospital clerk—what had happened to me, I stated that

I had been beaten by the police in the back room of the station. At the hospital, the cops told me when I asked that I could not make a telephone call until I was taken to court. I asked Dr. Hanse to dial a number for me, which she did on the telephone next to the bed, and I spoke to the party without the cops' knowledge. I was stitched up, my wrist and leg examined, and I was X-rayed: head, face, wrist, and then taken by wagon again with the same cops to the courthouse. In court, I observed, as did Chuck Cole, that Detective Blue Eyes had changed his sports jacket from a brown one to a blue one—he was so covered with blood after the incident in the station that this was necessary.

George Enos and the Baby Carriage

*by Howard Zinn with Dennis Blake
and Domenic Restuccia*

In the Boston area, Somerville is north of Cambridge. It is a place where mainly working people live, Irish and Italian, and other ethnic groups. Two Boston University students, Dennis Blake and Domenic Restuccia, investigated a case involving George Enos, Rose Faretra, Maryanne Barnard, and the Somerville police. They gathered statements from eyewitnesses, and, as they put it: "We socialized with George and his friends in the endeavor to better understand his plight. We attended the court sessions pertinent to George's struggle in the hopes of better understanding the state of law and justice in America, specifically Somerville, Massachusetts."

Blake and Restuccia report: "Suffice it to say, on three counts [two rude and disorderly, and one assault and battery] the effect of *juris prudence* [they deliberately separate the word] practiced in Somerville District Court was to find George Enos guilty before he opened his mouth."

It all started with an argument over a baby carriage on a warm summer evening. As the story was first told to them by Diane McDonough, on September 10, 1971:

"I bought a carriage for my children approximately one and a half years ago, and gave the same one to my sister [Rose Faretra] approximately three weeks ago.

"I was over Mother's house at 10 Pinckney Place, Somerville, when she got a phone call from the people downstairs from my sister—George Enos and Maryanne Barnard. They told my mother that Rose wanted me to come over immediately to identify the carriage because some lady [Diane Crane] was trying to say that it was hers, and my sister was trying to take it away. So I went right over.

"When I arrived, this is what I saw with my own eyes: one paddy wagon was on the corner of Skilton Avenue and Pearl Street, one detective car further down the street, and a cruiser car (Number 785) with two people in it. One was my sister Rose and the other was a boy being pulled out of the car and led to the wagon.

"I then looked at the house and saw Deedee [Maryanne Barnard] being carried out by two officers. I followed them with my eyes as they threw her in the car with Rose. At the same time I heard my sister yell and looked to her and saw that one officer had bashed her in the head and face. I went closer to the car and said, 'Oh, my God, why did you do that?' The cop said to me it was okay for her [Rose] to beat up a lady [Diane Crane] so we can do the same to her, right? I said, 'When my father sees this he is gonna want a better explanation than that.' The officer then said, 'Go home and mind your own business.' I said, 'It is my business.'

"Rose said, 'Go get Daddy and I'll tell him what the officer did.' The officer then said to Rose, 'You wouldn't say a fucking thing, lady, you understand? Not a fucking thing.' Then I said, 'Good mouth on you,' and walked away.

"As I left the cruiser I asked Maryanne Barnard if she had a camera and went into her house to get it, but when I came out with it they knocked it away from my face.

"As they drove off I went over to my friend's car, which was parked next to the detective's car. I told the detective that my father wouldn't like this and he'd be down the station with me. He said not to worry, that they will take her to the hospital. I said that they better and then I got into my friend's car and slammed the door and rolled up the window. The detective then got out of the car, came to the car that I was in, opened the door and said, 'Listen, lady, you better mind your own fucking business because you didn't see anything and you better go to hell home or you'll be right there with them.' I said, 'Go ahead and arrest me. I want to be with her to make sure they don't do any more to her.' Then he yelled out so everyone could hear, 'Stop using that profane language, do you hear?' But I didn't say any swear words at all. He grabbed me by the blouse front as he said it. I then got out of the car and went to my father's house and then to the police station."

Dennis Blake and Dom Restuccia talked also to Lucille Brissette, who lived at 207 Pearl Street, Somerville, and who gave them the following statement:

"My daughter returned from the scene of the incident and said cops were beating everyone in sight, they were swearing like troopers. When I arrived on the scene there was a girl in the patrol car bleeding [Rose Faretra]. I heard the cop say to Rose, 'Keep your fucking mouth closed—you ain't seen nothin' or heard nothin.' I was located right next to the police car when this took place. Pam [a neighbor] was standing next to me and heard the same things I did.

"My daughter reported to me that she had seen a cop break in the door to George's apartment.

"I heard the cops say to Maryanne Barnard, after finding out that she was pregnant, 'I don't give a fuck what condition you are in.'

"Diane McDonough said to her sister that she was going to call her father. At this time the police were in the car. They stopped, came back, and said to Diane that if she didn't want to join the others she had best remember that she saw and heard nothing. I heard the cops swearing like troopers, but I didn't hear the kids swear at all."

Blake and Restuccia reported that this witness, Lucille Brissette, "seemed very opinionated when it came to matters concerning the police. She claimed she had observed many instances of police brutality similar to the one alleged to have occurred on the night of George Enos' arrest."

What had happened inside George Enos' apartment before the street scene observed by Diane McDonough and Lucille Brissette, and by Lucille's daughter? Blake and Restuccia interviewed Maryanne Barnard (Deedee) of 10 Skilton Avenue, Somerville, who told them the following story:

"A few days before the incident I heard Rose and Diane Crane arguing about the carriage in front of our home.

"The night of the incident, George was in the kitchen upstairs playing cards. George then told Rose that a lady was taking off with her carriage. Rose, Barbara, and Linda went downstairs. I went downstairs about three minutes later. I saw Rose, Barbara, and Linda struggling with Diane and one of her girlfriends for the carriage. Diane told her girlfriend to call the police. The girls got the carriage back and I took it into my apartment.

"When the police arrived Barbara and I were on the porch. Rose then came downstairs. As Rose came out on the porch one of the officers walked by her and began to climb the stairs. Rose asked for a warrant. I then saw two kids fly down the stairs. Then the offier told Rose that she smelled like marijuana. Rose told him that he probably smelled the booze on his own breath. He then told another officer to lock her up for disorderly conduct. The second officer put Rose in the car.

"George was in the house. I then told the cops that the carriage was in my apartment. George told Linda, Barbara and me to come in. Before we went in, two detective cars pulled up with a paddy wagon. We then went into the house and someone banged at the door. George asked if they had a warrant. Then the door opened and an officer said, 'Fuck the warrant.' He called us fucking cocksuckers. He told Barbara and Linda to leave. They left.

"He then told me to leave. I said no, this is my kitchen. He told me to shut up or I'd get it too. He pushed the table across the room and cornered George. Seven other cops followed the officers in. Everyone was out of the kitchen and the officer told me to leave. He attempted to hit George but didn't at first. He then pulled George's hair and hit him. George tried to push him away but never hit him. I pulled the cop's hair and got him away from George. Two cops grabbed me. I struggled. When I got near the officer or hit him they hit me with their billy clubs.

"Three cops then picked me up and carried me outside abusively. Someone yelled out that I was pregnant. One cop replied that that was why they were carrying me. The officer said, 'I don't give a damn what fucking condition she's in.' He then pushed me against the car. I then told them to put me down and that I was capable of standing on my own. I then asked a cop why he was hitting George. He told me to shut up. They then took Ritchie [a friend] out of the car and put me in.

"I was in the car and watched the cops put George in the paddy wagon. Then one of the officers got into the car. I tried to tell Linda where the baby's diapers, etc., were. I tried to get out to show her. I opened the door and the cop said that we were not there for a chitchat party and that I was under arrest (I didn't know why yet). In the car he said that I was arrested for disorderly conduct, assault and battery, adding to the delinquency of a minor, and receiving stolen goods.

"When we arrived at the station he told Barbara Martin [a matron] to charge me only with receiving stolen goods. I went up with Rose. I got fingerprinted and signed a paper but I didn't know what I was signing. I didn't know my rights. An officer took me to have my picture taken and to be finger-

printed. He pushed me around. A detective on duty saw this
and told the officer that he would handle it. I was booked at
10 A.M. and was released at 11:10.

"I walked out and told the officer that Rose needed medical
attention. He refused to allow her this attention until 12:20
A.M. Two people then came into the station in regards to an
automobile accident and witnessed the fact that the officer
would not allow Rose to get medical attention.

"Then George and I left and went to the Somerville Hospital for treatment. Dr. Smith treated us. He gave me reflex
exams because of bruises I had in the back of my ear, three
bumps on my head, two bruises on my left arm, and one
bruise on my left leg. My bra strap was broken. I had been
picked up by it. We went to court at 9 A.M. and the case was
continued [postponed]. We then went to the FBI."

Dom Restuccia and Dennis Blake interviewed George Enos:

"I was playing cards upstairs. I looked out the window and
saw a lady taking the carriage. I told Rose that the lady had
taken the carriage. The girls then went down the stairs and
I went after them. The girls were at the car and the lady was
trying to put the carriage in the car. I then went back upstairs.
I decided to let the girls handle the situation. The girls then
came back and said that they got the carriage back and that
the lady had called the cops.

"Maryanne said that the carriage was in her house. She
said that it was in the closet. I then went down and took the
carriage out of the closet and put it on the back porch. I then
went out to stand on the front porch. By then the cops had
arrived.

"A cop then began to walk upstairs and Rose asked him
for a warrant. The cop then told Rose to shut up and that
she smelled like marijuana. Another cop then went upstairs.
I heard him yell out, 'Get downstairs, you fucking cunt.' I
then saw a cop holding Ritchie by the hair and dragging him
downstairs. Ritchie fell on the ground near the car and a cop

lifted him by the hair and threw him in the car. Ritchie then asked what was going on.

"Barbara, Linda, and Maryanne were on the porch. I told them to get into my house. I told them that the cops weren't going to get into my house without a warrant. I never swore. I went into the house, closed the door, and saw the police standing at the cars. Rose and Ritchie were in one of the cars. I then said again that nobody was going to get into my house without a warrant. A cop then yelled for me to come down. I said, 'No, so you can do to me what you did to the other kid?' I shut the door.

"I opened the curtains and the cops came up. I sat in the kitchen and told everyone to sit down. There was a bang on the door and I asked who was there. The cops said, 'Never mind, open the fucking door.' I said no, not without a warrant. The cops busted in and said, 'We don't need a fucking warrant, you fucking cocksuckers.' They told Barbie, Linda, and Maryanne to get out. Then one cop started to wave his hands at me as though he was going to hit me but he didn't. Then he started to hit me and told Maryanne to leave the kitchen. Maryanne said, 'No. This is my kitchen.' The cop told her to shut up or she'd get it too. Meanwhile the cops hit me. At times there were about five hands on my head. I then looked up and saw the cops hit Maryanne on the head with a club. They kept hitting me for about a minute and then carried me out to the paddy wagon.

"They never told me that I was under arrest or why. At the station I did not want to get out of the paddy wagon because I was afraid I'd be beaten again. A cop told me not to worry, that nobody would hit me. I was booked for rude and disorderly. I wouldn't sign though, since I was never told I was under arrest or my rights. Then they told me my rights.

"The cop that had been in the apartment came in and said very softly, 'I'm gonna kill you.' I told the Lieutenant. The cop denied saying anything. They put me into a detention cell until I'd sign. The cop asked me if I was scared. I said, 'Sure, why not?' I told him that he knew where the carriage really was. He said, 'Yeah. In the kitchen.' Then he admitted it was outside, but claimed that we had put it there because we knew they were coming. They then moved me from the juvenile detention cell to the adult cell. The cop started to punch me a little. Then the other cop came by and asked what was going on. I told him and the first cop denied it. He then threw me into the cell. After being released, I went to the hospital and to the FBI."

That George Enos and Maryanne Barnard went to the FBI after the incident is important. There is a faith that we grow up with in America, that while injustices may take place on the lower levels, there are wise and beneficent higher authorities that will redress them, that beyond the human beings wielding the clubs on the street there is the United States Constitution and the Federal Bureau of Investigation. Indeed, federal statutes, going back to post-Civil War days, make it a federal crime for policemen to deprive citizens of their constitutional rights. But blacks in the South found, in the civil rights struggle of the 1960's, that when they complained to the federal government, to the Justice Department, and to the FBI about local police abuse, they met a wall of silence and inaction. And so it is in any American city. The system we live under has a defense in depth, in which every abuse is referred to some higher authority, but, as in a nightmarish Kafka novel, the citizen keeps going from one authority to the next, seeking redress, and rarely finds it. There is no evidence that the FBI either investigated or acted on the complaints of George Enos or Maryanne Barnard, although it is the job of the FBI to investigate violations of federal law and to initiate prosecution where such violations occur.

How far and how long the citizen can go in the quest for justice depends on how much money, time, patience, and confidence he or she has. It takes years, and tens of thousands of dollars to get a case up to the Supreme Court. It takes time and money to sue the police. It takes courage and faith to lodge a complaint with the police department against its own policemen. Even if, as happens in very rare cases, a complaint gets as far as the Supreme Court (the Court only hears one out of twenty appeals that people make to it), and gets a favorable decision, that decision does not have immediate effect on the police or on the judges all over the country. They can still ignore these decisions, still do what they have been doing by habit, for so long, knowing that if you challenge them, you have to start all over again, climbing that long ladder of time and money to higher and higher authorities.

In addition, if you are poor and powerless, there is the threat that any complaint you make, any resistance you put up, will be taken note of, that you still must live in the same community, face the same policemen, who will keep an eye on you until they are assured you have acknowledged who is boss.

That is what George Enos found out, three weeks after the baby-carriage incident in Somerville. George and Maryanne Barnard had gone out to get some tea. He told the following to Dennis Blake and Dom Restuccia, who were still in touch with him:

"On October 4, 1971, at 12:30 A.M., we got out of the car at Dunkin' Doughnuts. On our way into Dunkin' Doughnuts a police officer came up to us and said, 'Screw.' I said, 'What? What did you say?' The police officer said, 'Let me tell you something. Get the fuck out of here.' I answered, 'I respect your badge, but I don't respect your language.'

"The police officer answered with, 'What are you here for, anyway?' I said, 'We came here to get a cup of tea.' He said, 'Your girlfriend should go into Dunkin' Doughnuts, and you stay here.' I said, 'No, I want a witness to what you're going to do.'

"Then we went into Dunkin' Doughnuts and he followed

us in. When we got inside, he said, 'Be quiet, don't make a scene.' I said, 'No! Why? Because there are a lot of people in here and you don't want them to hear what we say?' I said again, loud, so people could hear, 'I respect your badge, but I don't respect your language. If your wife were here with you I wouldn't use the language you used in front of my girl-friend.'

"He said, 'Keep it down.' I looked up at his badge and asked him what his number was. When he heard this, he said, 'You're under arrest.' While he was saying this he was grabbing at my shirt. We started walking out of Dunkin' Doughnuts. When we got outside I pulled away from him and ran. I eventually made it home. By the way, the police officer pulled my shirt completely off.

"When I got home I went to bed. All of a sudden, in my sleep, I felt someone punching me. When I felt the punches I said, 'What's going on?' There were three police officers punching me on the floor, pulling my hair. I yelled again, 'Leave me alone.' They picked me up by my hair and dragged me outside to the police car. I fell by the police car. I still really didn't know what was going on. I ran down the railroad tracks and they ran after me. They shot at me. I kept running and I hid. About twenty minutes later I worked my way back into the house. The policemen came back but I was upstairs. They didn't come in. I waited about an hour and went back downstairs. I am afraid, because I know the first chance they get they will do a job on me."

The trial that followed from the baby-carriage incident took place in Somerville District Court, and Domenic Restuccia tells about it:

"As I sat waiting for the trial to begin, I could not help noticing that the arresting officer was waving and nodding to everyone in the court. Then the trial began.

"The arresting officer was called up to the stand and told his version of what had happened. He never mentioned the brutality of the police nor the fact that the police had broken into the homes of these people. He only mentioned that he had found the carriage in the kitchen of Maryanne's house. After he finished his testimony, a detective approached the stand. Judge DeMarco then said that he did not want to hear anymore. [So there was no defense testimony!]

"The Judge said that the Enos family had a notorious reputation in Somerville. He then declared George guilty, put Maryanne on probation, and sentenced Rose to six months in the Woman's House of Correction for receiving stolen goods (but put her on probation assuming one year of good behavior). The Judge pondered whether he should give George six months or a two-hundred-dollar fine for "rude and disorderly" conduct. He chose to give him the fine. When George said he would appeal, the Judge said he knew he should have given him six months. This was the end of the 'trial.' "

The Complaint of Jamie Wickens

by Jamie Wickens

At 2 A.M., September 19, 1968, a Boston University student named Jamie Wickens was awakened by noises from the street and went to his window. What he saw sent him on a quest which took him many months. It was not an "important" case; no one was killed or permanently injured, except that injustice inflicts injuries which are invisible, permanent, and damaging in ways not easily recorded. What makes Jamie Wickens' story remarkable is that he did what many of us think of doing, but never do: to pursue a grievance as an indignant citizen who has witnessed someone else's victimization, and to pursue it to its very end, through all its detours, its impasses, its frustrations, past direct opposition and smiling condescension, ignoring kindly advice to give up. He was incredibly stubborn, persistent, indefatigable.

"Have you exhausted all administrative remedies?" the judges ask sternly when a citizen complains. Who has the patience? Jamie Wickens did, and his experience tells us something not only about the intricacies of personality and procedure inside a police department, but also about law professors and civil liberties organizations, about friends as well as foes. He spares hardly anyone, not even himself. It would

41

be hard to find anything more *real,* about law and justice.

Here is Jamie Wickens' report. . . .

The Scene: The deafening squeal of tires broke the early morning stillness, but the squeal was not momentary or instantaneous; it hung motionless and sustained a throbbing ring in one's ears. The patrol car and its victim (a 1962, baby-blue Corvair—Oklahoma plates) came to a raking, convulsive standstill. The Corvair lurched backward across the narrow street, lunged up on the curb, and fell silent.

And then the shot; also shrill and shattering, reverberating between the cavernous apartment walls in that narrow street. It was rather queer coming from such a small pistol, which exploded somewhat like a shotgun. And the cop, so young, certainly not more than twenty-six, pistol in hand, sprung hesitantly toward the Corvair, possibly unsure whether his weapon had found its mark. Pulling open the door, shattered glass tinkling to the street, he probably was still uncertain about his victim's condition, for the man indeed seemed numb as stone, as though drugged, shocked, drunk, and stunned all at once—frozen in the front seat.

The young cop, obviously scared, dragged him from the seat and stood him up against the car, arms outstretched on the roof. But then it was evident that the man was not necessarily drunk or drugged, for he stood absolutely still without the drunken sway or quiver; most clearly the victim of shell shock. The young cop played perfectly the role of the eighteen-year-old soldier in battle for the first time, as he frisked the man with his piercing, shaking yell: "Don't move, don't move; up against the wall." And indeed the man was still stonelike.

But that was hardly the end. Five other big cars pulled up around the corner: Perhaps ten police closed in on the man, flying elbows jolted his jaw, grinding knees in the groin, fists to his stomach, even a few gun butts ripped down upon his skull. It was much like a football scene with the awkward clumsiness of the cops knocking into one another in their eagerness to get at the victim. But he did not fall unconscious; the cops who dragged him away to the paddy wagon denied him that.

The remaining cops then examined the baby-blue Corvair, searched it, and slammed the driver's door closed again and again, until the shattered glass was strewn out on the street. I wondered at the time just why they were so careful about removing all the glass from that window.

On the street after most of the cops had left we (two other friends also witnessed the incident with me from my fourth-floor apartment) also examined the Corvair: the spattered blood on the roof, the bullet hole in the front side passenger window, and the empty, shattered window casing on the other side—how incredibly close that bullet had come to the man's head. We asked the young cop why he had fired at him. He looked astounded as if this were the last question he ever expected and replied, "Oh, I only wanted to scare him a little."

Standing beside the young cop was another young man. He immediately came to the cop's defense. "Hey! Lay off, will ya, buddy. Ya know what that damn bastard did to my new Buick, just a couple of weeks old? We were over at the corner of Massachusetts and Columbus Avenues at the light. All of a sudden that son of a bitch, who's in front of me, backs up and knocks out my front lamps. And then he just took off. Shit, if I had laid my hands on him, I would have busted him right between the eyes too."

"You mean, just because he backed into you and smashed your headlights?"

"Shit, man. My machine's brand-new."

A little later we were discussing the whole incident with a student from an apartment across the street who was also rather disturbed by the police brutality. But he was hesitant about serving as a witness or taking some other action, for fear of "getting too involved." In fact he was even rather surprised by our suggestion.

"How the hell can you take action against the police?" he asked.

In the early days of the case, during September, I was solely concerned with the man and how he could possibly be helped. My drifting fantasies often pondered what exactly would happen to this apparently poor man; what typical injustices would he suffer: the detriment of a court-appointed lawyer, the inability to post bail, etc. It was obvious that nothing could be done until we found out who he was. Then possibly we could contact his lawyer and act as witnesses for the defense.

One would think that merely identifying the defendant should be no problem. But when one's only source of information is the police, the matter is quite a bit more difficult.

A few of us began by seeking aid and advice at Boston University's Law School. We spoke to a law professor. He seemed genuinely disturbed by the behavior of the police in the incident and was apparently eager to be of some help. But soon he explained that criminal law was not his field, nor was he a member of the Massachusetts Bar; so he could not really directly assist us.

He did, however, introduce us to Professor M. and Professor K., both of the law school and active in the Massachusetts chapter of the American Civil Liberties Union. Professor M.'s immediate assistance consisted of directing me not to speak to anyone about the case in order to protect myself against possible police charges of slander. He further asked me to submit a detailed, written synopsis of the scene I had witnessed. I was a bit troubled by the professor's response, because I thought it very important to talk to other people about the incident, rather than keep my mouth shut for fear of being sued by the police.

Certainly though, he was quite right in asking me to draw

up a thorough description of the scene. It is easy for a witness to forget various facets of what he saw, and the result can be a very muddled and distorted account. The night of the incident I had taken fairly close notes so that it was not difficult reconstructing a coherent summary. But it was frustrating submitting a case summary so long before it would bear any results. Professor M., like nearly all the lawyers involved in this case, moved like a discreet snail, always intent on maintaining the dignity of his profession.

A week after the defendant's arrest, a small group of us, meeting after a Civil Liberties class, decided to act more directly on our own and visit the police station in the vicinity of the incident, located by the Prudential Center. I identified myself as a witness and intimated I was only interested in helping the police as a "good citizen." The on-duty officer referred us to Station Four (in the South End).

A couple of days later I reached Sgt. Jack Cronin by phone (Monday morning, September 30). He quickly surprised me by immediately recognizing and even identifying the incident before I finished describing it. Cronin said the defendant was a "long-time criminal" who had already been arraigned, tried, convicted, and jailed "for a good long time." ("So don't you worry, we took care of him.") Before I had time to respond to all this, he said he was on his way to court and therefore could not elaborate.

It was certain that Cronin, because of his thorough knowledge of the incident and the defendant, had been involved. Since, as Police Prosecutor, he was often at court, I wondered whether he had been the Prosecutor at the trial; indeed I later discovered that on the first day we visited Station Four, Cronin was in court with this case.

After classes that day, I again called Cronin to possibly find out more specific information about this case: primarily the defendant's name and the charges brought against him. Cronin was not keen on talking with me again. He said he could hardly furnish any of the information I was seeking, because he had no idea "whom he was speaking to," even though I had previously identified myself. When I suggested visiting the station to talk with him, he replied that none of this was public information anyway. I then asserted that I had been a witness and asked about the witnesses used at the trial or hearing.

Oddly enough, Cronin suddenly became more open and talkative. He talked of the testimony of two civilian witnesses; one of them was the owner of the car that had been hit by the defendant. I was astounded when Cronin said that according to the testimony of these two witnesses, the defendant had backed his Corvair up onto the curb and then plowed forward, actually striking the "young cop" on his arm. In other words, a clear case had been made at the hearing for the "young cop's" shooting in self-defense against the defendant's assault.

I then called Samuel Robinson, head of the American Civil Liberties Union's Police Practices Board, and explained the case and my conversation with Sergeant Cronin. I was disappointed with his reaction; he suggested that I file a complaint against "improper police conduct" at the Internal Affairs Division of headquarters. I discarded this idea because it seemed a very roundabout and hopeless way of getting immediate aid for the defendant.

A few days later, back at the law school, a professor advised that one possible way to find the defendant's name and other relevant information would be to obtain the docket file and court record on the case at the Boston Municipal Courthouse.

So the following day, with a classmate, Don Summers, I visited the courthouse. Browsing through the docket file, we soon discovered that without the defendant's name, it was impossible to identify the case. Inquiring at the Clerk's Office, we were told that the court records were not available to the public. "You just can't walk in here and snoop around for personal information about someone." We were not making much headway even in the relatively small matter of identifying the defendant, so how could anything effective ever be accomplished?

My pessimism was reinforced by a return visit to Professor M. to find out what use he had made of the case summary. It had in fact been circulated to various ACLU lawyers, and he was awaiting their suggestions. He advised me just to "sit tight for a while" and wait for some results; he even went on to say I had probably gone too far by talking to Sergeant Cronin and visiting the police station. I was surprised when he spoke of the Boston police as "the most competent and responsible in Massachusetts." In his view the best course of action was to let the police investigate the case themselves, and he was confident that any improper police conduct involved would be duly disciplined. What Professor M. was telling me was to leave the whole case in the hands of the police. This active civil liberties lawyer, like the police, did not want me meddling.

Another Boston University law student gave me the name of a City Hall police counsel and Mayor White appointee named John Fiske, who could act as a liaison with the police. So I immediately phoned Fiske, the police counsel, who totally agreed with me that Sergeant Cronin had no right to withhold the defendant's name. He would contact Station Four and speak to the Captain. But here Fiske added that, like most students, I was a bit too critical of the Boston police. When he first started his job, he said, he too was critical of police practices; but since then his view had completely changed. His parting words were: "You know, I really think this is another instance of a civilian witness coming in on Act Three of an incident and therefore not being aware of the full story."

I later called Fiske back and found that he had spoken to Lieutenant Dow of Station Four who was very apologetic for Cronin not making the police blotter on the case available.

Fiske then recounted some of the information from the blotter: defendant—James Finn; original incident occurred on the corner of Columbus and Massachusetts avenues; Finn received only a $100 fine for assaulting a police officer; lacerations on Finn's forehead resulted from the defendant bumping his head on the auto's roof in the course of the struggle. Fiske said that Dow "would be most happy to speak with me personally." I then called Dow and made an appointment to see him the following Monday morning at 10 A.M., October 21.

But Don Summers and I thought it wise to check the case in the Boston Municipal Court's docket file before seeing Dow. In the docket file we found four cards (each representing a separate charge) in the name of James M. Finn. Three of these charges were auto violations and the other was an assault charge. After duplicating the four cards, we went to the Clerk's Office and found out that Finn's lawyer was Joseph Sax, at 1 Court Street. Another clerk, checking the court record, reported Finn was charged on seven different counts; the three missing from the docket file were also auto violations: "going through red lights."

The docket card opened up some very intriguing questions about Finn's hearing. Though Finn was found guilty on all seven counts (his plea was not guilty for all of them), six of these dispositions were "placed on file." For the assault charge, Finn was given a $100 fine. This very light disposition was hardly typical of legal treatment for the poor. We thought of the possibility of some sort of "deal" at the hearing; but the mystery of why Finn received only a light fine for an assault charge, especially on a policeman, remained unsolved.

I reached James Finn's attorney, a few days later at his office. He made it very clear that the case was absolutely closed and he was not going to discuss it; he had more important matters to attend to.

In contrast to practically all the other policemen I met, Lieutenant Dow of Station Four seemed the epitome of the modern, liberal police officer. He brought public relations into his police work. He smiled at me as if to say, "I could not care less about your hair, or whether you're a hippie, Yippie, or SDS radical." He said, "Come right in here, boys, and sit down." Lieutenant Dow treated us as if we had no intention of criticizing but had just come over from a Boston public school for our eighth-grade civics project on "Police Benevolence." Dow readily agreed to discuss the whole case at great length.

He voluntarily furnished Finn's Revere address, and read the police blotter to us. The blotter's omissions were remarkable. For example, no account or explanation was offered as to exactly why Patrolman Doyle (the complainant) "discharged his revolver." We discussed the contradictions between the blotter report and my description of the scene and arrest. Dow reiterated the argument that Doyle fired out of self-defense. I quoted Doyle's own statement in which he said he fired only to scare Finn. Instead of calling me a liar, Dow admitted it was a careless remark.

When I spoke of the dozen policemen who molested Finn, Dow simply became evasive and talked about the Chicago Democratic Convention (1968), and the many hardships and abuses the police were forced to suffer continually. He had another appointment. If I was still dissatisfied, he said, I could file a complaint at headquarters.

This was exactly our next step. By this time, we were left with very few alternatives. There was no longer anything to be done for Finn himself, since a court appeal of the case was out of the question; his lawyer seemed intransigent, and Finn was probably content with his light sentence. Finn did not have a phone, and I was unable ever to contact him to discuss the case and the possibility that he might want to protest "police brutality." Most likely, Finn would have taken much the same position as his lawyer, and one could very well understand his desire to forget about the whole thing.

Since I could hardly file against the police myself and was at a loss for other effective means of protest, I was now filing a complaint merely as a formality, to exhaust the proper channels.

It was one of those gusty, raw, and rainswept fall afternoons in October when I arrived at police headquarters on Berkeley Street, where Don Summers and I were to meet.

We found the Internal Affairs Division, which is responsible for citizen complaints, on the fourth floor, in rather drab offices. We talked to Captain Connelly. "Well, boys, what's your problem?"

I described the scene I had witnessed. I questioned Doyle's right to fire at Finn and also the necessity of a dozen policemen "subduing" a passive victim. Connelly became defensive and argumentative. Not only was he unwilling to concede the slight possibility that there may have been some substance to my complaint, but he did not even bother transcribing it. He defended Doyle's use of his revolver by saying: "I don't care whether Finn actually assaulted Officer Doyle or not, I would have shot him also. In this business, we just can't take any chances."

I retorted that Finn could easily have been killed, and Connelly replied: "So if he had been shot—he is a criminal, isn't he?"

Connelly showed us a folder with Finn's "criminal record," which extended back to the age of thirteen (Finn was now thirty), and included kidnapping, various assaults, carrying a loaded weapon, etc. Connelly ended by asking if "this wasn't enough" to convince us about Finn.

I questioned Connelly about "the thorough investigation" theoretically conducted by the Division for the citizen who files a complaint. He replied: "Oh, don't you worry about that. We'll take care of everything."

The next morning I called the ACLU's Samuel Robinson at his law office and described to him in detail our trip to the

Internal Affairs Division. He responded by inviting me to that week's luncheon of the Police Practices Board at the ACLU's office. This was very pleasing because I had always thought that if only the ACLU were in some way involved in the case, our protest could become really effective.

At the ACLU luncheon meeting, I summarized the whole case, told of the conversations with Fiske, Dow, and Connelly, and answered questions. Gerald Berlin, the chairman of the Massachusetts chapter, was sympathetic and vocal. He thought this was an excellent specific case in which to challenge the effectiveness of the police department's Internal Affairs Division, which he considered a "total sham." The Massachusetts CLU had received relatively few "civilian complaint" cases against police brutality, and had had little opportunity to test the Internal Affairs Division. Robinson talked of the Boston Police Department's rhetoric about its readiness to investigate the complaints of citizens. Berlin and Robinson invited me to return to the next meeting, since John Fiske himself (the police counsel) was to attend. He periodically met with the Practices Board.

After this meeting, I realized the situation had suddenly taken a different tack. The ACLU was concerned with re-forming the Internal Affairs Division rather than doing something about this specific case. Berlin had explained to me that because I was a third-party witness, the ACLU would not have a court case of any substance; support and testimony from the defendant was imperative. So this case was "washed up," but maybe, for future cases, it was possible to change the Internal Affairs Division into a really critical, autonomous force which carefully protected the citizenry against police power.

In the week's time before the next Practices Board meeting, I again called Captain Connelly to inquire about the progress of the investigation. He became irate; no investigation had in fact begun. Investigators often take months or even years, he said, and he was very busy with other cases. (Fiske later told me that the division only investigates approximately five complaints each month.) Connelly had no idea whether my complaint was important enough to be investigated at all.

One of Mayor White's "top aides," was at the next luncheon meeting, as was John Fiske. Fiske agreed that Connelly was "unfit," but efforts to transfer him to another division were difficult because of Connelly's rank and many years on the force. I then suggested to Fiske that it was not merely a case of getting rid of Connelly, since the other police personnel in the division were no different. But in Fiske's view this was only because of Connelly's malignant control.

Berlin then made a point: How could this division ever be effective unless it consisted solely of civilian personnel, as in New York? According to Mayor White's aide, it was impossible to staff the Boston Police Department with the necessary civilian personnel because of severe funding shortages. The aide's position was always the same in the various discussions; he and the Mayor "totally agreed" with Berlin and Robinson, but they faced too staunch an opposition to act effectively.

In order to prod the Mayor, Berlin threatened to call a press conference, adding that this case could be very persuasive in arousing public support because I was an "impartial" third-party witness. The aide promised to confer immediately with White about a whole range of reform proposals for the police department and "keep in touch" with Berlin.

From the end of November through February, practically all activity on the case revolved around incessant phone calls, primarily with the Internal Affairs Division, Robinson or Berlin, and John Fiske. In contacting the Internal Affairs Division I usually spoke to Captain Connelly about the progress and results of the investigation. Connelly grew rather

tired of me and of what he construed as intentional harassment. He refused even to outline briefly the division's investigating procedures. It was as if I were insulting by merely
asking such a question, for this was classified information.
He drew a parallel with the FBI.

In still another conversation, Connelly informed me that
neither I nor any citizen had any right to know the results of
a police investigation. When I contradicted him by quoting
both Fiske and Deputy Superintendent Craigwell, he responded, "I don't care what they said. I'm running this Division."

During this period, I was in close contact with Gerald Berlin.
After some prodding, Berlin got from the Mayor's office a
proposal that he and another ACLU lawyer (Professor M.)
meet with Police Commissioner McNamara and three of his
deputy superintendents to discuss possible reforms on all
levels. Berlin confided to me that although Professor M.
favored this proposal, he suspected it was a delaying action.
He preferred the bolder tactic of calling a press conference
and creating public pressure. But he went along with Professor M. and the Mayor's proposal.

Thus began a series of weekly meetings with McNamara
and a rotating set of deputy superintendents. The result:
reform within the Internal Affairs Division. Captain Connelly
was replaced by another captain. The possibility of civilian
personnel was "being considered." The division now responded
to complaints more quickly and efficiently, it was said. Now
that Connelly was gone, the division's personnel was far more
courteous and polite.

Discussion of the Internal Affairs Division at these meetings
soon expanded into the questioning of general police practices
and the Boston Police Department's relations with students
and the black community of Roxbury. Berlin had no idea
what if any results would come of these meetings. Much of

what had been discussed and agreed upon "would have to be seen" before he believed it. A "Civilian Review Board" was a "dirty word" in the Boston Police Department.

Berlin told me that Police Commissioner McNamara and the deputy superintendents, at these meetings, were continually asking for specific evidence of police brutality. I was taken aback. What about the incident with Finn which I and others had witnessed? It was all like *Alice in Wonderland*.

Now that the Internal Affairs Division had undergone "reform," I wondered about the investigation of the Finn case. Sure enough, Connelly's successor, Captain Stapleton, returned my phone call. The investigation had been completed. Officer Doyle was "fully exonerated." He was in no way found guilty of "misconduct." When I then asked him to elaborate on the details and inquired about reading the report, he became indignant. "Who do you think you are? No citizen has the right to read this report or know the 'full findings.'"

I replied that I was really primarily interested in the testimony of the witnesses who supported Officer Doyle, especially since my testimony had been entirely neglected. Stapleton then retreated a bit and talked of the testimony of the policemen who "subdued" Finn who had not seen any shooting, and of the civilian who was in Doyle's patrol car at the time (whose car had been bumped by Finn). Gerald Berlin's suspicion about "reform" of the Internal Affairs Division as a result of pleasant "face-to-face meetings" seemed borne out.

I thought Stapleton might invite me to read the investigation report on the Finn case, just to get rid of me, so his refusal was a surprise. I decided to pay another visit to the Internal Affairs Division (IAD) and make a personal attempt to see the report. This time (Friday afternoon, January 31), as I was making my way alone toward those listless fourth-floor offices, I suddenly realized what a waste of time this all was. What could I possibly expect from the police? How could one ever take the IAD seriously? Just consider for a moment the idea of any police department establishing a division to investigate legitimacy of its own practices. It was ludicrous.

Furthermore it is probably exactly this tokenism which bewilders such traditional policemen as Connelly and Stapleton, who resent being turned to pasture in such a useless division; perhaps this accounted for much of their frustration and hostility. Stapleton, like Connelly, was not appreciative of my visit. When I asked to read the report, he said, "I thought I told you that the Finn report is none of your business. We've been very patient with you and all your insinuations and charges."

I politely replied (it was a strategy for survival) that "I failed to understand why a citizen was not allowed to read the report on an investigation that was conducted solely upon his instigation." Stapleton talked about the "classified and personal information" in the report which could not be divulged. I could not resist telling him that if this was the case, I saw no justification for the existence of the division. I suppose my politeness fell apart a little. Stapleton was angry and walked off to his office. Deputy Superintendent Donovan was not there to appeal to, so I too walked away. A few days later I had very much the same conversation, though less tempestuous, with Donovan.

In mid-February I received a letter from John Fiske requesting me to phone him at his City Hall office to discuss the investigation of the Finn case. Fiske summarized for me the "results of findings" of the police investigation:

As soon as the two autos stopped, Officer Doyle jumped out of his patrol car and ordered Finn to get out of his Corvair slowly with his arms raised. Instead of complying, Finn made a desperate attempt to run Doyle over, and Doyle fired at him in self-defense. At the same time he shouted to the civilian

(Rupp) in his patrol car to place a call for additional help, whereupon a dozen policemen immediately arrived. Finn had a long criminal record. He had committed no offense in eight years. But he "struggled violently" to resist arrest. It required all twelve policemen to "subdue" Finn. During the struggle, Finn bumped his head on the roof of his car, incurring forehead lacerations which were later treated at Boston City Hospital.

I thanked Fiske for this summary, but added that it was no substitute for the actual reading of the report. What of all the other citizens who similarly file complaints but know of no John Fiske to contact to learn of the results? Fiske said that he could not understand why Stapleton had not let me read the report, since he personally found it so convincing: there was clearly no police brutality. I questioned the bias of the testimony of Rupp, the civilian, Doyle himself, and the dozen other policemen. Fiske then agreed that Rupp and the other policemen were prejudiced witnesses. He also conceded that my testimony and that of my two friends should have at least been considered in the report. But Connelly had never even taken down my full complaint.

The conversation expanded to general police practices. I questioned "the Policeman's right to bear and use arms," especially in cities (I cited English bobbies, armed only with clubs). Fiske denied that policemen are generally "trigger-happy" as I asserted, and to the contrary, insisted that "practically without fail police revolvers are used responsibly." But he also knew of "accidents": a bystander was killed by a deflected bullet, and a black youth "accidentally" shot in Roxbury (the only instance where a citizen was permitted to read the investigation report). Fiske agreed that this happens every day in Boston, New York, and other large cities throughout the country.

Fiske thought the Internal Affairs Division could conduct

thorough and impartial investigations without civilian personnel. In his opinion, the only justifiable rationale for civilian personnel was the public's natural distrust of the police. In the end, Fiske told me not to be overly pessimistic. Widespread police reform could possibly begin in the spring or early summer, and he would surely do his best to see it through. When I asked again about reading the report he did not see how this was at all possible until "the general policy" was changed.

I spoke to Samuel Robinson and Gerald Berlin, both of the ACLU, about my conversation with Fiske. Robinson thought that the case had "worn itself out." No police reform could occur without adequate funds, which were grossly lacking in Boston. In five years, Robinson went on, we would be facing exactly the same problems, because in a sense they are eternal. Gerald Berlin admitted that the impossibility of combating police power left him frustrated and bitter. He knew the Civil Liberties Union was impotent against the police. The Boston Police Department, he said, could pacify the community indefinitely with such ineffectual reforms as establishing the Internal Affairs and Community Relations Divisions. To spend one's energy reforming these divisions is self-defeating, because they are effective sponges soaking up agitation and reform energy.

Thus my protest to the police was blunted into an innocuous drive for reform. The thought remains: how can police terror be effectively challenged?

I have made very little mention throughout this paper of my own continual fear of the Boston police. I have been rather dishonest in recounting many of the preceding scenes by implying a certain boldness and courage on my part; let me instantly deflate that. What was so frustrating about this entire case was that I was never really able to act upon "the courage of my convictions."

I don't know how much to blame myself and how much to blame a structure so overwhelming in its ability to keep itself intact that one person's courage, even if it exists, cannot be enough.

Triple Jeopardy

If you need hospital treatment, and if you are so poor that you must seek it at Boston City Hospital, and if you encounter the police at that point, you are in triple trouble. The police are likely to feel that if they abuse you, you are helpless to do anything about it. And they are probably right. Three Boston *Globe* reporters, Benjamin Taylor, Bob Sales, and Ken Hartnett reported on this.

One summer night in 1972, a Boston patrolman named Joseph Memmo was stabbed while fighting off three muggers, and was taken, in serious condition, to Boston City Hospital. Meanwhile, fellow policemen were searching through the South End for suspects. They picked up two black youths and brought them into Boston City Hospital for Memmo to look at. He pointed to one of them as an assailant, a twenty-year-old student at Northeastern University, Louis Ricketts.

Six months later, Ricketts was tried before a jury on charges of assault with intent to murder a policeman, and was acquitted on all counts. The *Globe* reportorial team says: "But a witness at the hospital says that police meted out their punishment to Ricketts that very night." They quote Dr. Jeb Boswell, Director of Emergency Services at Boston City Hospital: "He [Ricketts] was brought into an area where—it is alleged in writing by a witness—with his hands cuffed, he was beaten with fists by members of the Boston Police Department."

Ricketts was beaten and kicked and taken from the hospital without treatment, although he had a fractured nose. His attorney told the *Globe* reporters: "A security guard tried to stop it and they threatened him." Ricketts was a schoolteacher in New York City at the time the reporters were investigating the incident.

Blacks and young people at the hospital spoke of what they considered heavy-handed police treatment of patients who were troubled and therefore violent or insulting. One nurse talked about the police attitude: "They don't respect people. They use sheer force to deal with people because that's all they know."

The accident floor of Boston City Hospital is a very busy place. Every day, close to three hundred persons receive medical attention there, most of them poor people from Roxbury and the South End. Some are gunshot and knifing victims, some badly affected by drugs or alcohol. Often they are accompanied by distraught relatives and friends. Under these conditions, violence sometimes breaks out, and the hospital's security guards try to handle that. Sometimes they ask the police for help, and the police are helpful. But sometimes the police add to the violence, or initiate it themselves.

Dr. Boswell himself saw an incident where a young man was in a rage, screaming, and police had him face down on a hospital cart with his hands cuffed behind his back. He was completely under control, but when it came time to move him from the cart to a stretcher, the police jerked him off the cart with unnecessary brusqueness. Dr. Boswell spoke to the officers about this and was told to mind his own business.

Another incident was witnessed by Dr. Boswell, where a drunk spat on a policeman's uniform. The policeman said that the drunk would have to apologize after he sobered up, and he was whisked away by the police without medical attention. Dr. Boswell reported this incident. A Boston City Councilman, "Dapper" O'Neil, wrote to Dr. Boswell to complain about this report: "I am shocked to think that a report was made. In God's name, what would we do without the police. Support them, don't run them down."

The day after the spitting incident, the man who had been drunk returned to the hospital, and Dr. Boswell saw the imprint of a shoe sole on his chest. He wasn't sure where the imprint came from, but he worried about it.

Other incidents were reported to Dr. Boswell by hospital personnel. In one instance, a woman, arguing with a policeman, poked a finger into the officer's chest, whereupon he slapped her in the face. The hospital worker who reported the incident protested, and the policeman threw a wild punch at him.

In another case, a South Boston man, twenty years old, was in the hospital for treatment of a self-inflicted slash of his left wrist. He got into an argument with a policeman, and the policeman slapped him repeatedly. This was corroborated by a surgeon who saw the incident and heard the officer tell the patient he would break him in two.

Both these incidents were reported by the same hospital employee, a black man named Stephen Washington. This was daring of him, because few people in the City Hospital wanted to file reports on the police. The father of the young man who was slapped told reporters, "You put up a beef about the cops and you're down and out before you can get up."

Washington was being especially bold, because he had a record. In the fall of 1971 (a year before he filed these reports at Boston City Hospital) he had been brought into Dorchester court for nonsupport and was sentenced by Judge Jerome Troy to two years at Deer Island. He was then paroled, and hired by Boston City Hospital as an administrative assistant on the emergency floor. He had also been arrested in 1965 on a charge of attempted rape. Washington said this involved a prostitute, and the charge was dismissed.

On December 2, 1972, a week after Stephen Washington's report that police had slapped the young man from South Boston, Washington was arrested on a warrant charging him with rape. What was strange about the warrant was that it had been issued in mid-1971, a year and a half before, and had never been used to arrest him, although in the meantime he had been up before the courts on the nonsupport charge, sentenced, and paroled. When Washington was taken to the police station, he found City Councilman "Dapper" O'Neil there.

While under indictment, Washington, beginning to draw support from Boston's black community, was dismissed from his City Hospital job by the board of trustees of the hospital. Dr. Boswell said the effect of this would be to put fear into patients and hospital employees who might want to report encounters with the police. "I tell you, you are not going to hear about any more incidents for months on end because this thing with Steve Washington has had an excellent effect. A man has been put in jail. My people are intimidated. I'm intimidated. I'm impressed."

H.Z.

Aberration—or Pattern?

Police abuse of citizens is not a rare event. Even if one put together only the reports in newspapers it would add up to a recurring fact of everyday life. If one then considered how many incidents never make the newspapers, we confront a large phenomenon, of such great variety as to make dubious any claim that what we have are occasional errors, or the personality problems of particular policemen, or the characteristics of special neighborhoods. Note just a few of the instances reported over the past several years in Boston:

1. A man named Carl Battaglia wrote a letter to the Boston *Globe* on October 18, 1970, complaining of "police state tactics" he encountered, on a one-day visit to Boston from New York City:

"Last Friday night, somewhere around 8, I made the mistake of leaving an amiable group of my host's friends to help him shop for a late dinner. We drove to Charles Street, parked, entered Sharaf's and ordered the food. Within minutes, I heard shouts on the street and saw large groups of people running. I opened Sharaf's front door but was unable to get to the sidewalk because of spectators in my way.

"I had no sooner asked what the trouble was when I heard, 'Get him. Get him.' 'Who? Him?' 'No. Him!' In seconds, I was dragged through the crowd from the doorway by four or five city police, my arm wrenched behind my back. I was doubled over the front of a parked car, searched, told to 'shut up,' and, after some minutes (still doubled up), was pushed, yanked, and shoved to a paddy wagon, taken to a police station, and locked behind bars.

"Somewhere along the line my host had noticed my disappearance, came out of Sharaf's and yelled, 'What are you doing? That's my friend from New York City. He doesn't even live here.' The police told him to 'shut up' or he'd join me for a ride. During all of this, my comments to the police were: 'What are you doing?' 'You've made a mistake.' (If ever in a similar situation, avoid that one.) And 'Release my arm a little, you're hurting my shoulder.'

"I was charged first with sauntering and loitering, was later informed by my attorney that I allegedly called the Captain 'a fat pig' and by 12:15 A.M. I was released on bail and told to appear in court that morning by 9.

"At court I was told the charge now had been changed to idle and disorderly. I pleaded not guilty and the case was tried immediately. My testimony under oath was substantially the above recounting. In examining it, the city only posed the believability of anyone going to buy a dinner at 8:30 in the evening.

"A Lieutenant testified, under oath, to having asked me on three separate occasions to move, that I made disparaging and deprecatory remarks to and about his Captain and that my comments in general 'would have incited the crowd.'

"The Captain testified, under oath, that I had been 'instigating groups' and causing 'general disorder and dissension' on Charles Street from the twelfth to the nineteenth of this month. The general tenor of his testimony strongly suggested that I worked tirelessly at my task.

"Fortunately, evidence to the contrary proved I arrived in Boston the evening of the seventeenth. At this point the Judge rendered a verdict of not guilty."

2. In August of 1970, a Cambridge detective, Ronald Ellis, saw Steven Piorkowsky soliciting money from a pedestrian in Harvard Square, according to the detective. Piorkowsky, told that he was under arrest, ran off, allegedly knocking down motorcycle officer Arthur Yetman, who was coming to the aid of Ellis. Yetman and another officer, Benito Cappelo, caught Piorkowsky after a three-block chase, and, according to them, two men then interfered with the arrest, Lawrence McKinney, twenty-six, and Peter Main.

According to McKinney, he came out of his office in Harvard Square and saw seven policemen standing over a boy who was bleeding badly from a head wound. He said he asked a policeman what the boy had done and asked for the name of a policeman who had a foot on the boy's neck. They did not reply. He persisted, and was then seized by his hair and put into the police wagon. Later, he said, Piorkowsky, still unconscious, and Main, a photographer for the *Christian Science Monitor,* were thrown into the wagon with him.

The Boston *Globe,* reporting this incident, said Officer Cappelo was treated for facial cuts at a hospital, Piorkowsky was hospitalized with a concussion, and McKinney and Main were arraigned in Cambridge District Court on charges of disorderly conduct. Piorkowsky faced charges of vagrancy, assault and battery on a policeman, and disorderly conduct.

3. In April, 1970, the Boston *Globe* reported the following incident at Logan Airport:

"There was disorderly conduct yesterday at Logan Airport, but the students were the victims, not the perpetrators of it.

"It was a good group of students who gathered there to protest pollution. They were a very young group, disorganized, a bit silly, and naive.

"A crowd of newsmen and airline customers gathered around as the students sat on the floor around a half-dozen crude coffins. The kids sang (out of tune), threw flowers on the coffins and coughed a lot to emphasize their point.

"At all times they were polite as they handed out leaflets and if anyone was blocking the way it was the crowd of newsmen and onlookers.

"Most of the crowd was near the Trans World Airlines counter. TWA had courtesy men meet their customers at the door to make sure their tickets and baggage were processed. No one failed to make a flight.

"In the back rooms, behind the ticket counters, where VIP's usually are entertained, platoons of state police waited. They had been dispatched there earlier and were kept out of sight.

"Many of their fellow troopers and policemen had been injured, some quite seriously, just a week earlier in Harvard Square, and that involved students, too—one does not forget or forgive easily.

"From the back room all they knew was that a group of students was outside and they were there in case the students caused trouble. The troopers did not know how the kids outside were behaving. Perhaps it didn't matter.

"Then came the order to disperse. The portable loudspeaker would not work at first, so everyone yelled, 'Louder, louder.' When it did work many began coughing, but they got the message.

"The students were armed with flowers and words and leaflets.

"They began to move, en masse, as soon as the order was given. They had to pick up their coffins, with people in them, and this took a few seconds.

"Apparently it was not quick enough. The state police grabbed one boy by the hair. He had been carrying one end of a coffin. They pulled his head back and the coffin fell.

"Another girl, in a dropped coffin, was about to be hit when she yelled she was trying to get out. Apparently that was not fast enough either. She was shoved and dragged and arrested.

"Others, for no apparent reason, were clubbed and pulled by the hair. Most of the students, like most young people, have long hair, and a large patch torn from some one's head lay on the pavement.

"The sound of wood smashing into fragile skulls is frightening, sickening, and shameful. The police moved as would a pack of dogs against half-grown cats. There was random chaos.

"No one can say for certain how the violence started. Or why. Perhaps it was just one man who was tired and angry and impatient.

"What did happen was stupid and needless. It was hardly in keeping with the best traditions of the state police who, up to now, have had an excellent reputation for maintaining their cool."

4. Three young black people in a Jamaica Plain housing project, on August 31, 1972, claimed they were beaten by police, and filed charges with the Internal Affairs Division of the Boston Police Department.

According to their account, it all started when a group of white youths, drinking beer, came around late one evening to the housing project, shouting racial slurs and threatening to break windows. Police were called, and fifteen arrived, in seven cars. They began to clear the courtyard of the project, but, according to the blacks, were mostly chasing them away and making racial remarks.

Kevin Morton, a fifteen-year-old black youth, was carrying a table leg. Police took it away from him. He asked why they weren't chasing whites. Then, he said, several policemen responded by beating him about the knees with clubs, macing him, and handcuffing him.

His aunt, Yvonne Rushing, twenty-six, said she came to her nephew's aid when she saw he was being beaten, and then: "Police officers grabbed me and clubbed me in the back of the head. I was knocked to the ground. My hair was pulled and they were kicking me in the back of the head."

A sixteen-year-old black girl, Lynne Weekes, said a policeman clubbed her in the back of the head. An eyewitness said she saw Miss Weekes fly through the air and land on the ground, bleeding profusely.

5. In a high-speed auto chase that ended near Boston College, a fourteen-year-old Brookline boy was shot and killed by police, on August 12, 1970. Brookline police were reported to have spotted a stolen car, and began chasing it. They fired two shots. According to press accounts: "Details of the chase and shooting were sketchy because Brookline police declined to discuss the case and ignored questions by reporters."

6. In February, 1972, a traffic violation apparently led to the shooting of Cornell Thomas, a nineteen-year-old black Roxbury youth, by a black policeman. The policeman said that he stopped Thomas for driving the wrong way on a one-way street. Witnesses who were in the car with Thomas said that the officer pulled Thomas from the car and then shot him.

The inquest report on the case was kept closed, as were the records compiled by detectives from the District Attorney's office. A Dorchester District Court Judge, Margaret Scott, found the policeman had "justifiable cause" to shoot Thomas. An Assistant District Attorney, Newman A. Flanagan, handled the investigation and recommended that no action be taken against the policeman.

The dead boy's father, George Thomas, said the investigation was not a full one. He said that no investigators from the District Attorney's office asked to see the bullet-punctured jacket his son was wearing, and no one came to look at the car he was driving. There was nothing on the car to indicate that his son was in it when he was shot, he said. "It just doesn't add up. This seems to be an example for other police officers that they can shoot at will because nothing will happen."

Mr. Thomas said: "I raised that boy and had a lot of confidence in him and now they're telling me he was nothing."

7. Two "hot-pursuit" incidents in the Boston area: A police car chases a vehicle which has been reported stolen. It is

joined by other cars. In Braintree, the vehicle slams into the cement base of a utility pole and the fourteen-year-old driver is killed. . . . Two bank robbers flee in a car and are chased by an off-duty police officer. The officer's car collides with the side of the robbers' car, skids, slams head-on into a car containing a woman and her eleven-year-old daughter. Mother and daughter are killed. Police capture two men and recover $2,613.

Professor Robert Sheehan, of Northeastern University's School of Criminal Justice, speaks against hot pursuit: "Hot pursuit is a clear disregard for human life. We have a great tendency in this country to place property rights over human rights, a stolen car over the potential danger to human life."

8. What of the filing of complaints? In his unpublished essay, "Police Community Relations in Boston," Ronald Conheim writes that "in Boston, one may go to the police at their headquarters or district stations, the Mayor's Office of Human Rights, the Office of Public Service, and countless other community organizations." But, he notes, "all complaints are ultimately received by the Boston Police Department."

What happens when the police department investigates its own misconduct? Almost all the time—nothing. And sometimes, it is dangerous for a citizen to make such a complaint. Witness the case of Lawrence Jones, a black antipoverty worker from Dorchester, reported in the May, 1971, issue of *Docket*, published by the Civil Liberties Union of Massachusetts. Susan Bloch tells the story:

"One day in early March of this year, Jones and a friend drove from Dorchester into Roxbury on a shopping trip for clothing. On the way, they saw another friend, named Bob, who asked for a ride to a pawnshop, also in Roxbury. Since the clothing store was not far from the pawnshop, Jones agreed. When they arrived at the pawnshop Jones pulled up to the curb and Bob got out. As Bob began walking, he was stopped by a uniformed police officer and three plainclothes detectives and searched. The uniformed policeman took a 'B-B' shooter out of Bob's pocket. Bob was taken away by the three plainclothesmen.

"All this took place in plain view of Jones and his friend as they sat in their car. Though he is not a Black Panther, Jones was wearing two Panther buttons on his hat that day. His friend displayed nothing to reveal political affiliation. Just as Jones was about to drive away, he saw the uniformed police officer, now alone, approach the car. Without saying a word, the officer walked over to the driver's door, opened it, grabbed Jones by the arm, and pulled him out of the driver's seat. Together they walked around the car to the sidewalk, where the policeman placed Jones's hands on the hood of the car and told him to 'Spread 'em.'

"Jones did so and the police officer, now directly behind him, began to frisk him. Jones turned his head slightly to the right and asked, 'Hey, what am I being arrested for?' With that, the policeman billy-clubbed him across the bridge of his nose. Jones fell to the ground, stunned, his nose broken. The policeman then started to drag Jones toward the pawnshop. During the next few seconds the two men grappled with one another. Finally Jones was able to grab the policeman's billy club. The officer immediately drew his gun and commanded Jones to, 'Drop that billy or I'll kill you.' Jones dropped the club and was taken, under gunpoint, inside the pawnshop, where the policeman called for a paddy wagon.

"The incident was observed by at least forty persons, including Jones's friend, who remained in the car. But the trouble was not over. When Jones, now handcuffed, arrived at the Division Four stationhouse the policeman who had clubbed him now threw him out of the paddy wagon onto the pavement. Several policemen then proceeded to beat and kick Jones until he lost consciousness. He awoke in his cell only to be worked over by six or more police officers who, in groups of two, took turns beating and macing him, all the while switching hats to confuse Jones as to their true badge numbers.

"Jones was then booked and charged with assault and battery on a police officer. During the booking, a police officer standing behind him struck Jones across his handcuffed wrists. His left wrist was broken."

Then, what some might call a victory for justice took place. In Boston Municipal Court the next day, Judge Elijah Adlow found that no probable cause existed for stopping Jones and dismissed the charges against him.

Based on this, Jones then took two actions. He filed a suit under federal civil rights law asking damages from nine police officers. And he filed an administrative complaint with the Internal Affairs Division of the Boston Police Department. Two weeks later, he received a letter ordering him to appear in court on a violation of probation. It seems that the year before, Jones had been convicted of nonsupport of his wife and children and had been given an eighteen-month suspended sentence, on condition he pay fifty dollars a week for his family's support. He had not made these payments, and was now ordered to appear in Dorchester District Court.

The District Court ordered him to jail. On appeal, he was released until his case could come up in Superior Court.

There is no proof that he suddenly faced eighteen months in jail because he complained to the police department about his beating. But the coincidence is there, and he did receive an anonymous phone call offering to "go easy" on his probation violation if he withdrew the administrative complaint.

What happens when a citizen files a damage suit against police under federal civil rights law? First, it takes a long time for the case to come to court. Second, it is expensive, and complainants are usually not rich. Third, the results are rarely positive. In April, 1970, a federal court in Boston heard the case of two black soldiers from Fort Devens, Jackie Bellinger and Willie Patterson, who charged a patrolman of the Tactical Police Force with assaulting them. Bellinger received a scalp wound from an officer's nightstick that required twelve stitches. They sued for $100,000. The jury found that indeed, the policeman had beaten them wrongfully, depriving them of their constitutional rights and entitling them to damages. The Judge, Anthony Julian, then awarded damages of one dollar to Patterson, and two dollars to Bellinger.

H.Z.

Solutions

Here is the problem: In a country whose Constitution and laws pretend to protect us all from despotic power and grant us on paper all sorts of liberties, we are helpless, in our homes and on the streets, before the unrestrained power of the police. If we are poor, or if we are black, the chances of being abused by this power are much greater. But potentially, we are *all* subject to it, and it should be disturbing, even to a middle-class, substantial citizen of the community, that the police can maltreat him or her too if they choose.

What is the solution? We seem to put up with the abuses of the police because they are needed to deal with a much larger problem than their own behavior: the enormous, growing number of crimes committed by some citizens against others. And yet, the police are clearly not able to stop this shocking rate of crime. All they can do is single out a fraction of the most obvious offenders and put them behind bars, leaving at large all the basic factors in our society which breed crimes faster than any judge can sentence criminals. And the price we pay for this token protection is to make of our communities little police states.

Petty solutions are offered for a huge problem. Pay the police more, equip them better, enroll them in special classes, and so on. But none of this will change the fact that we live in a kind of society which breeds criminals like rabbits. A society that worships money, and yet deprives so many people of it. A society that advertises and exalts homes, automobiles, Caribbean trips, color television, and a million other possessions, and yet has not been able to organize its enormous wealth so as to give everybody a job and an income sufficient to get the things they want. A society that wastes hundreds of billions of dollars on instruments of death, that condones official violence on a mass scale, and then punishes individual violence on a small scale. A society that lets corporations legally take the wealth out of the earth here and abroad and monopolize it, and gives policemen guns to shoot some kid running away from a ten-dollar holdup.

We all live in an atmosphere of thievery and deception and violence, committed by the most powerful men in government and business. Why should we expect that youngsters growing up in the city slums will then obey the rules created by this government and business? And why should we expect that policemen will be able to avoid this atmosphere of violence and punishment which we breathe in from the time we are born?

So there are no small solutions, either to crime by private citizens, or crime by police.

But if the only solutions are big ones, which require changing the whole structure of society, of government, of business, changing the way of thinking about money and guns and human rights, what do we do in the meantime?

There just might be something we can do. Not on a national scale at first. That's too big. But locally, where we live, where people organizing together in a community might at least *begin* to create their own power to offset the power of politics, of business, of the police. Toward the end of this book we'll come to that.

H.Z.

Two: **COURTS**

Elijah Adlow's Court

by Howard Zinn with Arthur J. Kaufman,
Deborah Goldstein, Frederick Hayes,
Connie Galanis, Alan Bauer, David Sobel,
Arthur Werner, Mark Edell,
Susan Shalhoub, Judi Kaye, Thomas Kouba,
Richard Wayne, Joanne Taube,
Patricia Endel, John Racicot, Carolyn Jacoby,
John Carli, Joyce Harding

> The judge never looks up. He seems to sleep. But it is the sleep of cruelty.
> —Miss Madrigal, in *The Chalk Garden,* by Enid Bagnold

Judge Elijah Adlow retired in 1972 at seventy-seven as Chief Justice of the Boston Municipal Court. He had been on the bench forty years. Although he is gone now, he still epitomizes the justice that defendants have received, ever since any one can remember, and still receive, in the district courts of Boston. A newspaper item (the *Boston Globe*) of the fall of 1971 will introduce him.

> Chief Justice Elijah Adlow of the Municipal Court yesterday strongly criticized Massachusetts judges, the U.S. Supreme Court, hippies, and some prison reforms.
> Massachusetts judges, he declared, "have gone out on a limb to be lenient with criminals. . . ."

Adlow spoke at a luncheon meeting of the Executives Club of the Greater Boston Chamber of Commerce in the Sheraton-Plaza.

Dozens of my students sat in Adlow's court for days, weeks, months, and their reports were consistent with one another. His court was always an amusing place for court watchers, court officers, and a club of Adlow-admirers who came to laugh at the Judge's sallies. Arthur J. Kaufman gives an example:

"About an hour into the session His Honor rises from his chair, stands stiffly with his hands in his vest pockets and listens attentively to the testimony of a girl who had been the victim of a perverted purse snatcher. 'He asked me what color panties I wore and told me he wished I wore a black bra and black panties,' she says. 'Oh, he wanted a matching set,' Adlow responds. Laughter fills the courtroom. His Honor gives the offender a one-year prison sentence and then remarks: 'Why should young ladies be subjected to these experiences—they don't come out of it with a better disposition.' More laughter."

And Deborah Goldstein reports:

"Then there was the larceny case. A man was charged with stealing three sweaters from Jordan Marsh. As his case was being heard, I again felt how no one really gave a damn, and that a routine form was being filled in. The man spoke only very broken English and had a very heavy accent. He told the Judge that he spoke Hebrew. The man insisted that he had never done anything wrong, that he had not stolen anything, etc. He said that his wife had mistakenly put the sweaters in a bag he was carrying without telling him. This man was the first to whom Judge Adlow talked condescendingly that day, but he was by no means the last. Throughout the exposition of the case, everyone displayed a rather disgusting, patronizing attitude. As Judge Adlow gave the man one year's probation, he said, smiling: 'For one year you have to behave yourself. Don't take any sweaters.' And the people in the court laughed, which seemed to please Adlow immensely."

Frederick Hayes writes: "It is hard to take either Adlow or his court seriously when one enters it for the first time. The room itself is noisy, large, and drab, in contrast to Adlow, who is colorful, witty, and quite aware of the audience in his court. In fact Adlow not only looks a good deal like the late comedian Bert Lahr but seems to emulate him in the dispensation of justice as well. And it is quite true that Adlow is a funny man. Unfortunately, there is little humor to be found in sending people off to prison. So the jokes are used to thinly cover over the contempt that he has for anyone unlucky enough to come before his bench. Blacks and the poor fare especially poorly in this respect.

"At times, even his humorous veneer falls off and the man's blatant contempt for the defendant shines through. Three quotes that I personally heard:

"1. 'Well, you certainly look like a bookie.'

"2. (To a black man found guilty of pimping): 'If you want to do this stay among your own people.'

"3. (To another black man arrested for stealing): 'How often do *you* use drugs?' "

The new observer in Municipal Court is at first impressed with the number of times a judge, where there seems to be reasonable doubt about a person's guilt, where the evidence is puny, will not send the person to jail, but will put him on probation. After a while, the realization sets in that if this person comes into court again during the probation period, even if the evidence of guilt is weak, he stands a good chance of going to jail. In other words, two cases of dubious guilt become one certain jail sentence.

There is no time for deliberation in Municipal Court, and lives are disposed of, freedom is taken away—perhaps for years—in a matter of minutes. The same kinds of offenses come up again and again: drunkenness, theft, assault and battery, marijuana possession. As Deborah Goldstein says: "All the participants seemed to have the same bored look of having been through it all so many times before, and I got the feeling that it was all a game whose rules were prearranged and agreed upon and that had been often played by the same players. The Judge, however, seemed to be an amused spectator at times, surveying his domain serenely while stroking the side of his nose, or leaning back with a smile on his face."

A young black man was charged with being disorderly. He had been in a pizza place with what the police witness described as "known pimps and prostitutes." The man denied having bothered anyone. After finding him guilty and fining him $100, the Judge said, "You judge a man by the company he keeps." Deborah Goldstein comments: "This statement surprised me not a little. I had heard the saying before, certainly, but I had never heard it offered as an acknowledged part of legal philosophy. I guess I had always assumed that it was common knowledge that, at least, a man was supposed to be judged on the evidence in a given case."

The young black man protested the sentence. "I haven't done anything wrong."

Adlow retorted, "You haven't done anything right."

In all of the cases observed by Deborah Goldstein the lowest bail set was $1,000. Most were $2,500. "The Judge seemed to treat everyone as if he were a piece of dirt, but the lack of respect evident in his behavior was especially noticeable in the cases of the young (marijuana cases), the black, anyone who was *different*."

She kept referring, as so many of the observers did in the court of Adlow and others, to the rules and regulations of courtroom procedure, to the overwhelming atmosphere of subservience created by that procedure, giving everyone in the court (except those in charge) the feeling of powerlessness. What might seem trivial, she said, like being told when to stand up, when to sit down, not to speak, not to take notes, is important in creating that atmosphere. And while small things are made to seem important, the reverse takes place in that general loss of perspective: issues of life and death are pushed aside by petty technicalities. People arrested for protesting a war that has killed a million people are charged with "sauntering and loitering," and no larger issue than that is permitted to be discussed in the courtroom. As Deborah Goldstein says: "The result is that banalities become important, and things which are important become 'irrelevant to the facts of this case.' "

Connie Galanis wrote:

"Statistics just can't convey the experience of a court monitoring itself. . . . Adlow is something else. My friend and I were talking about the overall atmosphere of the courtroom. One day in court, when mostly everyone was laughing at one of Adlow's typical comments that was made at the expense of the defendant, my friend leaned over to me and said: 'You know those paintings of the French Revolution, where all the judges have on white wigs, and they are all sitting there pompous as hell, laughing hideously at the peasant before them? Well, that's what this scene reminds me of.'

"Is Adlow real? Statements like: 'Go back to the South, it's warmer there. That's where you belong. We don't need your kind around here,' spoken to a black prostitute . . . force me to acknowledge the fact that he is indeed real."

Four students—Alan Bauer, David Sobel, Arthur Werner, Mark Edell—sat in Adlow's court one day:

"A black man was being charged with attempted larceny. He was accused of attempting to steal a white woman's purse while mingling in a crowd at an MTA station. As the woman screamed, there happened to be a policeman in the crowd who instantly abducted the man. There were no witnesses involved and the purse was not even taken from the woman. It was only opened and nothing was removed. The black man had a prior record and in Judge Adlow's eyes the job he was holding was not steady. He was found guilty as charged and given two months in the workhouse. He certainly might have been guilty, but nothing was proven in court. He was judged completely on his color and prior record."

It is standard procedure in district court trials to discourage the defendant from appealing, in order to prevent clogging of the calendar of the Superior Court. This is done by the following formula, repeated endlessly in Boston Municipal Court and other district courts:

"Mr. X, you have been found guilty of——by this court and have been sentenced to six months in the house of correction. You have the right to appeal. Failing to appeal the case will suspend your sentence. Do you wish to appeal?"

Elijah Adlow, though he put his own peculiar personality on his court, was not alone. Nor did he represent a fading breed of judges. He represented a system of justice which we find, with different stamps of personality and locale, throughout the towns and cities and counties of the United States. It is more than a structural difficulty to be remedied by some reorganization, some new set of procedures. It is a state of mind about punishment, about people, about property, about human life. It is deep in our culture.

When, in the case of Sacco and Vanzetti, someone suggested a campaign to remove the Judge, the columnist Heywood Broun wrote: "Nor have I had much patience with any who would like to punish Thayer by impeachment or any other process. Unfrock him and his judicial robes would fall upon a pair of shoulders not different by the thickness of a fingernail."

Let's look at other district courts in this American city. Susan Christine Shalhoub writes:

"The first district courtroom I was ever in was the East Cambridge session, presided over by Judge Viola. The atmosphere was rather chaotic; much of what was said was inaudible from the spectators' seats. The Court Clerk, though, managed to speak in a loud, strong garble sounding for all the world like Cardinal Cushing saying the Rosary.

"Come to think of it, the Court and the Church have a lot in common as institutions go. Both have elaborate rituals which are piously adhered to; both find expedient the use of a formal language which serves to keep outsiders (defendants in the court, the congregation in the Church) in ignorance.

"I sat there five mornings in a row; it was not until a few days passed before I began to understand this three-ring circus before me is what passes for 'justice.' The actual judicial process, despite its outward confusion, is really rather mechanical. There is no time for it to be anything but—given the prevailing philosophy explained to me by an officer of the court: 'No matter what happens, everyone's gotta be out by noon.' "

Judi Kaye wrote:

"Where and how do I best relate my experiences at the Boston Municipal Court? Do I tell about the black man who was busted for possession of cocaine while his two white companions were found not guilty? Or about the unmarried mother arrested and sent to jail for being a common nightwalker? Do I question the shoplifting charge brought against a young mother caught shoplifting a pair of baby shoes? Do I smoke a joint tonight in honor of the two freaks busted for possession of marijuana. ('They were acting in a suspicious manner,' spoke the arresting officer. Nobody mentioned a search warrant.)

"Do I pity the drunk who staggered up to the railing of the dock to plead with the judge not to send him to Bridgewater? Do I cry for the black man charged with possession of a stolen vehicle and pleading his case before a white Judge?

"One gets tired of noting the number of times that a defendant was not adequately explained his right to counsel, given a fair bail, or given an explanation that he or she could appeal that bail. One wonders whether the man with the Spanish name even understands what the judge is saying. Each crime committed should not be determined by a defendant's previous record, yet many times the probation report is read before the finding is announced."

What many observers found in Boston Municipal Court others found in Roxbury District Court. There, in late 1972, a number of citizens petitioned for the suspension of Justice Samuel Eisenstadt for "his repeated illegal conduct in administering the law in the Municipal Court of the Roxbury District." The petition, addressed to Chief Justice Flaschner of the District Courts of Massachusetts, was supported by seventy-six affidavits and statements from lawyers, law students, witnesses, and citizen observers, covering cases over a period of nine months.

Mrs. Sarah Small, representing a community group in Roxbury, announced the filing of the petition and said: "The people of Roxbury are tired of being treated like dirt by Judge Samuel Eisenstadt. . . . Our observers have seen Judge Eisenstadt insult and verbally abuse defendants and witnesses. Our observers have seen Eisenstadt threaten witnesses with perjury and call them liars. We have seen Judge Eisenstadt make jokes out of the tragic fact that some people are drug addicts or prostitutes.

"The law of the commonwealth," she said, "is that a person is innocent until proven guilty beyond a reasonable doubt. But in Judge Eistenstadt's court it appears to be the other way around. In open court, Judge Eisenstadt has stated that when there is a question of credibility, he *always* believes the police."

Eisenstadt was accused of raising bail on defendants who claimed the right to appeal their sentences and of prejudice against black and Spanish-speaking people. The petition said he ignored the right of counsel in many cases, and in many cases never asked defendants if they wanted counsel. He also, it was charged, did not properly tell defendants of their right to remain silent, their right to produce witnesses, their right to cross-examine hostile witnesses.

In one case, where a stereo was stolen, the complaining witness and the prosecuting police officer explained to the Judge that the complainant had mistaken the defendant for another person of similar physical description. There was no evidence to contradict this, but Judge Eisenstadt insisted the defendant was guilty and sentenced him to two years at Deer Island.

In another case, a black cab driver and another black male were charged with kidnapping and assault and battery of a white woman. The complaining witness said she had been hysterical the night of the incident and couldn't remember what had happened, and the prosecuting attorney asked that the charges be dropped. But Judge Eisenstadt insisted on going ahead with the trial. Before the state had finished presenting its case, he said, he would call the licensing board and have the defendant's cab driver's license revoked. He also told the alleged victim that if she would not testify against the defendants he would send her to a mental institution.

As examples of Eisenstadt's lack of impartiality, the petition claimed that: the Judge addressed a male homosexual defendant as Miss, asked him why he did not get a girlfriend, suggested he might need psychiatric treatment, and laughed at him; in a case involving traffic violations, where defense counsel was explaining that the defendant was new to this country, Justice Eistenstadt suggested that someone ought to send him back to South America.

Eisenstadt, seventy-four years old, and on the bench since 1937, was retired—as was Adlow—by the Massachusetts law of 1972 retiring judges over seventy. But the pattern of less-than-justice goes beyond them. Touch any lower court and it is there. Thomas Kouba, spending a day in the West Roxbury District Court, reported on one procedural problem especially widespread in Massachusetts.

In Massachusetts, the district court trial is a kind of preliminary trial, which, if appealed, goes to Superior Court, and there is considered a trial de novo—that is, it starts from scratch, presumably, with all facts and arguments presented anew as if there had been no previous trial. Except, of course, that one outstanding bit of information cannot be ignored by judge and jury: the person standing before them had been found guilty in district court. But in district court, there is no requirement that a stenographic transcript be kept (if the defendant wants one, he must go to special lengths, and pay for it). As Kouba says: "This procedure does not encourage the defendant to appeal his case even when it is obviously justified. Without stenographic transcripts, the state's witnesses cannot be pinned down to what they have said."

"Reform" in the courts, as in the schools, often consists of erecting a new building. And so the dilapidated Roxbury Courthouse was replaced recently by a modern one. Richard Wayne describes his first trip to Roxbury District Court:

"To get to Roxbury District Court by public transportation you arrive at Dudley Station. Dudley Station is a relic of another era, a bus station and elevated train stop built over a half-century ago. The iron girds are drab green, encrusted with years of rust, making it appear like the forgotten hulk of an abandoned ship. Posters are pasted everywhere, graffiti is scrawled on the walls, broken bottles line the gutter. Dudley Station is dark even on the brightest days.

"Men wear loose-fitting overcoats covering their overalls. The young wear dungarees and sneakers. You don't see $40 boots and $200 winter coats. The women all look like working mothers, either coming or going to work. They look tired. You don't see white faces.

"The station is a little over two blocks from the court as you walk. On the way you pass four or five bars, a pizza shop or two, and the bail bondsman offices. There are a lot of people on the streets, but they don't appear to be going anywhere.

"As you look up from the narrow street, the courthouse appears. It is brand-new. It is made out of cement and glass on a big piece of property surrounded by a chain-link fence, a foot of barbed wire on its perimeter. The courthouse is alien to the composition of the community. The District Four Police Station is attached to it.

"Inside the courthouse you notice something immediately. The corridors are whitewashed covering the cold cement. It all appears unfriendly and sterile. Nothing except the doors are movable. The benches in the halls are bolted to the floor. Men in square-shouldered uniforms and men in three-piece suits talk rapidly as they bustle down the corridors. Most of these people are white. The people in the halls without the uniforms and suits are black. They're hunched over on the benches and leaning against the wall, sullen and quiet.

"The courtroom itself is white-walled and with no windows. The policemen in the court all sit over to one side, behind the prosecutor's table. A wooden rail separates the people from the lawyers and court officialdom. The judge's bench is set up high, overlooking the court. A court clerk sits directly below the judge's bench at a desk.

"Session in the District Court of Roxbury is scheduled to begin some time before ten A.M. A normal court day, however, rarely begins prior to ten. The morning session usually runs from ten to twelve and the afternoon session from two to four. This four-hour day is expected to carry the work of the court. In the recent uprising in Charles Street Jail it was pointed out that some people incarcerated there had been waiting for trials up to six months."

As for the trials themselves, Richard Wayne sees through his own eyes what others have seen countless times:

"Trials which take place in the district court deal either with crimes of property or are morals violations, crimes established as such by the ruling class, even though they are not specifically crimes against persons. They are, as social scientists have said, crimes without victims.

"Many people tried in district court are junkies. Their faces are old beyond their years, their eyes are bloodshot and drained. Their trials are often related to petty thefts which are committed to maintain their habits. A guilty plea is usually entered in these trials and the offender is released after a short detention. The sentence has nothing to do with curing the sickness that infected the defendant. The fact that this is a medical problem is not considered.

"Prostitutes are sentenced in a similar way, usually to ninety-day to six-month sentences. Not once did I ever see a pimp or male solicitor brought to trial.

"Brutality and violence characterize the presence of police in these communities. It was not once that we witnessed in Roxbury Court a defendant who appeared to be suffering lacerations on the morning of his arraignment. Without exception white prosecutors and smiling white defense attorneys helped sentence black men to prison.

"Those judges sitting on the bench who were black were more harsh than their white counterparts."

In a 1970 study by Stephen Bing and Stephen Rosenfeld, *The Quality of Justice in the Lower Criminal Courts of Metropolitan Boston,* the authors write about the juryless district courts that "the judge occupies, unchallenged, the most powerful position in the process." They also point out that police officers act as prosecuting attorneys in the district courts, and because of their lack of legal training, the judge often acts as prosecutorial questioner.

What Richard Wayne said about black judges in Roxbury Court was corroborated by Joanne Taube and Patricia Endel, sitting day after day in Judge Elwood S. McKenney's court. They say, "Judge McKenney enforces his authority by placing all of the participating parties in humiliating circumstances, by making personally degrading statements in open court. He establishes his absolute control in the courtroom.

"In the first instance it was the defendant who bore the brunt of Judge McKenney's short temper. The case in question was one of threatening an officer with a deadly weapon. After listening to various arguments Judge McKenney turned to the defendant and, before a group of thirty people, called him a child and said, 'You're not a criminal, you're just stupid.' "

Judge McKenney, they report, is obsessively conscious of the overburdened dockets and the lack of time to handle all cases. In his anxiety to save time, he often overlooks the defendant's rights, especially in not allowing the attorney (he *is* scrupulous about seeing that defendants are represented) enough time to talk with his client. He rarely gives the defendant's attorney an opportunity to present his case in full. On the other hand, they note, McKenney does give first-time offenders the lightest possible sentences or suspended sentences.

The oppression of the lower courts is such a mixture of big things (quality of counsel, prejudices of the judge) and little things (the atmosphere and procedures of the trial), as to make it defy any simple set of reforms; it demands change so fundamental in the whole culture as to bring with it totally new attitudes, new personnel, new institutions. Those "little things" which help cement the present system together are described with fresh, wondering eyes by John Racicot, who made thirteen or fourteen trips to the Third District Court in Cambridge.

He discovered, as so many others did, that it was hard to hear what was going on. The charges, read with auctioneer speed by a clerk, might be incomprehensible to the defendant. He found an average of five armed marshals in a quiet and apparently unthreatened courtroom. The atmosphere was one of intimidation, created by repeated "All stand" and "All be seated" depending on what the judge was doing.

More importantly, he found that "both the poor and minority groups tend to be convicted more often than whites or the rich." He was reminded of the maxim of ancient law: *"Luat in corpore, qui non habet in aere."* (Who cannot pay with money must pay with his body.) He did notice all the little things in court, but much more. "If only they were all little things! The truth is there are big things too. In the final analysis the problem with law and justice in America can be summed up in An-acharsis' words to Solon: "Laws are like spider webs; they hold the weak and delicate who are caught in their meshes, but are torn in pieces by the rich and powerful."

Carolyn Jacoby and John Carli, sitting in Roxbury Court day after day, took detailed notes. Here is one case they heard which suggests with what casualness, with what promptness, and failures of communication, human beings are sent off to jail.

Commonwealth v. Thomas Brown.

Black middle-aged male stands, faces clerk. Wears shirt and dark pants, moderately neat, holds jacket with both hands, fidgets underneath it.

JUDGE: Why didn't you appear in the court May the first, nineteen hundred and seventy-two, after having been released on a personal bail? Why didn't you come back?

DEFENDANT: I was sick.

CLERK: You were sick. *(Confers with Judge, who asks "What was wrong?" Time: fifteen seconds.)* What was wrong?

DEFENDANT: What was wrong?

CLERK: What was wrong? What is wrong?

DEFENDANT: Now?

CLERK: Now.

DEFENDANT: Nothing.

CLERK: You've been on default for almost a year, that's what the Judge wants to know. You said you were sick—what's wrong?

DEFENDANT: I was sick. *(Clerk confers with Judge. Time: twelve seconds.)*

CLERK: Court now orders that the Boston University Defenders Project represent you. *(Clerk confers with Judge. Time: twenty seconds.)* The court now orders that you recognize with sufficient sureties in the sum of two thousand dollars your appearance before this court February the second. You stand committed until this order has been complied with. You have the right to petition the Superior Court for reduction of this bail. *(The defendant is taken away.)*

Reporting on this and many other cases, Carolyn Jacoby, who was preparing to go to law school and had done a great deal of research on a number of questions of constitutional law, said: "What bothers me is, there's no hope for reform. You do a paper on constitutional due process—great, you're happy. Then you go into court, and all that falls apart."

The defendant becomes an inorganic speck in the judicial bureaucracy, devoid of humanity. Joyce Harding, after spending some time in Middlesex Superior Court, talks about this:

"The everyday life-and-death situation of the courthouses has become routinized and mundane to court officials. Day after day they see many cases of assault, robbery, drugs. They all become the same. The accused offender joins the ranks of hundreds of other such accused people. He becomes an offender, not a person. There's nothing special about him except to himself. He is an individual only to himself."

•

Gideon's Trumpet
and the Mass Defenders

by Paul Kaplan

> The right to be heard would be, in many cases, of little avail
> if it did not comprehend the right to be heard by counsel.
> > —Justice Sutherland of the U.S. Supreme Court
> > in *Powell v. Alabama*

Do poor people on trial get adequate counsel? They do now,
we are told. For a long time, they did not. But then came
Powell v. Alabama (1931) which established that in cases as
serious as murder, a defendant was entitled to adequate counsel. And then came *Gideon v. Wainright* (1963), in which the
Supreme Court insisted that even in lesser cases than murder,
indeed in all felony cases, there must be counsel. Lots of guilty
verdicts were overthrown, and those who see American history
as a continuous march toward justice pointed happily to the
victory of Clarence Earl Gideon, who had written to the Supreme Court from Florida State Prison, in pencil, on prison-
supplied lined paper. His case became one of the inspiring
success stories of America.

Seven years after the *Gideon* decision, Paul Kaplan, a Boston University student, went to work with the Massachusetts
Defenders Committee, set up for just the purpose of giving free
counsel to poor people charged with crimes. What he found
was that, in the real world of the lower courts, the *Gideon* case
did not mean much. The Mass Defenders (as the group is
known in Boston), although it is the chief source of counsel

for the poor, resembled "a mere legal formality to be met so that cases could be stamped by the court 'represented by counsel.' "

He writes about his year with the Mass Defenders in the following essay:

What is the quality of legal counsel provided for the poor today? For the tens of thousands of Boston citizens who are represented annually by the Massachusetts Defenders in court, the reply would be clearly: second-rate.

"Did you do it? . . . Do you have a record? . . . Are you on probation or parole now?" This is a typical conversation between a Mass Defenders lawyer and client, moments, if not seconds before the trial of a case in the district courts of Boston. Such a conversation may be the longest exchange the client would have with his or her lawyer.

Here is what I found in the Mass Defenders:

—Lawyers frequently went into court without interviewing their clients in depth; they took cases "on the fly," as the expression goes.

—What interviewing was done was mostly handled by students untrained in law.

—Few cases were appealed to the Superior Court.

—There were no black attorneys employed in the Boston office, although some 20 percent of the clients were black.

—The bail reform law recently passed by the state legislature was not utilized to the advantage of the clients.

—Administrative lawyers were often overtly hostile to people receiving welfare.

From my first day of work there, it was hard to find a lawyer who didn't believe that his defendants—who were referred to as "D's"—were guilty. The general feeling was: "They would not be here [at the Massachusetts Defenders office] unless they were guilty."

There were not enough lawyers, and too many clients. A

lawyer had an average of twenty cases a day, and so, not only were lawyers unable to interview the defendants themselves, but they considered themselves lucky to have time to read the interviews carefully. The lack of time to prepare cases not only diminished the attorney's efficiency; it also depersonalized the relationship between counsel and client. The result was assembly-line justice in a system that alleges the ideal of individualized justice.

When a young lawyer comes to work for Mass Defenders, his training is minimal, if any. One new attorney said: "I came to the office in the morning, I was given some cases and then told to go to Quincy District Court." Having been thrown out into the jungles of the district courts, the new attorney becomes a victim of Darwin's theory of the survival of the fittest—or, in this case, the survival of the perfunctory.

It is not surprising, in such a system, that clients should show distrust of their lawyers, especially those clients who, because they were unable to make bail, were held in jail. A defendant facing criminal charges would want a Mass Defender lawyer as much as a patient in a hospital who needed surgery would want a surgeon who averages twenty operations a day. Who would want to be the day's last operation?

One very hot day in August, 1971, I went to the Youth Service Board in Roslindale, where juvenile offenders were kept at that time, to interview a sixteen-year-old heroin addict, whom I will call Michael. I knew that Michael was charged with seven counts of armed robbery. I waited for him in the empty TV room, which contained one of the two fans on that floor, and which also seemed to be blowing the entire stench of the institution in my face.

The first thing Michael said as I introduced myself was: "I want a *real* lawyer, not any Mass Defender! You Mass Defender people work with the police." It was hard to get enough information from Michael to help in his own defense. Still, his case went forward in Boston Juvenile Court. The witnesses against him were seven cab drivers who claimed he robbed them. These were serious charges, and three of the complaints were turned into adult criminal complaints, to be tried in Suffolk Superior Court. Yet, the defense had no information except what it learned from the prosecution as the trial proceeded.

A young attorney, new with the Mass Defenders, who complained about the enormous case load, the lack of time for research, taking cases "on the fly," was told by one of the chief administrative lawyers: "We provide the defendants with free legal services; we don't have the time to hold their hands." Another was told that if he couldn't take it, he should quit. There were many lawyers on the waiting list who would like the opportunity to get court experience and to make contacts with the court personnel, judges, clerks, probation officers, and the police.

The Mass Defenders assumes that whether or not a defendant is entitled to counsel will be determined by the judge, and so it accepts only cases assigned by the court. This means that the defendant has to appear at his arraignment (his first appearance in court) without counsel, and only after the arraignment, when the judge has decided on counsel, has set bail, and has taken the defendant's plea, does Mass Defenders enter the scene. So that, on early, crucial determinations, the defendant is at a disadvantage.

Bail means freedom. The judge, in setting bail, relies on the probation department to supply the defendant's past record, the police prosecutor to describe the nature of the charge, and the defendant's lawyer (if one is present) to say something about the defendant's personal background. If, when the Mass Defenders enters the case, it tries to get a lower bail than has been set at the arraignment, it is placed in the position of challenging a judgment already made from the bench, rather than taking an affirmative part in the original decision.

The judge decides if the defendant can afford a lawyer, and

the procedure for deciding this varies from court to court. It may be: "Do you want me to appoint the Mass Defenders?" Or: "Oh, you were able to bail yourself out at the police station, I guess you can afford then to hire your own lawyer." It may take one to three weeks from the arraignment to the trial. At the end of the arraignment, the Mass Defenders lawyer, who has been appointed right there in the courtroom, will usually arrange for the defendant to be interviewed by a student, at the jail or at the Mass Defenders office. He may confer for a few minutes with the client, and in some cases do a partial interview. This brief conference is customarily the longest time the client has to confer with the lawyer.

Interviewing by an undergraduate student, who lacks a legal background, is at best a poor substitute for a trained lawyer. I did an interview with Mrs. G., who was charged with larceny of a $35 check (she cashed a check which was overdrawn). She had been deserted by her husband because of constant quarrels over money, and now lived with her five children in a $150-a-month apartment in Dorchester. She received $290.60 a month from the Welfare Department for the support of her children, so that after paying the rent she was left with $140 for food, clothing, electricity, and gas. At this time she was cooking on a single-burner electric hot plate, since the gas company had turned off her gas for nonpayment of bills.

Mrs. G. had cashed the check at a restaurant in Dorchester, and was willing to pay the $35 to the restaurant. She had been arrested at ten o'clock one morning at her apartment by a police officer who came there with a warrant. She was taken in a marked cruiser to court. She was not questioned, told of her rights, or searched. At court she was told by a court officer to plead not guilty; a Mass Defenders lawyer was assigned; the case was continued for nine days, when the trial would take place; and she was released without bail.

The interview disclosed that her husband, before deserting her, had given Mrs. G. a check for $35, and she did not know there were insufficient funds to cover it. Her husband owned and operated a small carpentry business, and a customer had given him this check.

If Mrs. G. had not been poor, her case would not have even come up in district court. People with money who cash checks with insufficient funds are able to handle such problems out of court. People without money have police come to their door and take them away.

The usual arresting procedure by police is done in less than a hospitable and courteous manner. It seems that one's treatment is contingent upon one's wealth and one's physical appearance. One person I interviewed was Freddy S., a thirty-year-old Puerto Rican who had been living in the United States for six years. Freddy couldn't read English, and barely spoke it. He was arrested in Dorchester in November, 1971, for driving an uninsured motor vehicle, without a license, and without an inspection sticker. He was handcuffed behind his back, brought to a police station, booked, and put in a cell overnight, before being taken to court. All this for motor vehicle violations that for someone else would have meant just a fine.

In the face of the discrimination and humiliation such defendants face before the police and the courts, it seemed uncalled for to me when one of the administrative lawyers at Mass Defenders said to me about the defendants: "Don't believe them, they would lie to their mothers."

The lawyers of Mass Defenders, usually of middle-class background and having gone through a process of education and training which inculcates middle-class attitudes and prejudices, were singularly unequipped to be sympathetic to lower-class clients. In this respect, they were like other lawyers, but shouldn't the defenders of poor people be of another sort? One lawyer's attitude toward his clients was: "These people on welfare are crooks. They're the prime reason for the spiraling tax rate."

Also, the system, by what it offers as rewards to promising young attorneys, encourages more conservative attitudes. One lawyer who left Mass Defenders entered the law firm of a district court judge in whose court the attorney had been assigned for several months. Another left to become a District Attorney. The distinction of being a District Attorney is a commonly sought-after position for a Mass Defender.

Employment at the Mass Defenders is considered by the lawyers as temporary employment and as a way of learning the trade—a type of legal internship. But the poor and black are the victims of these legal internships. For a recent graduate of law school, it is a good way to get courtroom experience. But since the salary paid by the state to the Defender is small, many maintain private practices.

Perhaps the Mass Defenders is only an extreme representation of the whole system of legal defense, in which there is always a gap between the background and interest of the attorney and that of the client, except that with poor clients, that gap is enormous. It may then be that the only long-term solution is to move away from professional attorneys toward organizations of people to defend themselves, pooling their resources and abilities and only using specially trained lawyers as consultants. For there is something fundamentally wrong in the way the defendant is treated as an object whose fate is decided by a corps of people—prosecutor, defending attorney, judge, jury—who seem to want to have little to do with the defendant.

In Camus' novel, *The Stranger*, the defendant Meursault says:

> It is always interesting even in the prisoner's dock, to hear oneself being talked about. And certainly in the speeches of my lawyer and the prosecuting counsel a great deal was said about me; more, in fact, about me personally than about my crime.
>
> Really there wasn't any very great difference between the

two speeches. Counsel for the defense raised his arms to heaven and pleaded guilty, but with extenuating circumstances. The Prosecutor made similar gestures; he agreed that I was guilty, but denied extenuating circumstances.

One thing about this phase of the trial was rather irksome. Quite often, interested as I was in what they had to say, I was tempted to put in a word, myself. But my lawyer had advised me not to. "You won't do your case any good by talking," he had warned me. In fact, there seemed to be a conspiracy to exclude me from the proceedings; I wasn't to have any say and my fate was to be decided out of hand.

The Rendition of Malik Hakim

From feudal times in Europe to black migration in the United States, people have come to the city to be free. They have usually been disappointed. The job in the city is enslaving; the housing is controlled by landlords; the streets are patrolled by the police on the watch for suspicious-looking people. Someone in trouble somewhere else, coming to the city in the hope of making a fresh start, had better watch out.

Anthony Burns discovered this in 1854. He had run away from slavery and came north to be free. But Congress passed a Fugitive Slave Law for people like him, and the authorities of Boston and the federal government were determined to abide by it (the national government had never been so scrupulous in enforcing the ban on the slave trade passed by Congress in 1808). They caught Anthony Burns, put him in chains, marched him over the dock onto the ship that would take him back into slavery.

Thoreau wrote at that time:

"I walk toward one of our ponds; but what signifies the beauty of nature when men are base? We walk to lakes to see our serenity reflected in them; when we are not serene we go not to them. . . . my investment in life here is worth many per cent less since Massachusetts last deliberately sent back an innocent man, Anthony Burns, to slavery."

Over a hundred years later, slavery was presumably gone—but not really for people sent to prison, and not really for blacks. And if you were both black and sent to prison, then what good were the Emancipation Proclamation and the Thirteenth Amendment and all the civil rights laws in the world? And if you ran away and went into a strange city to start a new life, to be free, your blackness would give you away, as in the old days. This is what Malik Hakim found out, in Boston, in the year 1970.

In the spring of 1971, Malik Hakim was a social worker in Roxbury, the black section of Boston, where he had arrived two and a half years earlier from Missouri. He was working with junkies, prostitutes, and street hustlers. He had just established the Malcolm X Foundation, to help young black people; he was a member of the Roxbury Crime Commission; he worked for the Joint Center for Inner City Change. The director of the Joint Center said of Hakim: "I don't want to lose him. He's a guy who's been on the trip, a guy you can have a nonjive relationship with. He keeps us dealing with realities rather than fantasies. You can't get another like him." He was thirty-seven, had found a wife in Boston, and was getting ready to bring his mother from Missouri.

The Ford Foundation, in early 1971, gave Hakim a grant to study Montessori education in Europe, and he went downtown to get a passport. He used his legal name, the one he had dropped when he arrived in Boston—Albert Bradford. A short time later, on May 13, 1971, FBI agents came to arrest him. One Albert Bradford was wanted in Missouri, they said, for a rape that had taken place on August 26, 1968, in St. Louis. That was the day he had left Missouri for Boston. Furthermore, he was wanted for jumping parole by leaving Missouri, where he had been paroled a few months earlier after spending sixteen years in the Missouri State Penitentiary on charges of rape and robbery.

Indeed, Malik Hakim was Albert Bradford. And he had

spent half his life—all of his adult life—in a Missouri prison
before he came to Boston. He had grown up in the St. Louis
ghetto, or, as Alan Latt [a student who investigated the Hakim
case] puts it, "the black ghetto, a place where hope is killed
before you are born and where despair is almost inherited."
At thirteen, he was into drugs, and soon he was "shooting
up"—an addict, a dropout, a misfit. ("Yes," Latt says, "another of America's living clichés.")

He was sixteen one December day in 1950 when, desperate
for money to buy dope, and armed with a gun, he got together with a fourteen-year-old friend, Clarence Bradley. They
started out on a robbery; in the course of it a white girl was
raped. Hakim later said: "I didn't take part in the rape of the
white girl. That was Teddie's [Bradley's] thing. . . . I was
a sixteen-year-old junkie and I was sick, man. I wasn't interested in no sex, black or white, giving it or taking it." He
said Bradley had raped the girl in another room, was tried in
juvenile court, sentenced to six years and served thirteen
months before being freed.

Hakim was persuaded by his attorney to plead guilty. The
attorney defended this later, saying: "St. Louis in 1951 was
a southern city. If we had let a jury decide, they would have
hung him." (Latt comments: "There's a man who fights for
his client.") The attorney went on: "If you put the prosecution through the expense of a trial in those days, they automatically asked for the toughest penalty. Here he had two
death penalties hanging over his head and the only way to
save him was the plea of guilty. He knew it and took it."
(Latt writes: "I want to vomit when I hear this. The money
it costs for a trial is equated with a man's life, and this is
justice, this is hell! There is no justice in law when to plead
guilty is the only road to existence!")

Hakim was told if he pled guilty he would get a twenty-
year sentence and be out in three. He was sentenced to three

life sentences, for robbery and two counts of rape. Latt wonders about this:

"A seventeen-year-old black boy, sitting under the pillars of the great white justice, looking at the judge, and the judge looking at him. . . . I wonder if you or anyone else would be scared? I wonder if your mind would be listening to every technical word that came out of your lawyer's mouth as he spoke, or if your eyes, mind, head, whatever would rather be focused on that judge and what he was thinking!"

In his fourteenth year in prison, Malik Hakim, now thirty-one years old, became deeply depressed. One day a guard found him hanging in his cell—he had made a rope from braided shirts. He was put under psychiatric care, then released, then sent to a training center, where he prepared for parole. In April, 1968, he was put on parole for the rest of his life.

Parole turned out to be a different kind of servitude. He was thirty-four, but he was told he could not live alone—he must live with his mother. He was given a job making $63 a week. He had learned to be a musician in prison, and was offered a job playing saxophone in a band, making $185 a week. He was not allowed to take it, because his parole officer said they served liquor where the band played. He wanted to play music for the kids in the park on Saturdays, but his parole officer said he could not because "he might start a riot."

Hakim had been visited in prison by Malcolm X, and had been enormously affected by their encounter. But now, he was not allowed to join any organizations, even the NAACP or the Urban League. All of these restrictions were working on him, and then came the final blow. He was told he could not get married, unless the parole officer approved of the woman, and if he married anyway, he would face parole violation and return to prison.

In August, 1968, Malik Hakim secretly left Missouri and

came to Boston. He began to work with young people, got a job with the Joint Center for Inner City Change, and then, two and a half years later, he was taken into custody by the FBI and held for extradition to Missouri.

He was released on bail and continued to work in Roxbury, while Governor Francis Sargent of Massachusetts made up his mind about signing the extradition papers to send him back to Missouri. The basic constitutional provision is in Article IV, Section 2:

> A person charged in any State with Treason, Felony, or other Crime, who shall flee from Justice, and be found in another State, shall on demand of the executive Authority of the State from which he fled, be delivered up, to be removed to the State having Jurisdiction of the Crime.

Congress in 1793 passed a law imposing this duty on governors, but a Supreme Court decision of 1861 ruled that no governor could be compelled to comply with such a court order. As constitutional authority E. S. Corwin has written, "governors of states have often refused compliance with a demand for extradition when in their opinion substantial justice required such refusal."

Between May and September, 1971, the black community campaigned to get Governor Sargent to refuse extradition. One leaflet was headed:

"WHO IS MALIK HAKIM?

"MALIK HAKIM, ALIAS ALBERT BRADFORD, IS THE DIRECTOR OF THE MALCOLM X FOUNDATION WHICH OPENED IN BOSTON, ON OCTOBER OF 1970. HE IS A FUGITIVE SLAVE!"

The new charge against Hakim was that, on the day he left Missouri, August 26, 1968, he had raped the woman owner of an art store on the block where he worked. The woman had been stabbed and beaten with a hammer, and had then staggered into the delicatessen next door, sometime between 4:15 and 4:45 P.M., according to Harvey Kopman, the owner of the delicatessen. Neither Bradford's employer nor a coworker remembered Bradford leaving his shop for any significant time between 2:30 and 5 P.M. This would seem to have ruled out Bradford as the assailant, but the police set the time of the attack as between 4:10 and 5:50 P.M., thus allowing time for him to have left work and committed the crime. Was this curious discrepancy between the recollection of the delicatessen owner and that of the police due to police overanxiety to link Hakim to the assault? The police said the victim identified Hakim from a photograph. But the photograph they showed her was eight years old, when his hair was different, and when he was without a moustache or beard, which he now had. Nevertheless, a grand jury indicted him, and the word went out over the teletype throughout the country, leading to his arrest thirty months later in Boston.

In late September 1971, despite the campaign, despite the pleas that Hakim had shown himself a good citizen during his three years in Boston, that he was a valuable member of the community, that he would not get a fair trial in Missouri, that his seventeen years in prison were more than enough punishment for anything he might have done, Governor Sargent signed the extradition papers. When the FBI came to arrest Hakim, he fled. Later, he said he didn't know who these men were—he saw a white man with a gun and he ran. In the chase, he jumped off an eight-foot ledge and injured both knees. He was then put in the Boston City Hospital, under guard, while work continued to make the Governor revoke his decision.

Hakim's wife went to see Governor Sargent. An aide of the Governor later said: "It was unbelievable. We had never heard anything like it before. She didn't beg or plead, she just put forth every conceivable argument. I think you could safely say the Governor was stunned by it." But he was not so stunned as to change his mind. His aide explained that in Malik's case (unlike a previous case where someone was wanted for parole violation and the Governor had not signed extradiction papers) these were serious charges. "To deny extradition the Governor would have to put himself in the place of a judge and jury."

There were more legal moves to be made, and Hakim's attorney, William Homans, a Clarence Darrow-like defender of poor and black people in Boston, succeeded in freeing Hakim temporarily because the Missouri papers were defective. When the papers were corrected, and the final order came through in early 1972 for Hakim to be returned to Missouri, this time with no delay, he had disappeared. As this is written, in June of 1972, he has still not been found. If and when he is found he will be returned to Missouri. The Constitution asks that, in 1972, a century after the rendition of Anthony Burns. The courts ask it, the Governor can explain it, and due process in our time will have worked its normal ways.

A man named Shahee, at the Malcolm X Foundation, told reporter Joe Klein of the *Phoenix* about how he'd met Malik:

"It was about three years ago. I was what you might call a wino. I was snorting dope and stuff too, but I was mostly drinking wine and hanging out on the street corner. One day this cat walks up and hands me a leaflet about this meeting they're gonna have. I ignore it, but two weeks later the same cat walked up and handed me the leaflet again and this time I decided to go.

"I went to the meeting, and he was talking about a lot of things, but mostly education. He said blacks had to be educated to their own blackness—and, you know, I never heard things like that before.

"I didn't convert all of a sudden, but I started coming around and listening to him. He taught me how to stand up and be a man."

Malik Hakim is hiding somewhere. But he is a man.

H.Z.

A Jury of One's Peers

> In all criminal prosecutions, the accused shall enjoy the right
> to a speedy and public trial, by an impartial jury . . .
> —Sixth Amendment to the Constitution

Can a jury be impartial if it is all white, and the defendant is all black? It is accepted now, at least in law, if not in the reality of actual juries chosen, that such a situation does not create impartiality. But problems other than racial have not been recognized. And one of them is that a jury of people over thirty may have difficulty being impartial when the defendant is young, and when his looks, manner, viewpoint, lifestyle are such as to antagonize a jury whose background is different. That, indeed, was the situation in the trial of Alan Lussier, young and weird looking, convicted of murder by a standard middle-aged jury, after a closing speech by the prosecuting attorney which was directed to the likely prejudices of such a jury.

Three Boston University students (not including any who wrote the report on the Lussier case) sat in on the Alan Lussier trial and took a special interest in the selection of the jury. They did some investigation of their own, and then they wrote:

"Phrases such as 'trial by jury' and 'judgment by one's peers' conjure up ideas of justice that have been instilled in us since childhood. However, in practice, the jury system is not what it professes to be in theory.

"The Lussier trial was the only murder trial that we had ever attended. . . . The Judge's power was all-encompassing. He was the godlike figure towering above everyone in a somber black robe, and the jurors respected him, cherished his power, sought his esteem. It seemed to us that he used emotional bribery in his relations with the juriors. He was their benefactor, and they looked toward him for guidance and instructions. They were made aware that their purpose was to reach a verdict.

"Because of the age difference and class distinction, the jury could not identify with Alan Lussier's rebellious looks and mannerisms. It may be, therefore, that the guilty verdict was inevitable.

"We did research for Attorney Lawrence Shubow's appeal of the case. His plea read: 'Now comes the defendant and moves that the court order the issuance of writs, and that the jury list does arbitrarily and systematically exclude young persons as a class.' "

The students came across a piece of field research done by Ed Warshauer, who was helping Jim Miller and Larry Shubow with the appeal. Warshauer wrote out an affidavit in which he stated that he had, on September 11, 1972, obtained a list of the array of jurors for the current sitting from the Suffolk Superior Court, Clerk's Office for Criminal Business. He then checked on 248 names and addresses on that list in the "Police Lists for Winthrop and Boston," available in the Boston Public Library, to find the ages of those people. He found 236 of the 248 (95 percent) were twenty-eight years of age and over. Of the 248, only one was identified as a student. The four students carried the research further and found that only two persons of the 248 (1 percent) were less than twenty-five years old.

Young people are a clear-cut group in the population and need to be represented on juries just like black people, women, working people, and any other kind of group from which one would have to draw jurors to give a defendant a jury of at least some of "his peers." The four students (Philippa Brophy, Dorothy Robinson, Nancy Friedman, Marcia Seligman), cited the Yale University psychologist Kenneth Keniston, who believes that young people growing up this past decade have had such a unique set of experiences as to give them a distinctive outlook on the world. Young people, the anthropologist Margaret Mead has said, are "natives" of the contemporary world, while their parents are "aliens" from another historical culture. Alan Lussier was tried by a jury which was completely alien to him, and which felt him alien to them. They decided he should spend the rest of his life in jail. Something is wrong.

H.Z.

The Unimportant Case:
José Gonzales

by John Flym

> . . . nor shall any state deprive any person of life, liberty or property, without due process of law; nor deny to any person within its jurisdiction the equal protection of the laws.
> —FOURTEENTH AMENDMENT TO THE CONSTITUTION

Criminal defense attorneys know that "unimportant" cases are the hardest to win. In a murder case, the defendant gets the benefit of all the technical rules of law. But minor offenses must be disposed of quickly—the system can't handle them all—and, to do so, judges and lawyers disregard the facts, violate the law, ignore the Constitution.

Judicial blackmail is used. A heavy penalty is held over the defendant's head until he agrees to "cop a plea" (plead guilty) in return for a milder penalty. Ninety percent of the defendants, fearful, feeling their powerlessness, do this.

In small cases, defense lawyers work mainly to negotiate such a plea between client and prosecutor, with little or no investigation of the facts or the law. When the punishment is less severe than life imprisonment, the truth is treated as unimportant. Lawyers who fight as hard in small cases as they do in big ones infuriate judges—they are clogging the system.

So, I was prepared to say no that day in the Turtle Restaurant in Cambridge when José Gonzales approached me to say he had heard I was a lawyer, he had no money, and he needed help. On top of all the other reasons, I was swamped with work—I had just started teaching in law school—and a small case may be as complex and time-consuming as a big one. When José finished telling me his story I knew it would be a complicated matter to handle.

We both knew that winning would be an uphill battle—a Puerto Rican in a small North Shore district court opposed by the police and the bureaucrats in an obscure case. And it would be hard to get a lawyer. For a few awkward moments, we measured each other's predicament—his desperation, my weariness.

Only one thing saved José Gonzales' case from getting the brush-off that almost all such cases get from lawyers (even "movement" lawyers): I decided to see if the seventeen members of my class in Criminal Procedure would agree to take it on as a group project. The next Thursday they listened to Gonzales tell his story and they decided to do it.

Here is what he told us, in brief:

José was a cab driver. On Sunday, February 4, 1973, he went to Plum Island with four Puerto Rican friends. On the way back, they noticed an empty wooden telephone cable spool by the roadside and thought it would make a good table. The spool was lying near a house owned by the Checkoways, Ocean Avenue, in Newburyport, people whom José knew. So he pulled over, walked up to the house, spoke briefly with Mrs. Checkoway, who said he could have the spool, and placed it in the trunk.

A quarter of a mile down the road, he was stopped by a police car, in company with an unmarked car. Police Chief Orfant was in the unmarked car and directed the activities of the policemen. Two more police cars arrived. José produced his license and registration, and then each occupant was required to show identification. When asked about the spool, José explained how he had acquired it, and offered to drive back to the Checkoways so that his story might be corroborated. The police declined the offer. They held on to José's license and ordered him to follow them to the station.

José waited at the police station forty-five minutes, and then the police announced that his license had been revoked in 1971. They now charged him with driving after revocation, and they kept his license. This was news to José; he had no idea his license had been revoked. As a cab driver, his job was dependent on that license.

After hearing José's account, my students went to work. They got an affidavit from the legal office of the telephone company stating that the spool was indeed abandoned. They got an affidavit from Mrs. Checkoway that she had given permission for José to take the spool. They got statements from the four Puerto Rican friends who were in the car with José when the police stopped him. They interviewed personnel of the Registry of Motor Vehicles about the alleged revocation in July, 1971; people at the Cambridge Hackney Licensing Bureau which licensed José in September, 1971; owners of the Brattle Cab Company where José had worked since then; and personnel of the Cambridge District Court regarding minor traffic violations in August, 1970, which seemed to be the cause of the revocation. Also, the students had to analyze the extremely complex provisions of the Massachusetts law on motor vehicle licenses.

Here's what they found out (and what lawyers handling such a "small" case rarely have the time to find out—unless the defendant is wealthy):

It all started in the summer of 1970 when José Gonzales, needing a driver's license so that he could get some sort of a job, obtained a learner's permit. Shortly after, he was stopped by a policeman in Harvard Square for driving an automobile without an inspection sticker, and it was noted that he was driving alone. A person with a learner's permit must have a licensed driver along.

That incident led to a chain of official actions which were so filled with improprieties and legal error as to make up a textbook case in bureaucratic nonsense:

1. When, two and a half months after the Harvard Square incident, José González received a summons from the Cambridge District Court, it violated state law (Chapter 90C, Section 2) which requires a complaint to be sworn within three days after the offense.

2. One of the complaints in that summons was false. It charged José with driving without a license, a more serious offense than what really happened, that he was driving with a learner's permit but unaccompanied by a licensed driver. (José pleaded guilty and was fined ten dollars on each charge.)

3. Three months later, in March, 1971, the Registry of Motor Vehicles issued José his driver's license. Since the law says a license cannot be issued unless the registrar decides ". . . the applicant is a proper person to receive it" (and the law requires that the Registry be notified "forthwith" by the courts of all traffic violations), presumably the registrar had decided so with José Gonzales. Yet, in May, the Registry sent José a certified letter notifying him his license might be suspended or revoked because of the August, 1970, traffic violations.

4. José had moved, and on the same day that the certified letter was sent to him, he went to the Registry to report his change of address. Apparently the Registry lost the 3-by-5 card on which a change of address was noted (although the records show he changed the address of registration of his truck on that day). The Registry also ignored the fact that its certified letter was returned unopened, and on July 12, 1971, sent him a notice that it had revoked his "right to operate" a motor vehicle. This notice was returned unopened. The Registry, again ignoring this fact, sent him another notice, on July

23, advising him that his "license" had been revoked, and this too was returned unopened. Under the law, as it stood then, a notice not received was invalid.

5. Although the notice to José in May referred to his learner's permit, and presumably the first July notice revoked that, there was no warning that his driver's license was being revoked. Yet the second July notice did just that, without warning or hearing. The Administrative Procedure Act provides that ". . . no agency shall revoke . . . any license unless it has first afforded the licensee the opportunity for hearing."

6. The May, 1971, notice of revocation gave as its reason that José, in the Harvard Square incident of August, 1970, had operated a motor vehicle improperly. There is much doubt whether the statute permits revocation in the case of a minor traffic violation (which by statute is punishable by fine only), and which had occurred nine months before.

7. With all these notices of revocation sent and returned, and José ignorant of them, he applied for a cab driver's license at Cambridge City Hall in the fall of 1971. The License Commission did its customary investigation, got the court records on his Harvard Square violations, checked with the Registry, and issued José his license. He began to drive for the Brattle Cab Company and continued, with no traffic violations, until February 4, 1973, when the arrest over the telephone cable spool took place. By that time, one and a half years had passed since his unopened notice of revocation, and by statute, a revocation in a case like this can be for only thirty days.

8. On top of all this, the arrest on February 4, 1973, was illegal—there is no statutory authority for police to stop automobile drivers without reason to believe a traffic violation is being committed. And so, by law, the "fruits" of such an illegal arrest (the discovery that his license had been revoked) could not be used against José.

On February 24, the trial of José Gonzales began in Newbury District Court. Twenty of us were there, a most unusual
defense "team" for such a case. We had witnesses, affidavits,
legal citations. We began to hook up our tape recorder (the
poor defendant's substitute for a stenographer) and the Judge
asked why so much fuss was being made for such a minor
charge. He called the attorneys on both sides to the bench,
decided it would be complicated, and said he would give
Gonzales "a break," send him back to the Registry of Motor
Vehicles for their decision, and set a new trial date for a month
later. Meanwhile, José would be out of work.

We went to the Registry. It was mobbed as usual, but we
finally saw a hearing officer, who listened, seemed not to understand the legal arguments, and said we would hear from
the Registry. Sure enough, a letter came from the Registry,
with a *new* notice of intent to revoke José's license, based on
his alleged failure in first getting his driver's license in March,
1971, to reveal his Harvard Square traffic violations.

Back to Newbury District Court. The Judge listened to our
legal arguments on the old revocation, shaking his head as if
in agreement. He then listened sympathetically to the argument that this new notice of revocation showed the Registry
considered José still had a legal license—otherwise what would
there be to revoke? And then he called the attorneys to the
bench, said he would give the defendant "a break," that we
should go back to the Registry for a hearing on the new notice,
and he would abide by the decision of that hearing, rather
than deciding now whether José Gonzales was guilty of driving
with a revoked license.

I declined his offer. Police Chief Orfant, who was acting
as prosecutor, urged that since the case "involved legal issues"
the Judge should "send it up"—that is, find the defendant
guilty in order that on appeal those legal issues would be resolved. The Judge found José guilty and imposed the mini-

mum fine. We gave notice of appeal. The Chief of Police was upset when I informed him that José would initiate a civil rights suit against him for the illegal arrest.

Back at the Registry a week later, for a hearing on the new notice. We asked that the hearing be recorded. The hearing officer refused. I produced a copy of the Administrative Procedure Act, which gives the right to have the hearing recorded. The officer said the only law he would go by was in a manual which he pulled out of his drawer. We left.

To date (May, 1973), no action has been taken on this hearing, so that it is impossible to appeal administratively. We could take aggressive civil action to force a decision. But it's too late. José was not able to drive, could not earn a living. After the second hearing at the Registry, he gave up. He went back to Puerto Rico, hoping to begin a small farm. He left without a penny to his name.

His appeal is still pending. He remains entitled to "due process." But he can never receive justice.

A "Prostitute" in Morrisey's Court

by Anne Wilson

I followed the case of a girl named Joann who found herself accused of prostitution. Her lawyer, Larry Shubow, suggested background reading for me. He asked me to be present during his conferences with Joann and the court appearances, and encouraged Joann and me to interrogate each other. Larry was always thoughtful and honest with us, which allowed the three of us to enjoy an unexpectedly trusting atmosphere.

This is Joann's story of the events leading up to her arrest. She had been at the Sugar Shack on the night of October 26, 1971. She had gone alone, but met some friends there, Michelle and Roberta. (She knew their names and addresses.) She left about an hour before closing time, about one A.M., and talked to Michelle outside for about ten minutes.

Then she walked alone from the Sugar Shack to the Auditorium subway stop area. She was walking on Newbury Street part of the way. It was a nice night and she was trying to decide whether to hitch home on Commonwealth Avenue or to take a taxi. However, she did not attempt to hitch. Near Auditorium station a man in a car pulled into the curb and asked which way she was heading. She answered that she was going out Commonwealth Avenue to Brighton. The man offered to take her and she got in. (Later she found out that this was Detective W. Donovan.) There was some small talk.

It was a private car with no radio. He propositioned her, asked her if she wanted a good screw. She played dumb and asked him what he meant. (Love or business?) He offered twenty-five dollars. She said, "That's interesting." She gave no positive response, but played along since she was getting a ride. He asked her where she was going again. He stated he was going to Commonwealth Avenue and Washington Street. She was planning on talking him into driving her home—a little farther.

At Charlesgate (near Kenmore Square) they stopped at a traffic light. In about a minute an MDC wagon [Metropolitan District Commission] also stopped at the light. Without saying anything to her, the detective got out of the car and called and signaled to the MDC driver, who was a distance away. (Joann does not think they were working together, because he was too far away.) The detective leaned back into the car (standing outside) and asked Joann what she wanted to be arrested for. She answered, "Jay walking," thinking he was joking. The detective then went to use the MDC wagon radio to call a Boston police wagon. It arrived about two minutes later. The detective never identified himself to Joann.

Detective Donovan took Joann's arm and "escorted" her to the wagon, which took her to District Four station. She asked the driver if he knew the officer's name and the driver told her. At District Four station she was booked and was permitted to make five phone calls (her baby-sitter was asleep). She was not told what the crime was or even officially that she was under arrest. Then she was taken to police headquarters (she was impressed by the "drive-in jail"). Although she had never been arrested before, she was not granted release on recognizance, but assigned two hundred dollars bail. The bail commissioner had to get out of bed. Instead of charging the usual 10 percent, he charged Joann fifty-five dollars, because, "That's what we charge the girls now." Joann was also fingerprinted and photographed. (She found it amusing when the photographers tried to take off a wig she wasn't wearing.) She was not questioned at either station. She was voluntarily searched. At approximately five-thirty A.M. she was released. Although she had asked several times, she still did not know the charges against her.

Joann is probably less vulnerable to the psychological strain of being judged by the "law" than most women in her situation. She reacts with cynical amusement to the courtroom "circus" and judges who "use women by night, judge them by day." Joann has friends who know various bondsmen, detectives, lawyers, and judges intimately, and she tends to think of them as part of the prostitution underground.

She thinks that prostitution should be legal and controlled by the government, which could set up health regulations like bimonthly medical examinations. She imagines a regulated quota of prostitutes, who would get licenses and pay estimated taxes like waitresses. When I asked her if she felt the present prostitution laws were unfair to women, she answered that they were unfair to both consenting adults; the law has no right to dictate conditions concerning sex. She added that the laws determining so-called "crimes against nature" were crimes against nature.

Larry's interest in the case was partially derived from his opinion that the prostitution laws are unfair to women, as it takes two to commit the crime, yet only the woman is prosecuted. Larry wanted me to find out if any women's groups would be interested in supporting and publicizing the issue. I talked to women in several groups in the area. None of their groups had absorbed many prostitutes and they therefore had no strong views on the subject, since they felt that the prostitutes should speak for themselves. This seemed like a sensible reluctance to take a stand on a problem complicated by the fact that some women feel terribly exploited in prostitution, while others feel freed by it.

Joann said that those women's liberationists who think that

the freest woman is a prostitute are wrong, because the freest woman is a whore (where money is not involved), who doesn't have to supply the demand, who can be discriminating in her choice. Joann is not sympathetic toward the women's lib movement. She thinks that the supermilitant ones have got sex problems. The abortion issue makes sense to her; she got one legally in Boston after fighting for it, but why should a fight be necessary? She's used to fighting and thinks the liberation movement is for middle-class white women who want their rights but don't expect to battle for them very hard as individuals.

Also Joann points out that freedom is a matter of getting from somewhere to somewhere and she doesn't trust the white woman's concept of freedom; it's too cold. Joann doesn't want job competition or to challenge men. She thinks first of sexual freedom and claims that the black woman has almost as much as the white man in this society. At any rate, she feels she has more freedom than the white woman.

Personal freedom is Joann's highest value. She's had experiences at different social levels. She knows what it's like to be on welfare. She also knows about activism; she has worked with SNCC (Student Nonviolent Coordinating Committee). A classless image of herself is accompanied by a sort of cynical existential curiosity—"experience for experience's sake." She loves to hear people out, discover their motives and "what goes on"; this usually involves playing at their games for a while. She did this with Detective Donovan. She admitted that if her mood, or the price, or his looks had been different, she might have complied. In other words, she dabbles in prostitution.

She also told me of an earlier occasion (she was eighteen), when she left her apartment to use the corner telephone and two cops started talking to her. They were playful, but they assumed she was a prostitute, took her picture unexpectedly, and told her she should have a "license," that is pay twenty dollars a night for as few hassles as possible. She let them deliver the whole speech. She was told not to worry about unmarked police cars, vice squad, narcotics squad, etc., because they (the cops) took care of them. They advised her to avoid freaks (they don't always pay), small foreign cars (they're not comfortable for business), and new cars (might be gangsters or pimps). "Your best bet is some old guy." They asked her for some money, but she had only three dollars. Since it was eleven P.M. at the time, they were suspicious and asked her if she was really in the business. She told them she was sort of sick, that she'd meet them later at three P.M., but never did. Her girlfriends say that there is a bulletin board of pictures and addresses of "licensed" girls in the police station. Joann was amazed and amused by this experience.

When Larry began working on Joann's case he hoped to make a motion challenging the present law which prosecutes only the female when both male and female are involved in the "crime." Joann's case was particularly suited to this plan because she had no prior arrests on her record. Irrelevant to the more ambitious goal, but nonetheless advantageous to the case was the possibility that the detective had not been on duty (no radio in his car), or that it might be a case of entrapment (solicitation by the police is an illegal arrest).

The familiar dilemma that Larry faced was that an attempt to improve the law would be detrimental to his client. She was likely to draw a harsher judgment if she made a decision to appeal the case to a superior court, a level at which Larry's motion had at least a chance to be taken seriously. If she pleaded guilty, she could get off with a minimum fine, while if she appealed (as far as possible) she risked paying out a lot of money, and perhaps receiving unwanted publicity, all for a very meager chance of success. When Larry and Joann discussed these problems, Joann seemed interested in seeing the law changed, but had no desire for martyrdom. She postponed her decision regarding appeal until the sentencing. However, she was determined at this time to plead "not guilty."

On October 27, Joann failed to appear in court because of illness. A warrant went out for her arrest.

On October 28, she appeared in court to have the default (for not appearing in court) removed and to have a date for a hearing set, but the clerk informed her lawyer (Morris Shubow, Larry Shubow's nephew) that this was not possible while the warrant for her arrest was still out. (It could not be located. It might have been in the mail.) Then Morris tried to find out through the assistant clerk what charges were being brought against his client. The clerk refused to give this information.

Morris reported this event to Joann and me, who were waiting in the hall. We decided on a new tactic; Joann, accompanied by Morris, went to the clerk to ask about the charges against herself. The clerk said, "I don't know who she is." Morris then identified himself as her lawyer and vouched for her identity. The clerk threatened to have Morris bodily removed and referred to him as a "fresh bastard." He added, as a helpful afterthought, that the bail commissioner might know the charge.

On October 29, the three of us waited in the hall again and learned that the warrant was still out. Although this was Joann's second voluntary appearance, she was still considered under arrest and had to appear in court from the dock, an event which statistically prejudices a judge against a defendant. Morris was finally given the official complaint, which was prostitution, the "indiscriminate offering of her body to men for hire."

A probation officer, an elderly woman, spoke to the Judge of Joann's "prior record"; that was her juvenile record, which is supposedly irrelevant in a district court. It seems that when Joann was fourteen she was arrested for "rioting." According to Joann, at eleven P.M., after a YMCA dance, she was waiting at a bus stop with about a dozen kids. Some boys had a fight. A cop ordered them to leave the bus stop and everybody did except Joann, who knew the last bus would be coming soon. They took her in.

In spite of the reference to her former record, the default was removed. This court experience was frightening for Joann, especially because in the dock a girl was coming down from heroin with constant screaming. Incidentally, these screams were mimicked or snickered at by cops, lawyers, the clerk, the guards, and Judge Francis Morrisey.

The trial was held on November 3. The first discernible event was the detective's reading of his official report. He said he had offered Joann a ride that night and she accepted. She had offered her services to him. He had said, "How much?" She had said, "$25,000." He had said, "So much?" She had said, "I'm a contortionist." (The courtroom was enjoying this.) They bargained down to $22.50. He stated that he had arrested Joann for offering her body for hire to motorists (note the plural) for $20.

Larry Shubow's first question directed to the detective was, "Did you at any time suspect the defendant was teasing you?" The detective answered that he thought she was dead serious when they got to $22.50. However, he testified that no money had actually exchanged hands, that he only assumed she would accept the money, and also that he had not seen her approach any other motorists. Larry reminded the Judge that evidence of the solicitation of one man does not legally constitute prostitution. Since the testimony differed from the written report, the latter was corrected to omit the plural.

The Judge offered to continue the case without a finding for a year or until the defendant and her lawyer could meet in the Judge's chambers and show that the defendant was on good behavior (that is, she has a job, and stays off the streets). At this time the charges would be dismissed. However, the record is not erased and would count against Joann in any future case. Larry wanted to appeal, but since it would cost Joann more than she would be likely to gain, and since she seemed happy with the Judge's offer, he advised her to accept it. She did this.

Although the courtroom regulars were amused at the detective's report, the high point of amusement occurred when Larry began to talk about the laws—evidently a ridiculous thing to do in a district court. It must have been a rare event, but it was obviously inspiring to one lawyer, who was the defense in a prostitution case that followed immediately in the same court. He tried to imitate Larry's performance, but he became overly emotional and began shouting (with the fervor I imagine our forefathers possessed) about the antiquity of the prostitution laws, which have not been basically altered since the 19th century. The Judge rolled his eyes toward heaven, rubbed his forehead and moaned, "God, am I going to have a rough morning."

Outside the courtroom a cop came up to Larry. "What are you trying to make a federal case for? She's just a whore." He gave a knowing wink and a pat on the back. Larry winced.

Meanwhile Joann was a few feet away and there was Detective Donovan with his arm around her. They were both smiling. He said, "Sometimes we have to play dirty." Joann said she didn't care anymore, because it was all over. But she wished he hadn't told "all those lies." He repeated, "Well, sometimes we just have to play dirty."

Detectives earn an extra payment each time they appear in court. Also, Donovan would probably lose his job if he didn't bring a certain number of girls to court each week. The post-trial behavior of the detective was very confusing to me. It seemed like hard-core sadism, but Joann seemed to like him; I guess it was that comradeship of the underground she'd mentioned earlier.

Joann told me many stories of courtroom sadism. She had

a friend who was on trial for nonsupport in Chief Judge Adlow's court. Both his wife and his girlfriend had just given birth to twins. Adlow looked down at the papers before him and announced solemnly, "I guess we'll have to amputate." The clerk seconded Adlow. Joann reported that her friend nearly fainted with fear. He had no reason not to believe what he had heard. After a pause, Adlow said, "I guess we'll have to amputate part of his salary every week." The courtroom burst out laughing.

Francis Morrisey, the Judge, has a comparatively liberal attitude toward wómen accused of prostitution; that is, he assumes them all guilty, fines them $100 to $300 and rarely sends them to jail. (He was once nominated by President Kennedy for a federal judgeship, but a question came up concerning the validity of his enrollment in a Georgia law school, and he voluntarily withdrew his name.)

The Judge had offered the "continued without a finding" outcome to Larry before the trial began, after looking at Joann's minimal prior record. Thus, he judged Joann guilty before the trial took place, and Larry and Joann didn't want to accept that. So they fought, in the impossible jungle of the lower court system, and lost.

Commonwealth v. Jones:
The Case of Pepé

by Phyllis Kachinsky

> Wherever the title of streets and parks may rest, they have
> immemorially been held in trust for the use of the public and,
> time out of mind, have been used for purposes of assembly,
> communicating thoughts between citizens, and discussing pub-
> lic questions.
>
> —Justice Roberts, in *Hague v. CIO* (1939),
> for the Supreme Court

The above quotation seems to fit a common-sense and widespread conviction among Americans that our Constitution
grants the right to speak freely and distribute literature freely,
especially in public places. "This is a free country." But it is
not the first, and not the last word by the Supreme Court,
which has made the absolute words of the First Amendment
to the Constitution ("Congress shall make no law . . .
abridging the freedom of speech or of the press . . .") relative and uncertain. Men and women have gone to prison in
this country for saying things, printing things, distributing
literature, and their imprisonment has been upheld by the
Supreme Court.

So the Supreme Court is not a dependable protector of free
expression. Furthermore, very few such issues even get to be
considered by the Court. Almost all of them are settled long
before that, by the policeman on the street, or by the lower

courts all over this country. And they pay little attention to the Constitution, or to Supreme Court decisions. If a policeman or a judge, or some power in the community respected by the policeman or judge, doesn't like what is being said, what is being printed, they can remove the freedom of expression, if they choose. Protesters and radicals are in special jeopardy in such instances. The excuses given by the policeman on the spot, and later in court, vary: disorderly conduct, blocking the street, loitering, failure to get a permit, or (as in one case where a group of young people were arrested for distributing antiwar literature in front of a high school just outside of Boston), "promoting anarchy."

Phyllis Kachinsky, a student of mine in 1968, wrote about the case of her friend Pepé Jones, as follows:

On July 3, 1968, David Owen Jones, alias Pepé (his nickname), was arrested in Harvard Square, Cambridge, and later tried for assault and battery on a police officer. This is an account of his arrest and trial.

Pepé arrived at Harvard Square about nine in the morning on July 3, 1968, with a bundle of two hundred copies of the *Daily World,* a left-wing newspaper, to sell in the area of the Harvard Coop. At about eleven o'clock, a Cambridge police captain came by and said that it was all right for Pepé to distribute the literature. At 6:30 P.M., Pepé was still there, and Officer Woodrow Curtis came by and told Pepé to pick up his papers and "get the hell out of here."

Since it was getting late, and he had sold many of his papers, Pepé decided to leave at the officer's demand. It took him a while to pick up his papers, because one arm was in a sling; he had had an accident at work. Officer Curtis, while watching Pepé trying to gather his papers, insisted, "Didn't I tell you to get out of here?"

Pepé answered, "I'm going."

According to Pepé, the officer then prodded him along,

pushed him into traffic, and told him to run. Pepé proceeded to run across Brattle Street, and the officer chased after him. Pepé said he turned around to see the officer unstrap his holster. Fearful, Pepé stopped, put up his hands, and dropped his remaining papers. On Boylston Street, two more police officers descended on him and began to beat him.

William Bunting (who, it turned out, was the son of the president of Radciffe College) was walking by. He saw the whole incident, went over to where Pepé and the police were struggling, and asked Officer Curtis for his badge number. Curtis told him to leave, but Bunting refused and continued to demand the badge number. Curtis began to beat Bunting, arrested him, and threatened to arrest his wife, who was standing close by.

Bunting and Pepé were both arrested. Bunting was charged with disturbing the peace, Pepé with being rude and disorderly, disturbing the peace, and assault and battery on a police officer. Later, the charge against Bunting was dropped, and the only charge kept against Pepé was the most serious one—assault and battery on a police officer. The assault and battery, Curtis said, consisted of the fact that before the chase across Brattle Street, Pepé turned around and spat at him.

On the day after the incident, July 4, 1968, the following article appeared in the Boston *Record American:*

The twenty-three-year-old son of the president of Radcliffe College was arrested on a charge of disturbing the peace last night by a Cambridge patrolman who was holding a prisoner in Harvard Square. William Bunting of 76 Brattle Street, son of Dr. Mary I. Bunting of Radcliffe, was released on personal recognizance after being booked at police headquarters. He was ordered to appear in East Cambridge District Court tomorrow morning.

Patrolman Woodrow Curtis on duty said he instructed a newsboy, David O. Jones, 24, of 18 Mt. Vernon Street,

Cambridge, to move a bundle of newspapers that Curtis claimed was blocking the sidewalk in front of the Harvard Cooperative Store.

The officer said Jones refused to move the bundle, yelled something to the effect, "Buy the newspaper the police don't want you to read," and then spit at Curtis and ran. Curtis said he chased Jones and lost his hat and glasses in the pursuit. He said he caught Jones on Boylston Street. While he was struggling with him, Bunting appeared on the scene.

Curtis said Bunting's "persistent questioning" concerning the arrest attracted a crowd and Curtis told Bunting to leave. When he allegedly did not, the Radcliffe College president's son was also placed under arrest.

Jones was charged with assault and battery and obstructing a public way.

On July 15, the first trial took place. The following description of the hearing is from the notes of Attorney Gabriel Kantrovitz, who handled the entire case.

Officer Curtis testified that on July 3, at 6:15, in front of the Harvard Coop, he found the defendant with his newspapers on the sidewalk. He told Pepé to stop yelling and remove the papers. Pepé walked away with the papers, calling "Get the papers the police don't want you to read." Curtis followed Pepé to the corner of Massachusetts Avenue and Brattle Street where Pepé allegedly spat in Curtis' face. A chase ensued until Pepé threw up his hands and dropped the papers. Two more officers came by.

Bunting testified he heard Curtis say, "Get the hell out of here." Bunting saw Curtis raise his arm and bring it down; he saw Pepé run. He saw Curtis with his hands on his gun but never saw the gun out of the holster. Bunting went up to Curtis and asked his name and badge number. Curtis told him to leave and when he refused, Curtis grabbed him and threw him against the wall. Bunting testified that Pepé's voice was lower than that of other newsboys and that Curtis' voice was the loudest. Bunting felt that Curtis was inciting the entire incident.

Mrs. Bunting testified that she came from the drugstore and heard Curtis say, "Get the hell out of here." Pepé walked to the curb and Curtis then said, "Didn't I tell you to leave?" Pepé answered, "I'm waiting for the lights to change." Mrs. Bunting saw Curtis raise his hand as if to hit Pepé.

Dr. Benito Rakouver, an administrator and teacher connected with thirteen black colleges, was another witness. He testified that he was at the corner of Massachusetts Avenue and Brattle Street at 6:15 P.M., waiting for the lights to change. He heard Curtis say, "Didn't I tell you to get out of here?" Pepé said, "I'm leaving." Curtis: "Get going." Pepé: "The lights are red." Rakouver saw the officer hit Jones across the back and prod him to run. Pepé's right hand was bandaged and Curtis seemed to be hurting him. He saw Bunting ask for Curtis' badge number and get thrown against the wall. Rakouver testified that he never saw Pepé spit. Rakouver was standing at the same corner at the same time that Curtis claimed the spitting took place.

Pepé testified that when he stopped running and put his hands into the air, Curtis came from behind and grabbed the back of his shirt and his bad arm and threw him against a car. The other policemen grabbed him and threw him onto the ground and started beating him and dragged him across the street.

Curtis testified that "the force at which I apprehended the suspect forced us both to fall against a car and subsequently to the ground."

Pepé was declared guilty of the charge, assault and battery on a police officer. He chose to appeal the case.

At Pepé's second trial, probably because Pepé had no past police record in the state of Massachusetts, the Judge offered him the following option: either be tried and accept the verdict, or go free and stay out of trouble for six months. If Pepé took the latter and if he happened to get into trouble within the allotted time, this case would automatically come up again along with the new offense. Pepé chose to be tried, trusting in the integrity of his witnesses, the ability of his lawyer, and the strength of his argument. Pepé also feared a six-month probation because of his political activism, which often caused him to be in situations where an arrest might take place.

The trial was scheduled on January 1, 1969, but was postponed because Pepé had to go to California, where his father had just died. It took place on May 29, 1969, at Middlesex Superior Court, Cambridge.

". . . What has happened to me is only a single instance and as such of no great importance, . . . but it is representative of a misguided policy which is being directed against many other people as well," Franz Kafka wrote, in *The Trial*.

The six jurors who sat at the trial consisted of a return material checker (foreman), a housewife, a warehouse man, an industrial engineer, and archaeologist, and an IBM supervisor.

The District Attorney opened the trial with these remarks: "Jones did intentionally assault Curtis in Harvard Square. Curtis will tell you how he told Jones to move along. Curtis walked with Jones, who approached the officer and spat in his face."

Officer Curtis took the stand, and in his direct examination by the District Attorney he repeated essentially the story he told at the first trial: There was heavy traffic on the sidewalk, so Curtis asked Jones to stop yelling and to pick up the papers. Jones did this in about four or five minutes, and then walked about ten or fifteen feet and yelled, "Get the paper the police don't want you to read." Jones went along, and Curtis walked in the same direction, telling Jones to stop yelling and walk along. Jones spat in Curtis' face and took off running. Curtis proceeded to chase him.

The D.A. asked him if he drew his gun. Curtis said no. He said he held his gun as he ran so that it wouldn't swivel.

When Curtis caught Jones, there was a struggle. Then a couple of people interfered. Bunting wanted the name and number of the police officer. When Bunting didn't leave, he was placed under arrest. Jones was put under arrest on Boylston Street when Officer Curtis caught up with him. Curtis lost his sunglasses and hat in the chase.

In cross-examination, Attorney Kantrovitz asked if Jones did not have a right to be there. Curtis said, "No. I told him to move along." He said he never hit Jones. Curtis said he took hold of Jones by his upper arm, placed him under arrest, told Jones his rights, and charged him with assault and battery and disturbing the peace.

Kantrovitz asked Curtis if he saw Jones crying. Curtis answered yes, but that he was holding Jones by his upper arm, not the bandaged part. When Bunting came along, Curtis told the crowd gathering around to move along or they'd all be under arrest.

David Owen (Pepé) Jones took the stand and Kantrovitz questioned him. Jones said he had been working in July, but had to stop because of an injury, a chip fracture of the thumb. On July 3, his thumb was in a splint and his right arm was bandaged. At 11:30 on that day he came to Harvard Square with 150 *Daily World* newspapers to sell for ten cents each. He had never sold papers before. There, in front of the Coop, a captain or sergeant walked by and said, "There are so many papers now, I can't keep up with them." He examined the paper. Jones asked him if he needed a license, and the police officer said not if he was over twenty-one. Before Curtis came, other policemen walked by without incident. Jones testified that he sold the papers the same way all day, holding four or

five under his good arm and calling out for people to buy them.
At six o'clock there were other newsboys around selling the
Globe, Avatar and the Boston *Free Press*.

Curtis walked by at one time prior to 6:30 and didn't say
anything. At 6:30, Curtis told Jones to pick up his papers and
go. As he walked away, a man asked Jones if the policeman
was preventing him from selling papers. Jones said maybe the
cops don't like the material. The man bought a paper. Curtis
was behind Jones until they reached the corner of Massachusetts Avenue and Brattle Street. There the light read "Don't
Walk." Jones asked Curtis if he needed a license or if he had
broken any laws. Curtis, Jones said, called him a dirty son of
a bitch.

Jones testified that Curtis hit him, and he stumbled into the
street. Jones never turned around and confronted Curtis as the
policeman had testified and so couldn't have spit at him. Curtis
pushed Jones into the street, and Jones kept walking. Then
Curtis told Jones to run, and he ran. He turned, saw Curtis'
hand on his gun, stopped running, and put up his hands. Two
other police officers, one of whom was a sergeant, approached
them from the side. The officers converged, grabbing Jones's
hand. He fell against a Volkswagen, where they hit and kicked
him, bent back his bad arm, and dragged him across the street.
Jones lost his glasses and papers in the struggle. He asked the
officers to let go of his bad arm and to hold him in another
place.

Jones asked why he was being arrested, but was taken to the
station without being answered. The first time the spitting incident was mentioned was in court days later. At Boylston Street,
as Jones was apprehended by the police, Bunting came along
and asked for the policeman's badge number and the reason
for arrest, as he had seen everything. Curtis told Bunting that
it was none of his business and to leave, and when he didn't,
put Bunting against the wall and arrested him.

Pepé was cross-examined by the District Attorney. Jones

said that besides calling him a son of a bitch, Curtis called him a Communist. (Pepé had been warned that any mention of his political activities might prejudice the jury, but probably in the tenseness of testifying, it slipped out.) The officers kicked him twice and hit him. He had injuries on his ribs and his forehead and had to go to the emergency ward at a hospital.

Dr. Benito Rakouver took the stand for the defense and was examined by Attorney Kantrovitz. At 6:30 P.M. he was in Harvard Square, standing at the corner of Massachusetts Avenue and Brattle Street, waiting for the lights to change. He was standing right next to Jones and heard Officer Curtis say, "Didn't I tell you to get out of here?" Rakouver saw Curtis put his hand to his gun, but only to hold it in place. He never saw Jones raise his hands or spit at Curtis. Rakouver noted that Jones looked frightened and Curtis angry. He saw Curtis drop his glasses and hat and finally catch Jones at 17 Boylston Street and drag him to the Wursthaus, where two other police officers joined them, grabbing Jones's arms. Rakouver said Bunting came over with his questions, and when he didn't leave, was thrown against a wall. Jones was crying.

Under cross-examination, Rakouver said that the only profanity he heard was Curtis saying to Jones, "Get the hell out of here." Rakouver saw the policeman holding the bandaged part of Jones's hand, but he never saw the police kick Jones. He didn't see Curtis raise his hand to Jones at the traffic light. But neither did he see Jones spit. Rakouver claimed he saw them during the whole time, except when Jones fell between the cars.

Mrs. Bunting testified, and Kantrovitz questioned her:

Mr. Bunting could not be present at the trial as he was taking a final examination at school. On July 3, Mr. and Mrs. Bunting saw Jones for the first time at the corner of Massachusetts Avenue and Brattle Street. She heard Curtis say "Get the hell out of here." Then Jones said, "I'm waiting for the light to change." She saw Curtis' arm in the air as if to hit Jones, but she never saw Curtis strike him.

In front of the Wursthaus, Mr. Bunting approached Curtis and Jones, and asked for Curtis' badge number. Curtis told him to get the hell out of there. Bunting told him that he had a right to know, and he would take it to the City Council. Curtis told him to leave or be arrested. Curtis then took hold of Bunting and threw him against a wall. He also told Mrs. Bunting to leave, and then Dr. Rakouver came over to help Mrs. Bunting. She never saw Jones strike or spit at Curtis. Jones, she said, was crying. Mrs. Bunting didn't hear any conversation between Jones and Curtis as to why Jones was being arrested. She added that she hadn't known Jones or Rakouver before the incident.

After the recess, Attorney Gabriel Kantrovitz summed up for the jury:

It would be inane and ridiculous for an individual with a fractured right wrist and with a bundle of papers under his left arm to provoke or assault a person, especially a police officer. During the seven hours that Jones was selling papers, a number of police officers went by, but the sale of the papers made no difference to them, on a hot July day. Curtis came by at about six-thirty and told him to pick up the papers and go. The defendant had the right to sell papers and was relying on his constitutional right to do so.

What happened at the corner where the alleged spitting occurred? No witness except Officer Curtis said that Jones confronted Curtis and spit at him. No spitting was testified to by any of the third-party witnesses.

Mr. Bunting was resentful enough to ask Curtis for his badge number. Bunting obviously felt something unjust was happening. He didn't know Jones. He wound up in a police station. His wife was threatened with arrest. Jones sounds like a rational person; it would have been irrational to provoke an assault on a police officer.

The jury must establish that, beyond a reasonable doubt, Jones did spit at Officer Curtis—or else they must return with a finding of not guilty.

The District Attorney concluded:

Bunting and Rakouver said they didn't *see* Jones spit at Curtis. That doesn't mean that Jones didn't do it. Bunting and Rakouver weren't looking at Jones at the time. Curtis didn't arrest other newsboys, so Jones must have been disorderly. On the corner, Jones said Curtis called him a dirty son of a bitch, but Mrs. Bunting and Dr. Rakouver don't recall any conversation. Dr. Rakouver didn't recall Curtis lifting his arm. Jones got permission to sell newspapers at 11:00 A.M. Perhaps at that time, Jones wasn't disturbing anyone or blocking the sidewalk. His own witnesses contradict Jones in other incidents also, for example the kicking. The D.A. asked the jury to believe Officer Curtis beyond a reasonable doubt that the defendent did approach and spit at Curtis. Although that doesn't seem like much of an assault, it still was an assault. Dr. Rakouver testified that Curtis appeared angry and Jones appeared scared. Curtis would have been angry if he was just spit on, and Jones would be scared because he knew what would happen.

The Judge spoke to the jurors: The closing arguments are merely recollections of evidence, not evidence itself. The jurors must determine the credibility of a witness. Assault is an unlawful attempt to harm someone. Battery is the success of the assault. According to the presumption of innocence, Jones is assumed to be innocent before the trial began. He can be found guilty only upon evidence produced in the trial. No suspicions or surmises are evidence. The Commonwealth must prove the defendant guilty beyond a reasonable doubt. The decision must be unanimous. The issue in question is: Did Jones spit on Curtis?

The jury leaves. The trial is over. We await the verdict.

At 2:27 P.M. we are back in the Third District courtroom. Pepé is sitting quietly in the defendant's chair. The jury is back. At 2:30, the Judge enters. The foreman rises, the defendant rises. The foreman reads . . . *"Guilty."*

Pepé was merely fined fifty dollars. But the question is not how he was punished, but if any punishment was justified. The Constitution provides for the individual liberties of its citizens and their right to speak out against the existing norms. Something has been corrupted. Or perhaps it was always corrupt, and from its birth possessed its inevitable failure.

Solutions

Court reform is always on the agenda in America. And Massachusetts is one of the more enlightened, reform-minded states. But tinkering with the system—getting rid of a particular judge or judges, changing rules of procedure here and there, streamlining the bureaucracy—will surely not touch what is fundamental to local injustice in the courts. It will not touch the culture of rich and poor, in which the rich or fairly rich judge the poor and fairly poor—or the race-consciousness that goes back to slavery and is still deep in all our minds—or the prejudices of age against youth, or of established citizens (or citizens who believe themselves established and in danger because they are told so regularly, by political leaders and the media) against radicals and troublemakers.

As with other issues, the rights of people before the courts cannot wait for the economic and social and cultural structure of the country to be revolutionized. There must be an interim defense for people against the system of injustice, beyond token structural reforms, short of total overthrow. We suggest that such a defense might consist of local communities organizing themselves, not depending on reform from the top or on the most beneficent of leaders, but standing as a constant force, to overthrow bad judges, oversee trials, overturn decisions. Local courts have always done their deeds out of sight, and thus have been able to get away with shameful treatment of anonymous people. To put the work of courts into public view, to end that anonymity, to create a collective self-defense for people in a community, is an enormous job, and yet it is workable. In the last part of the book, we tell the story of the campaign of the people of Dorchester against Judge Troy. That is at least a beginning of a hint of what might be possible.

H.Z.

Three: **PRISONS**

Punishment

Excessive bail shall not be required, nor excessive fines imposed, nor cruel and unusual punishments inflicted.
—EIGHTH AMENDMENT TO THE CONSTITUTION

If, as Dostoevski said, "The degree of civilization in a society can be judged by entering its prisons," then it seems reasonable to say that the degree of justice in a society can be judged the same way. And if prisons are *in themselves,* monstrously inhuman and cruel (even if not unusual), then as long as we have prisons, we live in an unjust society.

It is the courts that send people into prison, and it may be expecting too much that the courts should stop this practice, but long ago, the Supreme Court made a statement which, if carefully observed today, would end the practice of imprisonment. In 1879, in the case of *Wilkerson v. Utah,* the Court, interpreting the Eighth Amendment to the Constitution, said it was "safe to affirm that punishment of torture, . . . and all others in the same line of unnecessary cruelty, are forbidden by that Amendment." All we need then, is general recognition that to imprison a person inside a cage, to deprive that person of human companionship, of mother and father and wife and children and friends, to treat that person as a subordinate creature, to subject that person to daily humiliation and reminders of his or her own powerlessness in

143

the face of authority, to put that person's daily wants in the hands of others who have total control over his life, is indeed *torture*, and thus falls within the decision of the Supreme Court a hundred years ago.

We need then to ask one more question: to decide if a practice is torture, shall we ask the torturers or shall we ask the tortured? Are not certain conditions, by their nature, definable only by the people who suffer them? Who but a black person can decide if he is being humiliated? Who but a woman can decide if she has been sexually abused? And so, we will have to listen to the prisoners to decide if what they are living with is torture, and if therefore, not just because the Supreme Court once said it, but because human compassion demands it, the practice of imprisoning people to punish them for past actions must end.

"We have been kidnapped from reality and subjected to life in a vacuum," a prisoner in Massachusetts wrote.

"If we are what we are being treated as, then we should be shot," wrote another.

Timothy Currier was sent to Deer Island House of Correction September 30, 1970, escaped October 16, and turned himself in November 2. He wrote a statement:

"OK, I'm an escaped prisoner from Deer Island and I'm a felon, and to some, that's all there is to it. Yet that's far from just it. I'm a man, a human being with feelings, wants, needs, and desires as all of us have. Prison life, especially prison life at Deer Island, is a useless and fruitless one. Wasted are long, long hours of my life, wasted are time, money, and effort—all of which are expended to solely maintain the prison and the prisoner. I don't want to be maintained or supported, and I don't want someone to pay my way. I do, however need support. I need the opportunity to get myself together, to concentrate on changing some of my attitudes, hangups and such, and I try, I try daily, seeing change as I go on. But I don't need to waste years solely trying to cope with the hassles, frustrations, and restrictions that are so abundant in our prisons. That is 95 percent of an existence in prison—trying to cope with incarceration. It leaves little room for constructive and meaningful things that help me along toward rehabilitation.

"I left prison because I couldn't stand the nothingness—the loneliness each and every day, every hour, every minute. I'm returning because there is nothing to be accomplished 'on the run.' I'm returning now because eventually I would anyway and I choose now. The 'criminal justice' machine is determined that I pay. It cares little of what seems most important to me, and this is my rehabilitation—my ability to reenter society and lead an in-the-bounds productive existence. I feel the people want this. They want their prisons, their correctional institutions to be corrective; they want prisoners to be released ready, willing, and able to settle down into an acceptable lifestyle. They want this, yet sometimes fail to see what that takes, and what it does not take. Simply, some things are inducive to change, positive change, and others are not. What causes change in me is similar to, if not the exact same things, that cause change in everyone. Allowing an existence that has me staring out of a window for eight hours and laying in my cell for the other sixteen, causes me to be stagnant, depressed, and bitter.

"Right now I'd like to plead with the people, all people, to try and cast aside any misconceptions they have about the convict, the ex-convict, the prisons. Try and understand that some of your impressions may be wrong. I would, I am, pleading with you to become aware, to become involved with prisons, with their administration, with their inmates, and with ex-inmates. I pray you let yourselves be heard. You have a lot to say about how our prisons are to be run. Your city and state government represents you. If you are apathetic, unaware, they are apathetic and unaware.

"It's not easy doing this, but I feel it's best. As I was out two weeks I hurt no one, stole nothing, and in answer to District Attorney of Middlesex County, Mr. Droney's, statement that I and the majority of men in prison are animals— that was a very irrational statement—I question his sanity. I wonder how it is possible for a man in his social position to harbor feelings such as those about human beings. As is the case so often, he does not know the man, just a record that says very little; and it is easy to classify and categorize, but Mr. Droney could never ever justify.

"We are not animals, we are human beings subjected to a great deal of degradation that makes our attempts to 'get it together' sometimes impossible. We need your help. In a sense I'm asking you to set us free. Help us change such despicable places as Charles St. Jail and Deer Island. Listen if you will, though distasteful at times, to the convict, to the ex-convict. Who knows more about his needs than himself? Please listen. . . ."

Who are the people who end up in prison in Massachusetts? Timothy Currier talks above about "such despicable places" as Charles Street Jail and Deer Island. In Charles Street, 60 percent of the inmates are black, in Deer Island, 68 percent. In Boston, 16 percent of the city is black.

But blackness is only part of the story. The poor are the ones who inhabit the jails. Is it because they commit the most crimes? They are the ones who most often *get caught* committing crimes, because they have the least resources for getting away with their crimes, for covering up their deeds, the least resources for paying fines, arranging bail, hiring first-class counsel, making the right contacts.

Consider these statistics about crimes of the rich and crimes of the poor, given by the President's Crime Commission and a 1969 study done in California:

Only 14 percent of the prison population consists of people who have committed "white-collar crimes" (embezzling, fraud, tax fraud, forgery). Yet their thievery added up to $1.7

billion in one recent year, while the crimes of the poor for the same year (robbery, burglary, auto theft, etc.) added up to $608 million, less than half.

In 1969, there were 502 convictions for tax fraud, each case averaging $190,000. Burglaries that year averaged $321 and car thefts averaged $992. But of the 502 businessmen and clerks convicted of fraud, only 20 percent ended up in jail, with sentences averaging seven months. For burglary and auto theft, 60 percent of those convicted ended up in prison, with sentences averaging eighteen months for auto theft, thirty-three months for burglary.

In the Boston area, people from poor neighborhoods are far more likely to go to jail. People with money enough to go to college don't end up in jail as often. In 1969, of prisoners sent to Walpole, Concord, Framingham, and Bridgewater, only 1 percent were college graduates; 73 percent had received an education from the sixth to the eleventh grade.

Anthony Marino writes about being a prisoner at Deer Island, which he calls "Devil's Island."

"I was sent here two months ago by Roxbury District Court to serve a two-year sentence for possession of drugs and drug-related thefts. A rehabilitation program person was in court in my behalf but the Judge listened to his pleas with deaf ears and told me I would get all the rehabilitation I needed here.

"Well I can't buy this kind of so-called rehabilitation.

"We get up about 7:30 A.M. and are herded to eat a cold breakfast and a cup of lukewarm coffee. Then we proceed to various shops—paint shop, machine shop, electrical shop, cutting room, and construction. These are nothing but hangouts where the cons stay during the day. There is no machinery of any kind in these shops, no work or job training unless you happen to be one of the select inmates who work in the officers' mess, administration building, or work release. These inmates are predominantly white and conformed to the ideas of the administrators in return for good food (officers' chow), cigarettes, and other special favors the guards give to 'good' cons.

"When I get to my shop along with twenty-seven cons, I can either watch cartoons or various TV quiz shows on the boob tube, play cards, or just bounce off the walls, which I usually do anyway. I cannot leave the shop until lunchtime, when the special today is spaghetti balls and meatballs. Yeah! That's right, spaghetti balls the size of a grapefruit which you can only get at Deer Island because the spaghetti is so starchy it sticks in big lump balls. It really is a task sitting down and trying to make a meal of it.

"Then you have to fight for a spoon because of the spoon shortage. I have seen an inmate eat with his hands because he didn't want to hassle waiting for another inmate to finish with his spoon, then having to wash it, only to be rushed out of the chow hall because it was time to go back to his cell. The other night I saw a kid eat jello out of his hands.

"After lunch it is back to the shop for a repeat of the morning's activities. At 3:30 everyone goes back to the chow hall for the final meal which might be cold soup; but by the time your turn comes up on the line, they are out of metal bowls. So you either take your soup in a small metal cup or on a flat metal tray.

"After supper you go back to your cell, which is approximately five by eight feet with a tiny cold-water sink, a commode, and an old army bed and if you're lucky a wooden chair or table. Then you get to amuse yourself somehow because you are in that cell until 7:30 next morning (fourteen hours) unless you happen to sleep in the dormitory. About 30 percent of the population is allowed to sleep in the dormitory, but the first openings go to the 'good' cons who are also the ones with the good jobs.

"There is hardly any rehabilitation here unless you like to play horseshoes.

"The administration encourages friction among the cons.

Many cons use dope (snuck in through visits or corrupt screws). There are frequent fights between cons over dope. Recently a con got stabbed and another bashed in the head with a chair leg, all of this relating to a dope incident. The administration does not care if the cons kill each other—it makes it easier for them to run the joint. Cons should channel their hostilities in the right direction and stop this foolishness.

"Relations between black and white cons are uptight. White racist guards favor white cons and encourage racist attitudes in white cons. For instance, there is a lot of noise going on in my block on a certain night. A white guard comes by my cell and says, 'They're noisy bastards, aren't they,' nodding his head toward the cell next to me, which is occupied by a black brother. I'm supposed to say, 'Yeah. They sure are and they stink too.' etc., by this making friends with the screw. Now when he sees me he might acknowledge my existence and say hi or put in a good word to the deputy for me so that I might get a good job, etc. But instead, I give him a look like he just crawled out of the nearest pigsty and he will probably call me a punk nigger lover to the other screws and racist white cons. I have heard racist conversations among the screws and racist cons about blacks and Puerto Ricans often. The administration is racist and there are three black guards representing a black inmate population of over 50 percent. These black guards have little or no voice in the administration and have it hard bidding for good jobs in the institution. . . .

"I was locked up in 1969 (a previous commitment) for supposedly laughing at an officer. My sentence was 'five days on the boards.' The boards mean that you are put in a cell on a segregated tier, with no clothes, no books, no smokes, no lights. You get a filthy mattress and an equally filthy blanket (no sheets, and a pillow is absurd). You are allowed one meal a day, and water. (You used to sleep on a board, that is where the name originated.) If this does not 'straighten you out,' you can be sent to Bridgewater. All cons fear Bridgewater, especially DSU—Departmental Segregation Unit, MCI Bridgewater. . . ."

A woman whose husband was in prison wrote about the ordeal of visiting him. She called it "The Crime of Loving." Her name is Linda Camisa:

"I write this in order to give you a brief look at the agony caused by loving a man in prison. It is hard to face the reality that the man you love is for some reason put in prison. Even harder is the visit, because of the rules imposed by the prison system itself. Because then you are also treated as a prisoner when the only crime you have committed is loving this man. And that, to me, is no crime.

"The major problem is the guards. They are the ones who dictate the do's and don'ts. I know that on many occasions visiting my husband at Norfolk, I've been told by guards not to hold his hands, not to put my arms around him, not to even sit in certain parts of the visiting room because actually they didn't want to have to turn their heads to keep the eye on you. You are watched constantly.

"You are always aware of their eyes checking you out; now and then a wise one will even proposition you.

"You also have problems such as, if you don't smile in a certain manner, or if you comment on something, then you may even wait an hour before you get to see your husband. Does anyone realize what it's like sitting in a crowded (or empty) visiting room for sixty minutes, waiting? Well, I do, and when it happened to me I also had my two children with me, ages four and five. Let me say that after riding one hour up there on a hot summer afternoon, sitting for another hour in a crowded hot visiting room with my children was very nerve-racking and upsetting to the children and me. Finally, by the time I saw my husband, I felt so uptight I wasn't much good for his morale. . . .

"Plus there is the hassle of getting there. I'm lucky enough to have access to a car; some people don't. Imagine being broke and wanting, needing desperately to see the man you love. I've seen days when I was terribly depressed over matters at home, the house, the kids, and mainly welfare. When the car was broken down, I was broke and had no way to see my husband. It hurts deep down when you can't visit the one you love, the only one who might make you feel alive, and make you realize you're loved and that better days are in the future (hopefully!)."

What happens when prisoners, feeling alone and incapable of getting even the smallest of reforms connected with visiting hours or food, or medical treatment, decide to organize? Norfolk and Walpole are the two maximum security institutions in Massachusetts, and in 1971, Norfolk prisoners began to organize, tried to negotiate with prison officials to get changes. The guards union was angry at this, and insisted that certain prisoners be shipped out of Norfolk to other institutions, or they would strike. On November 8, 1971, armed guards and state troopers, in a surprise raid, moved into cells at Norfolk, pulled out sixteen men, and shipped them out. One observer tells about it:

"By the time I finish this letter, maybe it will hurt less inside. But right now I feel drained, hurt, betrayed, and filled with a sickening anger. I wish there were some pay-back, but I can't think of one. It seems that they have all the cards. All the time, and it really sucks.

"All through the demonstration, committee meetings, negotiations, etc. there was one overriding theme. Amnesty. . . . In spite of all the reassurances by more experienced cons that the kinds of changes that we have been initiating would not go down without some kind of retaliation, I believed. Foolish Youth.

"Between one and two last night I was awakened (I've been a light sleeper since Vietnam) and I looked out my window. There were troopers. And screws. Lots. Armed with sidearms, and big clubs. They were going into dorms and taking people, all kinds of people.

"The only man I saw who had pants and a jacket on was Mike Riley. All the rest were near naked, and nearly all were barefoot. It was cold last night. Damn cold. In some houses guys did give the screws and troopers arguments. A lot of people are locked in Isolation here in the camp. But over sixteen guys were shipped. Some natural leaders, some friends, and a few that just have big mouths. . . .

"They took a friend of mine and it wasn't till late this afternoon that he could talk about it. He was able to tell it, because they decided, after getting him all the way out front, that they didn't want him. Being pulled outside in your underwear, at 1:30, in bare feet by two troopers and a house screw. Looking at those troops, with guns, and masks and clubs, with the moon shining off the helmets and the hate that you could see in their faces. Thinking that this is where these guys live, with the guns and the hate, and the helmets and masks, and you, you're trying to wake up, flashing on Kent State and Jackson, and Chicago. And Attica. Most of all Attica. . . ."

At Concord Prison, a medium-security institution, leaders and organizers were also shipped out, November 11, 1971, and one of those men tells about it:

"I and five others like me were awakened by six screws in my room about 1:00 Monday morning. I was told nothing but to dress. They all wore helmets and face shields and carried clubs. One screw said that if I didn't hurry up and dress he would drive his club through my head. I was then handcuffed.

"I was taken outside my unit where numerous state police stood at attention with very large clubs. Again I asked what was going on and was told the club through the head story again.

"I was brought through the trap and was being pushed through to an awaiting van. There a screw with a list said I was to go to Walpole, no Concord. I mean Walpole, no Concord, and while he was struggling to read his list and stammer he rammed his club into my throat. Like it was my fault he couldn't read his list.

"I then entered the van to see a friend of mine already there. He knew as little of what was happening as I.

"Upon arrival here we were released from the van two at a time. I was the last man out of the van and the guard that struck me with his club was standing outside the van with a carbine on his hip (like he must have seen *Cool Hand Luke* twelve times). Out of the side of his mouth he said, 'Go ahead. Make a move.' He was intimidating me to move so that he could blow me away. . . ."

One of the young leaders of the prison reform movement at Concord was Jerry Sousa, who, with others, was taken out of Concord in the night and dumped into Walpole, where he was immediately put into one of the segregation units, Block Nine (this means twenty-four hours a day alone in a cell). Sousa had been in Walpole only a short time when he got a report out:

"We are writing with a somber report regarding the circumstances and events leading up to and surrounding the death of prisoner Joseph Chesnulavich which occurred here an hour ago in Nine Block.

"Since Christmas eve, vicious prison guards here in Nine Block have created a reign of terror directed toward us prisoners. Four of us have been beaten, one who was prisoner Donald King.

"Other prisoners in an attempt to escape constant harassment and inhuman treatment, prisoner George Hayes ate razor blades and prisoner Fred Ahern swallowed a needle. . . . they both were rushed to Mass General Hospital.

"This evening at 6 P.M. prison guards Baptist, Sainsbury, and Montiega turned a fire extinguisher containing a chemical foam on Joe then slammed the solid steel door sealing him in his cell and walked away, voicing threats of, 'We'll get that punk.'

"At 9:25 P.M. Joe was found dead. Another human life snuffed out by the system. Twenty-six-year-old Joe, who had served seven years of a life sentence at Walpole until the toll . . . the final payment . . . was extracted here tonight, by a cruel society that has turned her back on her brothers and sisters and children in prisons. Forced to serve part or all of their lives in cages, constantly in fear of being snatched from their bed in the middle of the night by blackjack-wielding prison guards, who stalk the corridors and cell blocks, seeking to vent their hostilities on some hapless prisoner. Prison authorities as well as news media will label little Joe's death a suicide, but the men here in Block Nine who witnessed this murder know. But are we next?"

An inmate named Don Sylvia wrote a poem: "The Man With No Identity."

When I was two years old
    my mother divorced my father for "cruelty."
When I was five, ten years old, I went to school, and the kids
    called me *"bastard."*
I went to court when I was thirteen (for breaking windows) and
    the "good judge" called me a "THUG."
When I was eighteen I got in a car accident
    (received some everlasting wounds on my head and face)
    and the "community" called me *"scarface."*
I grew a beard when I was twenty-eight, and
    society called me a *"hippy."*
I'm thirty-six, doing seven to twelve in society's prison, and the
    "District Attorney" calls me an *"animal."*
When I leave this prison and settle down,
    I'll be titled *"Ex-Convict."*
And when I'm dead, and laid to rest,
    I'll be an *"unknown soldier."*

                                                        H.Z.

Charles Street Jail

Boston, like all American cities, has a city jail. It is called the Charles Street Jail, administered by the Sheriff of Suffolk County, and it is not much different from other city and county jails in the country. This is a devastating commentary on the whole of our society, because Charles Street Jail is a filthy, dark, rat-infested dungeon, in which human beings are treated worse than animals in a zoo.

I first learned about Charles Street Jail, oddly enough, in Tokyo, where, in the year 1966, I met a Japanese philosopher named Tsurumi Shunsuke, who told me that, as a Harvard student when Pearl Harbor broke out, he was imprisoned by the United States Government because he refused to sign a loyalty oath to *either* the United States Government or the Japanese government, thus signifying to the authorities that he was "an anarchist."

"Where did they put you?" I asked Tsurumi.

"In Charles Street Jail."

Five years after that conversation, I was in Charles Street Jail myself, having been convicted for blocking the Boston army base entrance during an antiwar demonstration. I was there only two days and one night, and tried to imagine what it must be like to spend months, or years there. I couldn't wait to get out. Every ordinary act of living—sleeping, sitting, standing, breathing, eating, urinating, moving one's bowels—was a humiliation. Inmates were locked in their cells twenty-two out of twenty-four hours.

The food of Charles Street was a special cumulative irritation. It consisted of alternating varieties of nauseating indescribable concoctions, topped by piles of Wonder Bread, tasting like layers of absorbent cotton. The only seasoning was from the pigeons which flew overhead during meals and dropped their waste onto the food trays.

It was not a surprise, therefore, that, on November 13, 1972, inmates at Charles Street Jail tore up the place in uncontrolled anger, because of food. An inmate, writing in the Boston *Phoenix* as "Prisoner X," told about it:

"I was in the dining room on my side of the cell block about eleven-fifteen Monday morning when I heard a crash, an enormous racket from the other side of the block. Prisoners had thrown over their dining tables. People were finding worms in the pea soup. I went up to the serving area and found prisoners talking heatedly with some of the guards. Someone who seemed to be speaking in an official capacity said the worms were actually fried onions. A lot of prisoners said they were insulted by that story. The worms were definitely not onions.

"Sheriff Eisenstadt arrived on the scene after the commotion had begun. A group of perhaps seventy-five or eighty prisoners were standing in the serving area, waiting for a response from somebody about the food. Eisenstadt picked up a small cup, dipped it into a bucket of soup, held it for perhaps two seconds and threw it back into the bucket. He couldn't have determined anything from that dip. I heard later that at his press conference, Eisenstadt said he saw a 'microscopic' black bug. But that isn't what the 'bugs' were like at all; they were white, with lines across the top, tape worms, or maggots."

Sheriff Thomas Eisenstadt has been, for several years, administrator of the jail. He has admitted its unfitness, but has maintained it essentially as it has been since it was built one hundred twenty-one years ago. As Danny Schechter, a Boston radio newscaster, wrote: ,

"Anyone who has seen the Charles Street Jail from the inside is appalled by its decrepit condition. Anyone who has done time in it hopes that it blows up—or comes down. And anyone who has ever administered it concedes the harshest criticisms—and does nothing to change it."

Schechter discussed how the political career of Sheriff Eisenstadt was an institution in Boston, perhaps as invulnerable to dismantling as the Charles Street Jail:

"A majority of the men in Charles Street are black. Many are products of the Boston school system in the years when young Tom Eisenstadt sided with Louise Day Hicks to keep the ghettoes secure from integration. More than a few of the prisoners were sentenced to the jail by Tom's uncle, Judge Samuel Eisenstadt of the Roxbury District Court, now under attack from lawyers' groups for violating the rights of those appearing before him. Of those, at least some were prosecuted by Tom's own brother, Theodore, a former assistant D.A. of Suffolk County. Here is a family which runs its own judicial system. A number of famous 'families' have made their livelihoods from crime but the Eisenstadts' may be the first to live off prosecuting criminals."

Danny Schechter described the beginning of the trouble:

"The rebellion began as a case of indigestion. There was something yukky in the pea soup, what some prisoners said looked like worms, what guards insisted were probably only onions. As at least one prisoner shouted out through the windows when the prisoners still controlled the jail's main wing: 'This is it. We can't let this pass.' The soup bowls were thrown against the wall and shattered. There was rage, what the jail's 'Master' called 'an ugly mood' was developing.

"The men demanded to talk to the Sheriff. They wouldn't

proceed with what Eisenstadt would later call 'the orderly process of eating.' They wouldn't return to their cells. But there had been no major damage as yet.

"Enter the Man: 'I immediately went to the guardroom floor and addressed the inmates,' Eisenstadt said, 'and informed them that it is my policy never, under any circumstances, to discuss anything at any time while I am under duress or the object of threats. I did inform the inmates, however, that upon returning to their cells calmly and in an orderly fashion, I would be willing to speak to a delegation of five or six men of their choice and I would give them five minutes in which to do this. I returned to my office and waited approximately twenty minutes.'

"The men selected their committee but Eisenstadt then said he would talk to only two men of the six-member group. The prisoners insisted that he meet with the whole committee. It was after this exchange (or more precisely, nonexchange) that the jail was trashed. Eisenstadt had treated the men with contempt and now they would treat his 'property' the same way."

As "Prisoner X" put it: "When he told us that he was not going to meet with a group of six, the inmates felt cheated—we felt that he had gone back on his promise."

"Prisoner X" goes on to tell what happened:

"What followed during the next two hours was a frantic and courageous expression of rage, by prisoners who've been viciously beaten down for too long, and left with no other means to communicate deep-felt anger and frustration.

"We rebelled with the only resources available at the time, the bare physical rudiments in the jail itself. Tables were overturned, windows were broken, light fixtures smashed; radiators and plumbing apparatus were pulled apart, and benches ripped up. Primitive 'weapons,' in expectation of riot-equipped police, were fashioned out of the debris.

"We knew that we would be physically overpowered by the

cops, but also that disease, caused by poisoned food, was a less tolerable fate. And it wasn't just the poisoned food; it was, even more, the insensitive and racist response to our complaints by the jail staff, in particular Sheriff Eisenstadt. There were no 'hard-core agitators' who 'stirred us up,' as the Sheriff has claimed. All of us were reacting in unison to what we felt was a very real prospect—unless we do something, we may not live until tomorrow. We saw the whole issue, as a basic challenge of our survival. In response to our anxiety, Sheriff Eisenstadt in effect laughed in our face.

"I know there were many prisoners who felt, right then, and said literally, they were prepared to die if that must be the price, to convey their feelings of anger and resentment toward the intolerable conditions so long imposed on them. At one point, in exhilaration at the release of these feelings, the brothers liberated the canteen, to celebrate our very limited tactical victory. Cartons of cigarettes were passed around, and candy bars were consumed, hopefully to provide strength for the massacre all of us were expecting at any moment. Frequently, during the chaos and excitement of these two hours, I could hear other prisoners screaming, 'The Revolution will not be televised.' 'Dig it, brothers, the Revolution will not be televised.'

"The inmates were attempting, with a bullhorn, to explain through the open windows to onlookers, what actually had caused the uprising, and as I remember hearing my brothers from those very windows they broadcast, 'There were worms in our soup. There were worms in our soup.' We all wanted the public to know the real reason for our revolt. The smoke bombs effectively chased us from the windows, and the Sheriff had denied us what then was our only means to communicate with the outside world.

"The MDC [Metropolitan District Commission] police were the first to come in. I saw one of them in front dressed in riot gear, holding a dog on a leash. There were inmates in my tier standing next to their cell, trying to explain to the MDC policemen that their cell doors were locked. The MDC police beat a few of the prisoners in front of me. They didn't listen to the explanation that the doors were locked. They chased us down to the end of the tier and bunched us up. There were about fifteen or twenty of us down at the end of the tier. A group of about three officers held us there for about ten minutes.

"Then the word came that we were to be taken back down to the main floor, near the serving area once more. I was one of the first in that group of fifteen to be taken down. When I got there I looked back at the line of prisoners behind me. I could see them with their heads badly bloodied. At that point only one of them was taken to the hospital. They had been hit with clubs and I don't know what else. The police were calling us dirty mother-fuckers.

". . . the rest of us were ordered to strip naked, and for about the next two hours we stood there, naked, waiting for instructions or whatever, to go back to our cells.

"During this period, we all witnessed one very brutal assault by the MDC police. A few prisoners in the south wing had never left their cells for lunch, or had returned to their cells immediately after lunch. The MDC were sent after them. We saw a prisoner in the first cell led out by about three officers. He took about two steps from the cell and was immediately clouted, very hard on the forehead by another officer. When he fell over, obviously unconscious from the blow, the MDC police began jabbing him with their clubs and yelling for him to stand up, apparently believing he was faking it. When he didn't move, they ordered the dogs on him, and the brothers standing next to me, all watching in horror, whispered, 'We gotta do something.' But, all of us standing naked, and with another force of MDC officers in front of us, clubs and dogs at the ready, of course we were helpless. But it was really despicable, the way that brother was attacked. When he began waking up, with the police dog chomping on his foot, he was prodded with clubs to stand up and was finally pushed and clubbed down the stairs to join the rest of us, his face a bloody mess. He was not taken to the hospital.

"Finally, they called the cell numbers off individually as they were cleared by MDC policemen standing on the tiers. When my cell number was finally called and it was my turn to go back, I climbed the stairs from the serving area back to my tier and there was a group of about eight guards waiting for me. It was perhaps fifty feet from the top of the stairs to my cell. I was beaten by guards on the tier who jammed a billy-club in my gut as I held my hands over my head. When I keeled over, the guards yelled at me to keep my hands over my head. I did that, and they jammed the billy-club back in my gut, and pushed me into the cell. Three guards worked me over in the cell for about five minutes, hitting me in the back and stomach with their clubs and fists. . . .

"I could see Jail Master Langlois watching the beatings along the tiers as well. It was Master Langlois who was calling off the cell numbers, for us to be taken back individually to the cells.

"It was very cold. For a long time we were in our cells without any clothes. And of course the windows were broken and the cold was coming in. . . . Then we heard the shouting of the guards. They were calling for two more prisoners to be taken to Cell Number Eight. Every few minutes somebody yelled for 'two more' in Cell Eight. About thirty seconds would elapse after they called, and then we heard screams. We knew that they were systematically beating a whole series of prisoners. . . ."

Danny Schechter wrote: ". . . the prisoners' rebellion has been characterized as a destructive, animalistic orgy. No one has mentioned, or apparently is interested in, the pattern of brutal reprisals against the rebels that began to form as soon as the uprising ended." Sheriff Eisenstadt denied the beatings. Jail Master Langlois denied the beatings.

Eisenstadt called a press conference to explain what had happened. The television crews did not have to bring lights with them because Eisenstadt, when he became Sheriff, had repaneled his private office and installed his own set of color TV spotlights. He had joked about the bugs in the soup to the prisoners, telling them, "Why there are bugs in the soup of the finest restaurants of Boston." And he told the press:

"They are those little black bugs that invade everybody's house. As a matter of fact, just two weeks ago, they got into my pantry and my wife gave me soup with those little black bugs in it. But I didn't riot. I didn't dare. I wouldn't dare. She felt worse than I did. So these are things that happen everywhere."

Eisenstadt told the press conference: "If it had not been the pea soup, it would have been something else." And Danny Schechter commented: "He's right on that account."

Eisenstadt refused to let Schechter or any other newsmen into the jail to talk to the prisoners. Schechter commented: "As I left the jailhouse, that scene from the beginning of Eisenstein's movie *Potemkin* came to mind. The meat aboard the good ship is crawling with maggots. And those maggots sparked a revolution."

H.Z.

Walpole

Walpole, about fifteen miles from Boston, is the maximum security prison in Massachusetts. Tension has always been high there. Around Christmas, 1972, a crisis situation developed which lasted for many months. As a disciplinary and security measure, the Acting Superintendent, Raymond Porelle, ordered a lockup—the prisoners were to be kept in their cells, not to be allowed out for work or recreation, not to be allowed visitors, not to communicate with the outside world. There was rebellion by inmates, messing up of the prison as they threw their food outside their cells and the guards refused to clean it up. Because of all that, Porelle was taken off the job by John Boone, the black, reform Commissioner of Correction, and a twenty-four-hour vigil inside the prison was permitted, for several months, to a group of citizens concerned with prison reform.

Here are notes taken during one of these eight-hour observer periods—from 3 P.M. to 11 P.M.—in one of the two segregation units at Walpole, Block Nine.

The lower tier of Block Nine holds prisoners who have asked for isolation in their cells, who didn't want to be in what is called "population"—the minimum-security area blocks where prisoners can socialize with one another outside their cells for part of the day. One of these prisoners told about himself.

"I'm a gypsy. I wanted out of population because I need quiet so I can write. I'm writing a book about gypsies—who knows about them?" He showed a thick sheaf of pages on which he had already written.

He was in good humor, and he began to tell stories about his boyhood as a gypsy which kept the inmate in the next cell laughing—they could not see one another, but clearly they were friends. He told about how when he was twelve and a half his mother called him in from playing in the street, and introduced him to a thirty-seven-year-old woman and told him this would be his wife. His wife had a son from a previous marriage who was in his twenties, and he told how one day the son slapped his hand as he reached for a piece of meat on the table and said, "Dad, you're not bringing anything into the house—and you eat more than anyone." Whereupon his son built a shoeshine box for him so he could go out and earn some money.

His neighbor in the next cell was convulsed with laughter by this time. The gypsy had a radio in his cell, and he stopped talking suddenly as he heard the Governor's voice on the radio. Governor Sargent was talking about Walpole. The guards were threatening to go on strike. They did not like Commissioner Boone. They did not like the citizen observers. Their authority was being undermined. The Governor said that if the guards went on strike, state police would enter Walpole and stand guard.

The gypsy shook his head: "There will be a massacre at Walpole." His mood suddenly changed. "Last week the guards took a prisoner right out here [he pointed to the area outside his cell] and put him up against the wall [his voice suddenly broke into a short agonized sob] and they beat the shit out of him." I saw in this prisoner something that I would see again and again in these eight hours in Walpole, something I was not quite prepared for, and perhaps a result of prison movement of the past few years: an intense concern by prisoners for their fellows.

On the tier above, where those in segregation were not there voluntarily but were being given special punishment, the cells and corridor were in a shambles. Many of the cells were dark, because the lights were controlled from outside, and when the guards deliberately kept them on at night, the prisoners smashed them. Outside of the cells, against the wall that faced them, were heaps of garbage, the accumulated remains of food thrown out of the cells over a period of weeks. The garbage heaps were blackened here and there, where the prisoners had thrown matches to burn up some of it, to reduce the stench, and keep the rats away. They said that the guards, angry because of the resignation of their man Porelle, had not come around to take their food when they finished, and so rather than keep it in their cells where the rats would then come, they threw it out against the walls. These heaps of charred, decaying food were a constant, visible source of hostility between inmates and guards.

The men in these isolation cells were let out only twice a week to take showers. They could have a TV set in their cells if they could get the money to buy one. A Puerto Rican fellow on this tier, they said, had asked for a TV set, had the money, was ignored, kept asking for one, and was put in the "Blue Room" for two days. The Blue Room was a special cell at the end of the corridor, with no bed, no light, no bars, but a solid steel door, only a stone floor and a hole in it for a toilet.

What were these men here for? Drugs. Breaking and entering. Armed robbery. One of them stood against the bars in the faint light and told me about himself. Frederick Ahern. Five years ago when he had done ten years of a twenty-year sentence, he had been paroled. He was then thirty years old, and had spent all his life but one year since he was fifteen behind bars. "Why don't they take me out and shoot me?"

After ten years in jail, they had let him out on parole with fifty dollars. He took his mother, his sister, and his girl to a meal at Howard Johnson's. "That blew half of it." He was sent to a halfway house, where every four hours he had to make a personal appearance, and every two hours he had to phone in. He once went out to Lowell to see his mother, returned seventy-five minutes late, and was put on restriction for two weeks, at a time when he wanted badly to see his girl. He finally committed a robbery. "The cops came. In the middle of the night. They put the twisters on my arm, and walked me out of the halfway house, back to prison. You see, out there, who did I know except cons? I wasn't ready for the streets."

At the end of the corridor, a committee was meeting to go over the records of the prisoners in Nine Block. Prisoners complained that they were put in isolation without hearings, a violation of prison rules and of Supreme Court decisions. So now, although some of them had been in Nine Block six months, the committee was meeting. Ahern said bitterly, "They've got my folder out there. But what's in that? It's not me."

Last month, Ahern was beaten by guards, and had five stitches over his left eye. "Five screws handcuffed my hands behind my back." He once had swallowed a sewing needle, desperate to get out of isolation. He was taken to Peter Bent Brigham hospital, but right there in the hospital, the cops taunted him, then smashed his face down into the floor. A nurse saw it and called a doctor, who stopped it.

This was not the first time he had been beaten. Back in 1966 he had been sent to Norfolk Hospital. They had broken his nose, busted his head with a billy-club, held him over the tier, naked, the guards threatening to drop him onto the stone pavement three tiers below. That was right after a "pill riot" —a riot over having to stand in line at the hospital to get pills. He had spent five years in Ten Block, the other isolation block, and had been here in Nine since November. "I should be bitter, I should be a raving lunatic."

How did it start? He was from Lowell, got five-to-seven for armed robbery. "I was twenty, trying to build a rep as a hard rock. What are most robbers? Poor. My father was a truck driver. A drinker. Fist fights. At thirteen I was out of the house. I was one of sixteen kids. Who cared?"

On December 20, in the midst of much commotion at Walpole, and much desperation, he and others grabbed a guard, held him as "hostage," asked to see Boone. They didn't harm the guard. In fact, the guard testified on their behalf at a later hearing. Ahern was promised in the Dedham court where he and the others were tried, that if he pleaded guilty as the main culprit, the others would get off, and he would get three-to-five. But instead they gave him fifteen years, to start after he finished his current twenty-year sentence. "It's all force, and force breeds force."

In the cell next to Ahern a black man was sleeping on the floor instead of on his cot. He explained that there was a vent over the cot, and last week guards had sprayed a fire extinguisher through the vent—they often used the vent in each cell in this way to harass and punish prisoners. He sleeps with the light on, because otherwise rats come into the cell. He had been in this cell for two months, before that in Block Six for five years. They sent him here because they said he kept pornographic literature in his room. "I was reading a black *Playboy*-type magazine. *Playboy* is allowed. Prisoners can get it in the mail. But black *Playboy* is no good."

He spoke about the Puerto Rican guy in this block who had been put in the Blue Room because he raised a fuss when his visitor was not allowed in to see him after she had been waiting all day. "Let's be truthful about these concentration camps. They're not for rehabilitation. They're for punishment. If they were for rehabilitation, they would have to start *years* ago. They give me one-to-three, then three-to-five, then fifteen-to-twenty. Is this rehabilitation? Why don't they take the thousands of dollars they pay to keep me in Walpole and send me to school? *That's* rehabilitation.

"I was in court on a bank robbery. I can speak as well for myself as some bum who doesn't care about me." He got help, however, from a fellow inmate, serving a life term in Walpole, William "Lefty" Gilday. "Lefty Gilday helped me. The court asked me did I have a lawyer. I said, 'I have one in mind. He's in Walpole.' The Judge asked: 'Is he a member of the bar?" I said: 'What kind of bar? That's all bullshit! Lefty did more for me than a public defender, who will only tell me to plead guilty.' The judge didn't like me using the word *bullshit* and wanted to send me to Bridgewater.

"I have never harmed anybody. I was one of fourteen brothers and sisters. My father worked all his life and had a heart attack. I can't see working for nothing. I was in the service for three years, learned to be an aviation mechanic. But when I got out I couldn't get a job. So I got to take what I need. My father was a railroad worker on the south shore, around Plymouth. He died at fifty-two."

He was back again talking about the Puerto Rican fellow in the next cell. "His girl came from Holyoke to see him, waited all day, then they sent her home. They told him that, and he got mad. They shut his outer door, you know, so he couldn't see out, all steel in front of him. He said something to an officer, and they shot a fire extinguisher into his cell. First they shot it into this cell, by mistake I guess. Then they put him in the Blue Room."

The black man continued. He'd been having stomach problems for a year, but they wouldn't X-ray. "The prison doctor is full of shit. He's for the system."

He talked about the inequality of the law. "In that Pentagon Papers case they want to give that man a hundred years. But look at Watergate!"

Suddenly his talk switched to the Indians. "It's not Ski-Nose's country—not Nixon's country—it's their country."

Since Attica, he said, people were thinking differently. Prisoners were fighting back. People were defiant. If they only knew their own power. "What if people in Boston said: We're not going to work. For one day! What could they do? The people's tax money built these prisons and that money keeps us here—so the people have a right to come here and see what's happening."

Two cells over was Jerry Sousa. We recognized one another. I had given a class in labor history at Concord Prison some months ago, when he was there. Since then, he had been shipped out of Concord as a troublemaker and leader, shipped right into Block Nine at Walpole.

His arrest had come as a surprise. He was at his wedding reception. It was the year 1963. He was cutting the cake, when police walked in with machine guns and shotguns and arrested him on charges of armed robbery. During a holdup, the café proprietor had fired at one of the robbers, who got panicky and shot him. Sousa had a witness who placed him far from the robbery scene, and his codefendants said he was not the third man with the gun. But he was found guilty, sentenced to life, had now been in prison nine years. He could not be paroled. Only a commutation by the Governor could get him out.

A ruling had come to Concord—everybody over twenty-seven must be shipped out. They brought Sousa to Walpole, and the wagon backed right up to Block Nine. I remembered Jerry in our discussion at Concord. He had strongly expressed a belief in nonviolence as the only way to make revolutionary changes.

Earlier in his sentence he had been at Walpole, and one night at 10:30 P.M. he had been beaten by guards for being drunk. He entered suit in federal court against them and this was still pending. It set an example, and other prisoners filed suit, and the authorities didn't like this. He was sent to Bridgewater DSU (Departmental Segregation Unit)—the most feared place of all—for six months. Then back to Walpole in "population." One night blacks and whites were talking about not being set against one another, and he gave a speech on black-white unity which the guards heard. They came for him, said he was inciting a racial disturbance, put him in Block Nine. Then to Concord. And now back to Block Nine.

"There is this reclassification committee meeting out there at the end of the corridor. But it's just a pacification group. No one has been released from Block Nine yet.

"We hear the rats squeaking out there at night. When it gets too bad, we set fire to the garbage in the corridor.

"In Concord, we really got that joint together. Everybody was like brothers. You could lie down in the yard and close your eyes. If guys can learn here not to tip each other off, when they get out, they'll be okay. We got to start practicing brotherhood here. They don't want us to unite against them."

Jerry Sousa talked about the organization they had formed, the first prisoners union in the country as far as he knew: The National Prisoners Reform Association. In Walpole, 85 percent of the inmates were members. They had an inside executive committee and an outside executive committee. They were now negotiating with prison officials to get people who had had no hearings released from Block Nine.

Another prison leader, Anthony Carlo, had been in Walpole four years. Why was he in Block Nine? He had yelled at a guard for shining a flashlight in his face. Then, at two in the morning, he was awakened and put into Block Nine. He was the coordinator of the Massachusetts Prison Reform Association in Walpole. "That's why I'm here. They wanted to get me out of population."

Carlo had done three years for breaking and entering, then was paroled, and had been out on parole for a year and a half when they swooped down on him and put him back for a parole violation.

"What was your violation?"

"Association."

"What does that mean?"

"Association with an ex-felon. That's grounds for parole violation and sending you back."

Carlo reviewed the events at Walpole. On December 29, Superintendent Porelle had started the shakedown of the cells. Searches. People locked in their cells all day. "It was the start of a reign of terror. They wanted to start a behavior-modification program and end all the self-help programs that were being started. Their total stress was on security and control. It had all the tones of psychosurgery."

The guards harassed them. "They play games with us. Spitting in our food. Or they'll deliberately miss someone with a meal. They'll tear-gas your room, then close the metal door. We were all locked up for thirty-five days. No visits. Our mail was tampered with.

"But instead of people coming out broken, they came out political activists."

He spoke about a man I had heard yelling in the next corridor, a big man named Peter LeDetto, in for murder. He was returning from a hearing before the committee meeting at the end of the corridor, waving a piece of paper, shouting, "What does this mean? Who can understand this! Listen to this, men! What does it mean?" The paper, in complex language, denied him a return to population out of Block Nine.

Carlo said that last week guards had beaten LeDetto with clubs, unmercifully. "He's like a big kid, he doesn't harm anyone, he yells, talks foolish. But aside from raving, he's no threat to anyone. But they beat him once before, when he was in population, and when Boone [the Commissioner of Correction] came by one day he talked to Boone about his beating and pointed out the head of the goon squad. So when

Boone left, they took him out of population, and dragged him here, and all the way down the corridor they beat him with clubs." Carlo's voice was anguished. "I was never worked up so much in my life. We all had to watch that. We were yelling and screaming. It was our pain. I tried to get through the bars, I was so desperate, so angry, so helpless. I couldn't sleep that night, because I had hurt my big toe kicking at the bars while they were clubbing LeDetto.

"It happens all the time here. A guy from Five Block was taken up here, beaten, had a concussion, was thrown into the Blue Room. One month ago, a guy died. They tried to say he committed suicide with a belt. But he had welts on his head. They killed him." Carlo gripped the bars tight. "That's why guys were ready to die to stop that. I would have been ready to die, and I'm getting out this year."

H.Z.

Journal from Hell—Jimmy Barrett's Diary in DSU [Departmental Segregation Unit]—Bridgewater

America doesn't know or recognize Jimmy Barrett. But he knows America, and he is a legend at Walpole Prison. In December, 1972, in the midst of much tension at Walpole, Jimmy, who had served nine years of his life sentence, and was just over thirty, decided to organize a Christmas fast. To dramatize the fact that poor white and black people all over the country did not have enough to eat, prisoners—yes, *prisoners*—would fast.

So Jimmy typed out, with two fingers, sitting in his cell, copy after copy—he had no carbon paper—of a message to prisoners: "WE PRISONERS ARE EXPECTED TO PAUSE AT CHRISTMASTIME WITH THE REST OF MIDDLE AMERICA. TO EAT AND BE MERRY AND GIVE THANKS. . . . BUT THERE ARE MILLIONS OF PEOPLE IN THIS COUNTRY WHO DO GO TO BED HUNGRY AND COLD AND SICK." He stayed up all night. He typed up over a hundred statements. He got them distributed to all eleven blocks at Walpole. And visitors took them to Norfolk, Concord, Framingham (the women's prison).

On Christmas Day, more than a thousand prisoners at the four institutions refused to eat dinner—more than half the inmates in the state penitentiaries. A historic moment, the first time the four prisons had acted together.

A few days later, Jimmie was shipped out of Walpole, indeed, out of the state, to Atlanta. Eight others were shipped out too. It was a time when the Walpole population was locked up in their cells, and so it would be hard for them to protest.

Jimmy had been shipped out a year before, when there was trouble at Walpole, sent to the dreaded DSU-Number 10 at Bridgewater, and it was there that he wrote his remarkable diary.

In his entry for January 25, 1972:

"And it kept eating on me, this is the road to insanity, doing all these months and months and months locked inside a cell without love, without being able to show my feelings. And it seemed to me to be ridiculously simple: I wanted something ALIVE in my cell. That was it, that would save me. And I didn't dare tell anyone for fear they would think me crazy, but I wanted something in that cell with me, something alive and full of life, and that I could love and have crawl on me and show me affection. I jumped up and started hollering and banging, I wanted to see the priest, get the priest down here. I gotta tell him something important. And I know that all ears are perked, wondering what's with that guy and I am pacing back and forth wondering how in hell I can explain that I want something alive in my cell. The priest came down. Look, Father, I know you're going to think I'm crazy or something but I've been locked up for years and . . . And I tried to tell him that I needed something, a bird, a kitten, a puppy, that I could feel myself dying day after month and positively needed something full of life and love. I have to have something to which I can direct my feelings. And he came on, hmmm, I daresay you have an interesting point. Point, schmoint—bring me in a kitten."

Before we give more of his diary, it might be good to know a little about Jimmy Barrett. In *The Real Paper*, January 24,

1973, Joe Klein wrote about the Christmas fast, about the shipout to Atlanta, and about Jimmy himself:

"Last Monday, Jimmy Barrett's sister Peggy stood outside the prison in the cold night air with about one hundred others, protesting the lockup and the shipouts. She shouted across the walls from a sound truck. She taunted prison authorities, cursed the system, cursed the walls, promised that Jimmy Barrett was coming back. And the lights in the cells began blinking on and off like a Christmas tree in response. People began hugging each other and crying when they saw the lights start blinking. 'We get your message, fellas,' Peggy shouted. 'We love every last one of ya.' She began calling out messages for individual prisoners from their wives and girl-friends. And now the men inside were screaming, loud an-guished cries, so loud that the one hundred or so outside the walls could hear them. And Peggy went on, shouting at the elephant walls of Walpole. . . ."

Just before, she had spoken of another wall. The wall of the Home for Catholic Children in the South End, where she and Jimmy had spent six years of their childhood. The kids from outside would climb the wall, sit on top and laugh at them. At the orphans.

But the Barretts weren't orphans. In a sense they were worse—a court had ruled their mother wasn't fit to keep them. Their father had run off, and their mother was a waitress in a bar. She drank a lot and wasn't around much.

"Most of Peggy's memories of Jimmy involve his getting beaten by someone or other. The nuns at the orphanage beat him when he snuck out to buy her some candy. His stepfather dangled him out the window and then beat him. The blacks from Roxbury beat him in gang wars. The guards in prison were always beating him—Attorney Joe Oteri once came back and told her Jimmy was beaten so bad at Walpole that blood was coming from his penis, his ears, his mouth—every opening in his body. . . . Sure, he fought back. He was good with his fists, having won a Golden Gloves competition in the South End. But the odds were always crummy.

"And then it was Jimmy against Steve the Greek. This was a classic confrontation, the kind of vendetta you see in the movies. Steve the Greek was a crud, one of the most hated men in the city of Boston, a loan shark and a strong-arm man. He and Jimmy had a misunderstanding over money— the exact story is unclear—but the result was that the Greek began hounding Jimmy.

"After several months it came to a head: On Sunday, Steve the Greek tried to run Jimmy over with his car. On Monday, he split Jimmy's head open with a lead pipe. On Tuesday, Jimmy bought a gun. On Thursday, he was walking into a South End saloon as Steve the Greek was walking out. They were both startled. But there they were, and Jimmy shot Steve the Greek four times before Steve could shoot him.

"The police caught up with Jimmy at Peggy's house. He admitted to killing the Greek and one of the cops shook his hand. He told Jimmy he'd done the South End a service as they hauled him off to jail.

"It was not his first felony. Years earlier, Jimmy had been caught breaking into a market, trying to get food so a crippled woman in the Cathedral Park housing project could feed her family. He was nabbed with $40 and a shopping bag full of baby food.

"They offered Jimmy Barrett a sentence of five to seven years if he would plead guilty in the Steve the Greek case. But he figured that no one could ever find him guilty of anything more than self-defense, so he refused.

"He got life. In October of 1963, at the age of twenty-four, he was sentenced to Walpole State Prison on a charge of second-degree murder.

"His two most immediate priorities upon arriving at Walpole were: 1) get into a fight so everyone would know he wasn't one to be pushed around and 2) escape. He was incredibly naive about the latter. He had this strange idea that there was an escape committee—like in the old prison movies —and he went around asking people if they were on it.

"As naive as he seemed to the older cons, Jimmy had one thing very straight in his mind from the beginning: It was him against the system. He hated the guards. He refused to take their most picayune jibes. When he saw a guard beating up on someone else, he'd be the first to jump in. This would usually result in a busted head or winding up in segregation or both. There was a period in the late sixties when he spent thirty-two of thirty-six months in segregation. He was accused of all kinds of assaults, attempted escapes, and in one case, murder. He was cleared of the murder, but was hung with several of the others.

"Early on, he began organizing. In 1965 he organized a campaign to have prisoners sign up for service in Vietnam— luckily, the army refused to go along. In the pill riots of 1967, when there was a mass attempt to liberate pills from the infirmary, he helped organize a legal defense. He hadn't been in on copping the pills—Jimmy is well known for his abstinence—but, typically, he'd gotten involved when he saw a guard beating a guy in the aftermath.

"Still, there was no politics to his organizing. He fought back because he was a tough kid from the South End who didn't take any crap. He organized because it came naturally. He was a leader and was well respected. He was known as one of the smartest guys in the joint. But he was still a racist—he believed blacks should be transported en masse back to Africa, for their own good and ours. And he was still a rebel without a cause.

"The change was gradual. He read. Especially George Jackson's prison letters. He listened to other cons, and slowly turned radical. A friend says, 'He had always been radical in his heart. Finally, about two years ago, he began to get his head together.' The turning point came in December, 1971. He was locked in segregation once again. This time, he and others in Block Ten rebelled for a different reason: the blacks, sick and in pain, were denied medical attention. Jimmy was shipped out to Bridgewater, DSU 10."

Here are some pages from his diary:

JOURNAL FROM HELL—DSU Bridgewater, 1972

I came here on January 5 from Walpole's DSU—Block Ten. We were, each in our separate cells in Block Ten, punched around and then dragged off to the paddy wagon in chains and leg irons. There were ten of us upstairs in Ten Block demonstrating for the previous twelve days against the conditions we were living in, especially the medical mistreatment and the blatant racist baiting from certain guards.

The real trouble started on December 23 when Ralph Hamm's war-wounded knee became painfully swollen. This followed on the heels of Teddy Miller's neglected pain from his bayonet-ripped stomach. Hamm and Miller are blacks. To be black in prison often means to be hated and shunned. But to have your face rubbed in this alleged sin by guards' sarcastic remarks about niggers and spooks is too unkind. As a white, to me it became outrageous. When these guards then displayed obvious satisfaction in teasing the sick prisoners, losing their prescribed medication, forgetting to call the prison clinic, then the situation became for everyone what it long had been for the suffering blacks. Intolerable.

On December 28, I swore aloud that, come what may, I for one am prepared to go to the wall. I had had it. Then, one after another, each man stood at the cell door and stated his position, how far he was prepared to go. We were as one heart and mind. And we then struck back as best we could. We banged and clanged, broke up whatever we could and waited for the heavy reprisals. It was a long wait too, because, this being the first time in history that an entire tier stood shoulder to shoulder, the officials were playing on time for defections and modified stances. Meanwhile, I wrote and wrote and encouraged, cajoled, argued the others into doing so. On January 4 we issued our Position Paper. And waited.

January 5, 1972

Today it was quiet. Telephone rings. Whispering from the guard area. Stop the bullshit and let's get on with it. We knew it was coming. And I thought again of the times I had been gassed and beaten, and again I checked out my preparations: folded blanket at the ready, towel tied into a hood with only eyeholes, two containers of cool water at the ready. And me, nervous.

Everything I was shooting for, down the drain. But I knew it was the same with the others: they too had sacrified what little they had going for them. My only real concern was my law materials, the books and papers and letters. Years of research and note taking crammed into two boxes: my key to freedom. What will become of my case? For three years, since my arrest and indictments for attempted escape, I had worked on the law. The federal courts had become my tunnel, case comparisons my shovel. And now . . . Oh God, without a reversal, I will never ever get out. Warden Moore's screamed threats to me seem hauntingly real.

We heard the truck pull up. There was no attempt to surprise us: I guessed that twenty were coming up the back stairs with their shields and chains and grunts.

Down came six of them, directly to my cell. I was the last on the tier, knew I would be first to fall. The guard near me—the pig who at any time could have resolved the block problems, but who chose instead to aggravate them. . . . now he was signaling to the far away guard to pull my bar so he could slide open my door. The bastard was going to come in himself. How many rigs has this man stomped, how many days' Good Time has he deprived us of. I'd have just one shot. I was scared and nervous. For a second again I thought about ramming his face with the broom handle, breaking his ugly sneering face. He hated me, this pig. Okay, Barrett, step out. What for, I'm waiting to see the Board; where'm I goin'? STEP OUT! And as the gas man stepped around him to aim, the tough guy guard stepped into the cell. I dropped my hands at my side, feinted him by reaching for my law papers and, when he reached for my hair, I hooked him with a left and buckled him with a driving right. I took a step back to hoot him and it was all over: they swarmed into the cell, arms, legs all over me, I couldn't move, couldn't breathe, legs, arms twisted; who was trying to smash my head? And then I saw stars and went limp.

When I recovered seconds later it was to a feeling of hopelessness, defeat, and then the guard was all over me, trying to get a good shot at me and his helpers were in the way. I would have laughed at him if I could afford the breath. Instead, I hugged in closer, and with no other weapon on hand I bit him. Bit him as hard as I could on his chest, and when he jumped aside I laughed at the blood and spittle that scarred his uniform. And then I was dragged along the floor, cuffed and chained and hustled out to the wagon. The others followed. Beaten as well.

Chains cutting and dragging, we were hauled through the DSU itself, past the five gaping cell figures, men whose faces were lost to the shadows and large flat bar behind the small peepholes.

Strip was the first and soon to be familiar word after the chains were undone. Arms up. Feet up. Bend over. Spread 'em. Wider. Then into a cell, naked, armpits sweating, wondering if I am going to get clothes, staring at the crap-stained pot and recognizing now all the odors and smells of the thousands before me. The cell is just as I heard it would be. Back comes The Paunch with clothes and more rules. We'd be here for two or three days with the pots and pitcher of water. After that we'd be taken downstairs with the others, into regular cells with toilets and sinks and smoking privileges.

That day and evening and night were the longest in my life. The hours dragged by. Time itself seemed to stop to look closer at its newest offerings, toying, playing with me, time backward and sideways, like a cat with a mouse. There was no escape by sleep: instead, the snatches of dozed minutes here and there between my staggered senses only added to my lostness in Time. When I knew it was at least 8 P.M., it was only 5. When I swore, ached for it to be 11 at night, it was yet 7. Oh God, don't let me falter here. The fight hasn't even begun. Try not to think, just lay here and go into a stupor. But always, it was the awareness of the cell and the smells and me and the awful surroundings and the fear that was eating into me, the awful uncertainty of what would happen to me, what WAS happening to me; and then of the others back in Ten, probably being gassed and clubbed right now, and the wish that I had rammed that guard with the broom, at least it would have been a more meaningful defeat. And then there was another day.

There is no such thing as a new day in the DSU: when time reaches here it is like an old gutless whore—something that steals in, battered and worn out, used and abused and discarded and drained of all that was fresh and good and promising, and full of disease and heartache and frustration for any who dare take her up to kiss hope into her.

January 6, 1972

In the morning we were taken downstairs one at a time to empty the pot, fill up our plastic container with water, and wash up. The room—the shower room I learned later—was filthy. I emptied the smelly pot, rinsed it out, then stripped naked to wash in the same sink. The others, they said, just washed their face and hands. They didn't want to strip in front of the five guards. Fuck 'em. The guards I mean. That's their morning entertainment, seeing dirty prisoners shy away from washing. Later, when I tasted the water from the pitcher, it stunk of chlorine: they had let us take it from the sink that feeds the shower: with chlorine-treated river water. This is a sick game the guards play, and they score many many times before the convicts find out the rules and byplays and their rights and privileges.

Another agonizingly long day. I was determined to not use the pot except for urinating. That added to my discomfort.

Lights go out at ten. The doctor had been by, giving us a cursory look-over. I told him of my headache. He said I'd be all right. The other two resisters put in for their medication. Something to sleep by. Escape by. They could have it. The state eagerly medicates its recalcitrants. Everyone is blissful that way. And the state, the guards, then have an almost-ultimate weapon.

In midmorning, after emptying the pot and gathering up the bedding, we were taken downstairs and given cells. I got Number 3, the worst in the corridor: a suicide cell with fine mesh steel screen for a low ceiling, obscuring some of the light from the bulb. The other cells have like a grate about seven feet from the floor as a ceiling and, though there are shadowed X's across the walls, the light is a whole lot brighter. I can see I am going to have a reading problem. And a living problem: my cell is directly opposite—about 8 feet— the cell that has been fixed up to serve as the lounge room for the correctional officers.

Music is piped onto the corridor from a loudspeaker connected to the radio in the office at the end of the tier. The tier is on ground level. Corridor, I mean. WJIB is on. The choice is that station or WHDH-FM. Music to milk cows by, the kid called over to me. For now it was relaxing. I used the flush toilet, flushed it a few times to test it, and then put it to work.

That afternoon, Mike Haroz visited the three of us, offering to take up our cause in the courts. Beautiful. We had been hoping that he would visit us down here, and he certainly didn't waste time drawing up papers for an injunction. The situation is unchanged in Ten Block. And now the remaining resisters were refusing to see the disciplinary board. Good.

Friday-night showers. A room with a hooked-up shower. Heavily chlorinated water. No curtain or anything. In fact no shower-room period. You just stand in the center, turn a knob and do the best you can. Five guards staring. I hated every second of it.

January 8, 1972

Worldly traditions are followed—some of them—even Down Here. Frankfurters and beans. What good's a week anyway if it can't be tucked in with frankfurters and beans. One of my favorites. The beans were awful, half-cooked. But I eat all I can, of everything I can stomach. I have seen too many men return from here as shells of their former selves. Eat.

How good it was to shave today too. I swiped half the shaving soap without anyone noticing it, so things are looking up.

This afternoon I was by the door as the guy comes by passing out bread. Two slices, sometimes four. And I had a cellmate right there, shoulder to shoulder, ready to take it in. He wasn't very big but I can't stand them, their wiggly antennae and ugh, so I got some toilet paper and kinda picked him up and flushed him. I searched the beans looking for others. There was no cockroach but I found a couple of hairs. I'd rather not think about it.

January 9, 1972

Sunday. Same as any other day. Once I looked up to see the prison chaplain come by. I got up to the door and said hello, asked how he was doing. He was big, about forty, in football condition, and looked tough. Like a cop. For the minute he stayed I couldn't help thinking that he was cold-looking, no smile. He said he would be back to talk to me later and I said Good, glad to have seen you, Father. Then Ray Rich said he was a dog. That he looked in on Ray after he had been beaten up and put into a straitjacket, and just walked away without a word.

January 10, 1972

A man named Pierce was by again today. Last Friday he said he'd see if there were any lawbooks around. He forgot them. It is a drag waiting for a guard to pass the ball-point pen back and forth between me and Ray Rich. They just ignore us like we weren't there, walk by and look right through us.

January 11, 1972

Every day I ask: I still can't seem to get a haircut. Except for Ray Rich (who's going sorta bald) and myself, all the men, prisoners, here have quite long hair. The guards still go about with their GI haircuts of course. And their lapel flags or small handcuffs as a tie clasp. The guards hate hair. It is evil, filthy, sinful. What is so much more: it is un-American, undemocratic, unthem. The only time I grew all sorts of hair was after they killed George Jackson. A private protest against the pigs that be. George Jackson shook me up as few revolutionaries ever could. He swung me over.

January 12, 1972

Wednesday. A whole week. That meant I was entitled to twenty minutes of walking in the yard. We go out by two's, along with four guards and an army of watchers and signals and phone calls. This is what adds meaning to their jobs. All the idiotic security procedures.

I wore two sets of underwear. Two guards felt me all over with their paws, but didn't skin-shake me. When I returned

I saw that my papers, what few I have, had been scrambled about. I don't keep carbon copies for that reason. The guards are commenting now on my writing and typing so much. Staring in at me. The guards are not adjusting well to the communistic business of sealed, uncensored letters. That is a personal affront to them.

The sinks have two push buttons. One works. It releases tepid water. Neither hot nor cold. The kid hollered, hey it's nice now, whataya think, you're in a hotel or something, the water's beautiful for washing, that's what I'm doing now. I'm running for cold, he's running the same button for hot.

January 13, 1972

Ray Rich went to court today for the A and B indictment he picked up in the old DSU corridor. Twelve guards beat him senseless and, when they knew he was asking how to file charges, they had him indicted. He got beat up because he banged and yelled when another guy was being beaten.

I made out tremendous today, bookwise. Not only did I get the law book. But the schoolteacher came by with what I asked him for: a ball-point pen, a little typing paper, a German grammar, and an algebra book. What more could a man want!

And I put the PEACE plea on the back of my letters too. A little thing, I know, but that had me feeling uneasy. I wrote to Mollie, telling her the score but asking her not to be frightened off. She tried to write me in Walpole, a very charming young lady, from all I hear, and the officials, without a word to me, returned her letter, saying she could not write me, wasn't on my approved correspondence list. It has been eight years since I even wrote to a girl. I mean someone close to my age (should I write, someone I can sexually identify with?). She is a friend of my beautiful cousin Ruthie.

There is a guard who works the night shift, I don't talk to him or anything, but I hear how he stops to rap with the young kid next to me, and the guard sounds like a swell guy. And if someone else asks for something, he is very nice about it, casual and polite. There are a few like him in Walpole. And they are unpopular with their brother officers.

January 14, 1972

We were walking, rapping, and John exclaimed, Look out! Bomb attack! and ran close to the wall. I looked up and there were at least 150 seagulls swooping overhead, splattering everything and everyone under them as they cruised by. I never saw anything like that before: the immediate sky was full of huge birds, all—or seemingly all—relieving themselves. I was laughing, watching us all scoot for cover. I didn't get hit but they didn't miss by much. There isn't much to soil around here.

When I went back in the cell today from the yard, the odor was so unpleasant that I nearly vomited. . . .

These inmates who carry in food and sweep up: they are from the drunk side. They are all trained to say nothing to us, not a word, to completely ignore us. It is pathetic, too, to see them toe the mark. Broken men. I got a haircut today from one of them. What a stink of body odor. Awful. Some of these guys are like zombies. This afternoon, an old man, tall and stiff, came in carrying the inmate-plumber's tools. He had this vacant stare. Empty. Later, John told me that the poor devil was afraid to even look at him, and then, when John kept prodding him to speak, the man said, very slowly and painfully: "This is where they put the boys who don't behave."

Tonight Artie was crestfallen because Mike Haroz wrote that the injunction was denied. Why the brat thought it would turn out otherwise, I don't know. I'd like to talk with him, explain some things to him, but I can't in this setup. It doesn't look as if we are ever going to get out in the yard together. I tried to assure him that we have won, that all the punishments and court decisions cannot erase that fact. That we knew before we started on this campaign that the written victory would be theirs. But that there are times when men are in such situations, as we were, where the very fact of resistance is victory. How many dare do what we, as a ten-man team, did? We lost, but as men.

Our task now is to keep up the heat, lament the plight of the remaining seven, and do all we can to stop the pigs from rubbing our faces in the setback. He says he understands, but at heart he is taking it hard. With a forty-year sentence in front of him, he had better start now realizing that prisoners often fight just on principle. There are no laurels. Seldom even a pat on the back from the cons around you. He'll lead with his heart for just so long, and, if he doesn't take cover behind an amorphous beyond-reach code or become a cynic then there is not much left. He can tuck tail and run (which most of us do) or he can play the diplomat (God forbid) or he will crack up. Or kill himself.

That's what Bull Martin did. Jimmy Parker. Rod Harrington. Brave men, each of them. They refused to compromise their standards. Rather than submit to the state, they killed themselves. Tell the old-timers here that they were "cowards" and they will smash your face. Jimmy Parker was a poet, a warrior-poet. I read him in 1964 (he killed himself in Bridgewater in 1962) and nearly wept with rage. There was no out for him. He refused to coast along complying.

January 18, 1972

Today John and I went for the yard exercise and saw the priest. John has been asking him for over a month for a pad of lined paper.

JOHN: "Howyadoin', Father! If you think of it, send me over that paper, will ya?"

PADRE: "Your request has already been recorded."

After eight years of sexual suppression—eight years of

denying any and every urge other than release by masturbation which, some time ago, itself even dulled into nothing more than a clinical process, a ritual which is drummed up and performed only because it seems like the time has come —the subject or idea of sex, sexual performance, adequacy, the ability to do all I want when I get out, things like that, they are not dwelt on too much. Because after eight years in here I know I am not "normal." I can't suppress love and affection and longings and dreams for so long and not have it take its toll. And in prison—an all-male, so naturally homosexual atmosphere—sexual images, in time, become distorted. Just how much so I am not sure. How can I be? But I am not even talking about that because, though I am not one, there is certainly nothing wrong with a healthy homosexual life.

I am afraid of all the suppression. I lay in bed this morning, about 6:30, thinking that since this whole shebang got off the ground twenty days ago, I hadn't even thought of sex. I have been so wrapped up with the Block Ten showdown, the first week's struggle to get adjusted in here, and then the relentless letter writing: 54 in 10 days, that my mind didn't even "relax" into a sexual fantasy. That isn't normal. That is what frightens me, makes me so very bitter with prison. How can a normal man not have an orgasm in twenty goddamn days, and not even think about it. So I thought of Sophie, my dear Sophie of long-ago days, and had a clinical process. . . .

January 19, 1972

Once I came to prison I never again heard from J. Her mother saw to that, writing to Warden Scafati. I don't blame her. I suppose it was her "mother" thing. And there are other reasons for keeping a rein on my feelings: I am not sure I know how to handle them. . . . In eight years I have never embraced a girl, kissed her, laughed and flirted with her. It is too long to go without expressing love, without even being told by someone that you are loved. Without feeling love, a personal love, for someone.

Lover or not, I can't seem to shake this three-day head-ache. I guess it is from long writing in the dark.

February 5, 1972

A month here today. I read some, not much because of my weakening eyes; I exercise some, not much because of these mild recurring headaches; but I write a lot: 117 letters in 30 days, plus this journal. Still though, this has without doubt been the longest month in my life.

Here is something I must confess, something that is a joke to the few people I am really close to: the biggest event in my prison life, one of the main things I look forward to, is going to court. It is an event. I put my whole heart into it. Bridgewater trips are awful, but I am talking mostly about the trips to Cambridge, to Boston, even to Dedham. Every time out I fall in love! I fall in love with all the hustle and bustle, the kids, the romping dogs, the bicycle riders, the hitchhikers, the countless pretty girls. I fall in love with life. I like to look into faces while we are stalled in traffic, and if someone smiles at me in return, I am magnificently turned on, my day is complete.

Solutions

We must talk about prison reform. But before we do, we should consider carefully what George Bernard Shaw once wrote, in his book *The Crime of Imprisonment:*

"Imprisonment as it exists today is a worse crime than any of those committed by its victims; for no single criminal can be as powerful for evil, or as unrestrained in its exercise, as an organized nation. Therefore, if any person is addressing himself to the perusal of this dreadful subject in the spirit of a philanthropist bent on reforming a necessary and beneficent public institution, I beg him to put it down and go about some other business. It is just such reformers who have in the past made the neglect, oppression, corruption, and physical torture of the old common goal the pretext for transforming it into that diabolical den of torment, mischief and damnation, the modern model prison."

Prisons cannot be reformed, any more than slavery can be reformed. They have to be abolished. And yet, they will not be abolished until society is changed, until people *think* differently about punishment, about law, about crime, about violence, about property, about human beings. They will not be abolished until our society works differently: until wealth is equally distributed, and people don't live in slums, and the motivations for crime and punishment become very weak, and the desire to live cooperatively with other people becomes very strong.

Then are we on a perpetual seesaw, between tiny, deceptive changes, and utopian impossibility? And are we dealing with one of those frustrating puzzles, where every time you get one piece in line, another goes out of line, and there are too many pieces to deal with at once: the frustrations and brutality of the prison guards, the violence of the prisoners, the complacency of the public, the caution of politicians?

We have to *begin*. And the only way to begin is from below, with the prisoners themselves, with their families, their friends, people in the community who begin to care. It is they—we— who need to organize, to resist, to pressure, to demand, to persuade, to jolt people into new ways of thinking by confronting them with the horror and unworkability of prisons, the need to abolish them, and what that means for changing so much else. We need to have immediate reforms, even while we refuse to fool ourselves about how reforms are not enough, how fundamental change is needed.

It has to come from below, because change that comes from the top, from national laws, from legislators, has no staying power unless pushed by an incessant force of those who care most, and who don't stop. Organized people, at the immediate, local level, who do not get discouraged when they lose, and don't disband when they win, and who have a long-range view of what is needed—that may be the best solution there is, because there is no perfect one, to the dilemma of petty reform or utopian revolution.

Massachusetts is a leader in prison reform. In October, 1972, a Correctional Reform Act went into effect, providing for prison inspections by the Public Health Department, work-release and study-release programs, furloughs, and other provisions. Even before the act was passed, the state had closed its youth institutions.

But it is the old story of much heralded reform as a spray

of chlorine into a poisoned well. Walpole, Norfolk, Concord, Deer Island, the Charles Street Jail, remain very much as they are. The reform Commissioner of Correction, John Boone, wants to make changes, and is harried by the guards, by the politicians, by the whole punishment establishment, by those who oppose him because he is black or because he is a reformer. (As this book is edited, he has just been dismissed by Governor Sargent.) It clearly takes more than one law, more than one man, to end the crime of punishment in Massachusetts, or anywhere else.

The prisoners themselves, their families, their friends, have begun to organize. One day, one hundred and fifty persons marched outside Concord Prison to support the demands of inmates. Through the first months of 1973, citizens stayed inside Walpole for twenty-four hours a day, on three eight-hour shifts, to create a kindlier atmosphere, to try to make sure terrible things did not happen.

At the heart of this process of change were the prisoners themselves, affected in some indescribable way these past years by the revolt at Attica, by the death of George Jackson, by the war in Vietnam, by the general rise of protest in the country. In this process, men, who had not gone in as "political" prisoners, who had been what we call common criminals, began emerging *rehabilitated*. But not in the way the government talks of rehabilitation, not obsequiously taking their place in the accepted, legal criminal order of things. Rather as rebels and organizers, as thoughtful, militant men ready to devote their lives to abolishing prisons along with that complexity of conditions that makes prisons seem logical.

H.Z.

Four: **HOUSING**

Justice Is Having a Decent Place to Live

by Howard Zinn with Thomas G. Leahy,
Mark Stern, Merle Berke, Janice Marin,
Merrie Mitchell, Jordan Stitzer,
Joseph Caruso, Ned Epstein

> This is still a free country. Under free enterprise, a landlord
> can set a certain rent and the tenant may or may not pay it,
> and can seek quarters elsewhere.
> —Attorney representing landlord before Brookline Rent
> Review Board

We live in a society where how much money you have determines the most basic facts of your existence: Do you have
a place to live? Do you have to worry about being thrown out
of your house and looking for another place? What is it like
to live there? Do you freeze in the winter and swelter in the
summer, or are you comfortable? Is the air you breathe foul?
Is the street pleasant and tree-lined or rutted and garbage-
strewn? Is your house overrun by vermin? Mice? Rats? Do
you have to worry about your children being bitten by rats?
Does a couple have sexual privacy? Does an individual have
space and quiet for work, for relaxation? Do you live in a
place obviously vulnerable to fire and have to worry about
you and your family burning to death?

Behind the word *housing* is all of that, the most essential matters of everyday life. And how can one talk of a just society, what do "constitutional rights" matter, if there is not justice every day in where and how one exists, sleeps, wakes up, has a family life?

In the nonindustrial countries, in Latin America or Asia, we know how vital land is to the people, and we see clearly the injustice in those places, where a tiny fraction of the population, the wealthy, own 80 or 90 percent of the land. In industrial America, it is less obvious, but living space is similarly controlled by those with the most money, especially in the cities. The rich have no problem. The middle class can buy homes or rent high-priced apartments and struggle to pay for them. But the poor cannot afford that, and so they live without comfort, without security, worrying about paying the rent, about keeping warm in the winter, about their kids growing up in noise and dirt and confusion.

The "free enterprise" system described by the Brookline attorney, in which the landlord is free to charge what he wants and the tenant is free to pay or move elsewhere is not freedom, because the tenant does not have enough money to pay, and there aren't enough other places to move to. Census figures show that about 40,000 of the 220,000 housing units in Boston are substandard. It was estimated in 1969 that 10,000 low-income housing units were urgently needed in Boston, but in the first half of that year permits were issued for 1379 units and 1012 units were demolished, so the net increase was 367 units.

There are not enough places to live. So the real estate people and the banks take advantage of this to make huge profits. The rest of us must pay what they ask or go homeless. What gets built is decided by how much money is to be made by real estate people. They make more money from high-rise luxury apartments, so that is what they build.

A Boston *Globe* reporter, Janet Riddell, did a survey in

1970 on the housing problems of low-income families, and reported on three cases:

"Mr. and Mrs. Robert Grenham and their seven children live on the second floor of a three-family house in Hyde Park which lies in the path of the Southwest Expressway. They were supposed to be out in November. But they can't find a place to go. . . .

"Mr. and Mrs. Lawrence Breadmore and their nine children are crowded into a five-room Dorchester apartment. The bank foreclosed on his former landlord and issued eviction notices to all tenants last July. He was asked to be out by December 1. But he can't find a place he can afford. . . .

"Mr. and Mrs. John Leach and their four children live with a faulty furnace, $70-a-month heat bills, and rats in the hallways of their Dorchester apartment. They want to move. But they can't find a better place that they can afford."

There does not seem to be money available to build housing for people who desperately need it. But there is plenty of money for highways and office buildings and fancy hotels. Shortly after the *Globe* report on the lack of low-income housing, the same newspaper carried a front-page headline: "$300 MILLION BUILDING PLAN FOR PARK SQUARE AREA." The first paragraph said:

> Plans for initiating a long-range rebuilding program for a 35-acre section of the Boylston Street-downtown Park Square areas of the city for high-rise apartments, hotels, office buildings, and entertainment facilities were announced at a press conference yesterday by Mayor White.

It is expected that real estate people would put profits before human need. But the *government,* we have assumed ever since the New Deal, would step in and take care of the poor, with all kinds of housing programs. Not so. Yes, some low-income housing has been built, but nowhere near enough. Most government aid has gone to banks and big builders, guaranteeing their loans, subsidizing their construction efforts, assuring their profits. And the local government agencies have worked closely with highway and financial interests and politicians to favor the rich and ignore the poor.

For instance, the Boston Redevelopment Authority was supposed to carry out the federal urban renewal program with its goal of "a decent home and a suitable living environment for every American family." But Thomas G. Leahy, doing a study of housing in Boston, concluded that BRA "is primarily concerned about institutional, financial, and business interests rather than providing a decent home for every Bostonian. Increasing the city's tax base and building luxury apartments such as Charles River Park in the West End, the Prudential apartments, and the 'window on the world' waterfront apartments, take priority over low-income housing."

In this, the poor suffered. "The BRA's major undertakings for the poor, barring the Washington Park project in Roxbury, have been negative; that is, removing low-income housing to make way for priority projects but not replacing the housing it destroys. The former residents of Scollay Square, the West End, and the neighborhood where the Prudential Center now stands certainly do not presently reside in the apartments that replaced them. Even in the Washington Park project, 3,510 housing units were removed and only 1,550 new ones constructed."

This was the BRA story for the decade of the sixties: tear down low-income housing, replace it with profitable office buildings and luxury apartments.

Another example of how the federal government has done more to enrich real estate people than to help homeless people is in the use of Section 221-d3 of the National Housing Act. Mark Stern investigated "221-d3" housing in Boston, which accounted for much of the low- and moderate-income housing built in Boston in the sixties. An alliance is formed between government, banking, and realty interests, in which the realtor builds a low-income development by borrowing money from a bank at the current rate of interest (7 to 8 percent). But the realtor actually pays the bank only 3 percent, and the government pays the rest.

This is supposed to enable the construction of low-rent apartments. But at one of these developments (Camelot Court Apartments, in Brighton), rents which were set at $45 a month so poor families could pay, jumped in four years to $145 a month. The 221-d3 developers, Stern found, were supposed to invest 10 percent of the capital themselves, mortgaging the rest, and then were permitted to make a 6 percent profit on their investment. But if the developer had his own construction firm, he only had to put up 2 percent. So if a project cost $5 million, instead of putting up $500,000 himself, he could put up $100,000, and would be allowed a profit of $30,000 (6 percent of $500,000), so that his real profit would be 30 percent.

But the big money, Mark Stern discovered, was made in federally subsidized housing by tax breaks. The owners of 221-d3 projects could claim on their tax returns that their property was rapidly decreasing in value, when it would probably be increasing. And then they could sell shares to other investors who want such a tax break, and make a lot of money that way. So in the end the 221-d3 developers can make more money than in nongovernment projects, and yet have government backing and less risk.

Furthermore, to increase the profit, poor materials were used in construction, and the housing deteriorated rapidly. The plumbing began to leak, the ceilings began to disintegrate, rats and roaches appeared, and in one of these projects in Roxbury (Academy II Homes) the roof of one building blew right off in a strong wind.

Refusing to pay rent increases under these conditions, a group of tenants in one development (Castle Square in the South End) took to the courts to compel the Federal Housing

Authority to hold hearings before granting rent increases. They then learned which side the law was on. The Circuit Court said:

"Applying the constitutionally relevant test, therefore, it seems to us that the government interest in summary process for approving rent increases outweighs the tenants' interest in greater procedural safeguards. . . . The National Housing Act does not provide categorical assistance to those in need of housing, nor does it erect detailed statutory safeguards to protect their interest. . . . Review would discourage the increased involvement of the private sector which is the goal of section 221-d3 (*Hahn v. Gottlieb,* 430 F 2d)."

It could hardly be put more plainly: the goal of that section was to involve "the private sector," which means making it profitable for them. And that means, don't let the tenants have a say about rent increases.

It seems the way the system works, the landlords do very well no matter what happens: if the slums are replaced by luxury apartments, there is money to be made there; if the replacement is government-subsidized low-income housing, the rate of profit is high; and if nothing is done, if the slums remain, there is profit in that.

The profitability of slums was investigated by a team of Boston University students in 1972: Merle Berke, Janice Marin, Merrie Mitchell, Jordan Stitzer. They looked into a section of Boston called the South End.

Once fairly elegant, the South End today is a melting pot in which nothing melts except the dilapidated walls of the houses, in the fires that have scourged the area and destroyed one out of five buildings there. The inhabitants are a mélange: old-generation Irish and Italians, Greeks and Syrians, blacks and Puerto Ricans, new immigrants like the Portuguese, and lately, college students, transients, alcoholics. The sound of police and fire sirens seems never to end. The crime rate is very high. Unemployment is 75 percent above the city's average; the incidence of tuberculosis is six times the Boston average; the infant mortality rate twice as high. The streets reek of uncollected garbage. There are roominghouses without fire escapes, where high-voltage cables have frayed insulation, gas fumes pervade the basement, and there is one bathroom for the entire building.

The team inspected the rooms in one roominghouse: "The rooms were cold, small, and dimly lit. They contained a shallow closet, and a small sink and mirror mounted on the wall of peeling paint. Shades for the window are not included, but cost extra, for each used, shredded shade. An old inefficient steam radiator and a two-drawer dresser with a mirror were the only furniture included besides the bed containing a single sheet and blanket. A room such as this costs sixteen dollars per week, sixty-four per month."

Another room was advertised in the newspaper as a "furnished side room" with refrigerator and light housekeeping. The team describes what it found:

"The windows in the front of the building were smashed. There was no heat. Once inside one must wait until his eyes are adjusted to the dark because the hallway is lit by only a single fifteen-watt bulb. Climbing up the cracked, winding stairs, one had the omnipresent feeling that the building was about to collapse, as large cracks covered the length of the walls.

"Inside, the floor was ripped apart with pieces of linoleum and boards scattered about revealing the underlying cross beams. The bed had two broken legs and contained a sheet and one soiled blanket. The light housekeeping included a clean sheet 'usually' furnished every week. The refrigerator was small and had no electric cord. Besides this there were no closets, sinks, dressers, or other furniture except for a broken chair. The room reeked of urine. Not only that, but the door was cracked down the middle and had a broken lock.

"The building contained one small bathroom consisting of a flush toilet (working!) and an old-fashioned four-foot dirty bathtub which was filled with a few toilet plungers, assorted metal pans, and some boards. Half of the fire escape was missing. The building had no telephone or even a mailbox."

The team discovered how the inspection laws are dealt with, when something as serious as a missing fire escape is involved. The landlord, promising to build a fire escape, gets a temporary inspection certificate, and then keeps renewing the temporary certificate annually. Or the boardinghouse is technically listed as an apartment-dwelling residence, which by law is only inspected upon a formal complaint.

Slums are profitable, the team found. As an example, they took one building assessed at $5,000, with 15 out of 20 rooms rented constantly at $15 per week. Total rent: $11,700 per year. Costs for the landlord: $800 for property taxes, and $200 for maintenance. Profit; $10,700. Multiply that by several buildings and you begin to get the picture.

Perhaps if tenants faced landlords in direct combat, tenants would know the need for organization, pressure, militancy. But there are all sorts of intermediaries who pretend to be helpful to the tenant: investigating committees, rent control boards, political leaders, laws and courts. These create a defense in depth for the landlord system, which exhaust the energies of those seeking change.

For example, there was the legislative committee that was set up in early 1971 to investigate a fire that destroyed a building on Peterborough Street in the Back Bay section of Boston. Eight people died in that fire.

The chairman of the committee was Mario Umana, the Majority Leader of the State Senate, and a campaign manager for Boston Mayor Kevin White. The committee's report blamed the tenants for the fire, although it had been determined that the starting point was a sofa placed on a first-floor corridor, which on three occasions the tenants had asked the superintendent to remove. The committee found absolutely no fault with the owner of the building, one of the richest landlords in Boston, a man named Maurice Gordon. Indeed, his name appeared nowhere in the report.

A reporter for the Boston *Phoenix,* Charlie McCollum, did some investigating when the report came out. Eight people had died because the fire raced up through the building in a few minutes. Tenants who did not have a second exit or were unable to reach a window to be rescued by firemen were doomed. What caused the rapid spread of the fire was clear: inoperative fire doors, lack of sprinkler systems, highly flammable plywood paneling in some corridors, false corridor ceilings, lack of prompt rubbish disposal, non-fire-retardant paint in stairways and corridors.

Tenants had filed over a dozen complaints with the Housing Inspection Department in the year before the fire. Indeed, the building had been condemned in 1961 and again in 1965. The defects were never corrected, but the condemnation notices had been revoked. Fire doors, it seemed, could not close because the rear wall of the building created a warp, and in 1961 the building department had noted this. In early 1970, the fire department had noted "defective fire doors in the corridor." The State Sanitary Code requires two acceptable exits for each dwelling unit, but twenty of the forty apartments in the building did not have a second exit.

Maurice Gordon, the owner, had a history of easy relations with the courts. When, in 1963, there was a fire in the Sherry Biltmore Hotel which killed four people, an investigating committee recommended an overhaul of the Boston Building Department and criminal action against Maurice Gordon. Gordon was allowed to plead *nolo contendere* for a technical violation of the building code and was fined $500. At another time, a bench warrant was issued for his arrest, but never served, and then Judge Elijah Adlow dismissed the case against him upon the request of Gordon's attorneys.

The failure of all the intermediary institutions to bring justice to the tenant was discussed in the spring of 1971 in an editorial in the Boston *Globe,* after a series of articles exposing the housing mess in the city. It talked about "a system of favoritism to the landlords, beginning with inspection procedures that are often a farce, going on to lower court proceedings that are often a disgrace." Of seven hundred cases filed in court against landlords, only twenty resulted in fines, and ten of these were removed on appeal. "The city has the power . . . to arrest and imprison landlords after court proceedings. But it has never done so."

Enforcement of the law, which seems to work like a vise when members of the lower classes commit a crime, does not seem to operate well with landlords. Two students at Boston University decided to fight the widespread practice of landlords insisting on "security deposits" before renting an apartment, and then finding an excuse not to give it back when the lease is over. They took their case into Small Claims Court and won the right to get their $165 security deposit back. Then they spent nine months trying to get the decision enforced and actually have the sheriff collect the money. They were still working on this when I spoke to them in 1972.

The desperate helplessness one feels before this intricate system of defenses was expressed by one young man, Joseph Caruso, who had spent thirteen years of his life in a low-income housing project:

"In a country where all men are supposedly equal, why is it that some people can't afford their own house to live in, while other people own houses all over the world? Something is not right here.

"I have a friend whose father is what you might classify a slum landlord. He owns a few apartment houses that should have been condemned long ago, and he rents rooms out mostly to students, young people, and blacks from Haiti who speak little or no English. . . .

"Now the guy that owns these apartments seems like a nice guy. He is friendly, personable to talk to, but he is money hungry. He doesn't see anything wrong with what he is doing. He feels as though he is doing the people that live in his apartments a service by providing them with a place to live, and at the same time he's pulling in the cash.

"This is the kind of person that the American system produces. They see nothing wrong in making money in almost any way they can. Why should someone make money off of another person's need for a place to live? Why should people be forced to live in places like this? All of this is perfectly legal in America.

"On the news the other day I heard about a woman and her four children who were evicted from their apartment last year and still have no place to live. Mostly they sleep in their car in the parking lot of an all-night department store. This is totally unbelievable. . . . people are going hungry, going without a place to live, forced to live under subhuman conditions in the most prosperous country in the world. . . ."

Another instance of the intricacy of the system, defying the ability of ordinary people to make their way through it, is described by Ned Epstein, who lived in Brookline and began to organize tenants there. Alpine Associates owned many buildings, kept raising rents and threatening tenants with eviction. Tenants in Brookline got together, campaigned for rent control and to stop evictions, and at a stormy town meeting in September, 1970, passed a rent control bill. This rolled back rents to the March, 1970, level and required a certificate of eviction from the Brookline rent control board before a tenant could be evicted.

Immediately, the Brookline Landowners Association filed in court for an injunction to stop the enforcement of the rent control law by the rent control board. It was granted. Alpine Associates refused to tell tenants what the March, 1970, rent levels were and insisted tenants pay the customary rents. The tenants, organizing, decided to put their rent in an escrow fund. But many were afraid of eviction. Technically, the injunction did not cancel the law, but prevented enforcement of it, so there was a legal impasse, but, Epstein reported, "some people still felt that it was us who were breaking the law if we did not pay the rent Alpine was asking for."

He commented: "It's totally incredible what the socialization process has done to some. They feel that bucking the system is illegal when the system blatantly breaks its own laws." Still, their fear was real: "For many of the older people, living on fixed incomes and having no other place to go, joining escrow meant possibly being blackballed by Alpine. With families it was much the same. 'We will be kicked out on the street and then what will my children do?' "

Nevertheless, sixty-two housing units and over $17,000 dollars were withheld from Alpine. Alpine retaliated by deciding to issue parking permits to tenants with cars. Then they did not give permits to those who had placed their money in escrow, which meant that cars might be towed off the streets by police.

The tenants took their case to the Board of Selectmen, crowded the meeting, made a powerful plea, and the Selectmen granted emergency parking on the streets overnight. Finally, the injunction was lifted, and the rent control eviction law stood. What Alpine then did was to use a tax-escalation clause in the leases to raise the rent about as much as they had done before the law was passed. Epstein was bitter: "There is always a way out for the Lord and never much of an alternative for his serfs."

The Eviction of Peter and Catherine Hannon

by Timothy McMahon

I am writing this report in early 1972. On June fifteenth, Peter and Catherine Hannon plan to take their daughter Cristine and leave this country, possibly for good. The reasons for the move were complex and difficult to define. As Peter told me, "I can't point to one specific thing that made us decide we had to get out of this place. I guess it's a combination of a lot of things, physical and mental. The apartment hassle was just the thing that freed us to get moving." Peter was referring to their eviction from their apartment in January of this year. For them both, it marked their first real encounter with the American legal system.

Peter Hannon is thirty-two. He is a sailor by profession (he works for a Norwegian shipping line), and a painter by desire. Raised in Cleveland, he attended Western Reserve University for three years until he dropped out. He saw the "objectivity" of the classroom as sterile, nonintellectual. Peter's beliefs could be called idealistic, although his manner is rarely righteous. He has never had a great amount of respect for authority, being of the opinion his life is best run by himself. Most of Peter's life is now centered around his family, his painting, and his sailing, although he also finds tremendous satisfaction in music and carpentry.

Catherine Hannon is twenty-four. Since she had Cristine

almost one year ago, she has devoted herself mainly to the occupations of mother and housewife. Catherine graduated from Boston University in 1969. In the summer of that year she traveled to Holland, where she met Peter. Together they toured Scandinavia, later returning to Boston, where they set up a household together. In September, 1970, Catherine became pregnant. She gave birth to Cristine on June 20, 1971. On October 12 of the same year Catherine and Peter were married, at least in the eyes of the state.

Catherine has described herself as somewhat sheltered, although caring for herself and then for Cristine while Peter was away at sea has exposed her to the problems of urban living the past three years. She has learned to adjust to her new situation quite well, being an extremely stable and understanding person. "I'm always a little depressed for a few days after Peter leaves, but I'm no longer frightened by being alone as I was at first. I've just come to trust my instincts and let them decide what I do. I always try to treat people decently, like I'd want to be treated. And if they don't reciprocate I try to find out why, but sometimes I have to write someone off as just a plain bastard."

All these points tell something about Peter and Catherine, but even together they don't fully describe who or what they are, that is, what makes them individuals unlike any other human beings. And yet, that they are individuals, like you and me, seems so extremely important to keep in mind. For too often, in discussing law and justice in this country, the human element is obscured.

In September, 1970, Catherine and Peter moved from their first apartment in Cambridge to a new one located on Park Drive in the Back Bay area of Boston. Prior to making the move, both had inspected the apartment and noted several repairs which would be needed. Included in the list were the replacement of an antiquated bathtub, the repair of a toilet which did not flush properly, a badly cracked wall, the replacement of ceiling plaster in the bathroom and bedroom, a missing freezer door in the refrigerator, a badly leaking kitchen sink, the replacement of a broken front window, the installation of more electrical outlets in the living room and bedroom (both had only one), and putting in new window and door locks (only one window completely locked and the door's lock rested on a wooden block wedged between the door and frame). When these repairs were mentioned to the owner, Frank Walters of Walters and Sons Realty, he assured them the improvements would be made before they moved in. They accepted his word and signed a standard Greater Boston Real Estate Board lease, for $190 a month as husband and wife.

As might be expected with a verbal agreement with a landlord, the repairs were not made before they took possession of the apartment on September 1. However, they decided to ignore this fact for a few weeks, as the process of moving created for them enough difficulties to keep their time well occupied. Once settled, Peter called Frank Walters to question him on the delay. Walters apologized profusely, claiming there had been a fire in another of his buildings over the summer and all his workmen had been tied up since in making the place "fit for habitation." The matter was again dropped, this time for almost two months, while Peter was away at sea.

A number of new discoveries were made by Catherine during this period. First, the kitchen and bathroom were heavily infested with roaches. Peter and Catherine had naturally expected some, but the size of this insect offensive was a bit hard to take, even for these Boston apartment veterans. And second, there was no hot water in the mornings and often at night as well. Again Walters was called, and this time the new developments were included in the list. He told them his men would be there the following day, adding that he had received similar complaints on the water and roaches from other tenants and that both matters were being cared for.

In what were now daily attempts to reach Walters, Peter

and Catherine were repeatedly told Walters was not in. After one of these calls, Peter phoned again saying he was from the Mayor's Office. Within minutes he was talking to Frank Walters. One week later workmen did arrive. They replastered the cracks in the bathroom and bedroom, replaced the broken window, and attempted to fix the sink and toilet. Both attempts proved unsuccessful, neither men being plumbers, as one man admitted on a return visit at a later date. An exterminator finally did arrive, but his efforts were also unsuccessful. Peter and Catherine made several more attempts to reach Walters but were repeatedly put off. And so it went for the remainder of the year. Peter eventually bought the tools and equipment necessary to fix the toilet and sink, replace the door and window locks, and install a makeshift freezer door.

Despite these difficulties, Catherine and Peter decided to renew their lease for another year. As Peter told me, "From past experience and just talking to some friends we realized our case wasn't an isolated one. I mean, everyone has landlord hassles. Besides, we'd fixed up the apartment pretty much the way we wanted it, and made friends with most people in the building. That was fairly important from my standpoint, especially after we had Cristine. I mean, I was away so often with my job, it just made me feel better knowing they were among friends. And besides, it was a good location and a relatively safe one." So once more they signed the standard lease, but this time they wrote into the lease the remaining needed repairs.

Once again Walters failed to make the repairs. And once again Catherine and Peter were finding it almost impossible to reach him by phone. "I guess," said Catherine, "by this time we were really making a nuisance of ourselves. Every time I called, I talked to someone different, but the answers was always the same—No, Walters isn't here and no, I don't know anything about any repairs. Wow! Sometimes they were really hostile, like they were doing me a favor by just talking to me."

In spite of the difficulties, the Hannons were fairly well settled into their apartment routine. Although they couldn't take baths (Catherine at least, always used to take them), and the toilet occasionally backed up, and they were constantly blowing fuses as well as losing the battle of the roaches, they entered that second year in fairly good spirits. Said Catherine, "I guess we were just happy living together, and of course the baby made that even more so. I was really worried when I got pregnant. Peter and I had decided to have a baby but I wasn't really sure how it would be once she arrived. For some reason I just couldn't picture Peter as a father. But I have to admit things have really been beautiful. I don't care what anyone says, I really love being a mother. And Peter, he's amazing! I mean he really loves Cristine. You know, when we first brought her home from the hospital, he'd just sit there, sometimes for hours, just staring at her like he couldn't believe she was real. . . . Well anyway, you asked me about that night. It was sometime last September. I went to put Cristine to bed, and then I saw these two roaches in her crib. Well, I was pretty upset, because those were the first ones I'd seen in the bedroom, so I called Peter. When I told him, he really flipped out. I mean, he was yelling and swearing, and then Cristine started crying, and I started yelling for Peter to shut up—it was really a bad scene."

To make matters worse, Cristine became ill a few days later. Catherine immediately took her to the doctor, who diagnosed it as a mild virus, treated her, and gave instructions to keep the child warm and quiet. Catherine again, "I don't know if you remember, but that was around the time we had that brief cold spell. We brought Cristine home from the doctor's and put her to bed immediately. Well, the heat didn't come on that night, and I mean it was really cold. The story was that the furnace broke down near the end of our first year, and we complained, and the other tenants complained, but he never fixed the damn thing. Well, Peter was furious, I mean he started to get violent. I was scared to death. I'd never seen him that angry. I can tell you this now because he isn't here: If Walters had been in the apartment that night I seriously think Peter would have killed him. That was the night we came to your place, remember?"

Peter: "That was the last straw. I simply decided that I wasn't going to let Walters eat at me any longer. I looked at it this way—this is my home and my family and there's no reason they should suffer because of that son of a bitch. So I decided, if he's not going to make the repairs, I'm not going to pay rent."

When Peter discussed his decision with Catherine, she felt it might be best to follow the legal guidelines for withholding rent, but Peter resisted. He was tired of doing that which was proper. Instead he would do that which was right. As he said, "Why should I put my money in a bank until he makes the repairs? He gets the rent in the end anyway, and what do we get for the time we spent in the apartment before the repairs? Nothing—no cutback in rent—nothing. The hell with that." In the end Catherine sided with him.

And so, when October rolled around they refused to pay rent. And again in November. By this time Walters was sending people round the clock daily, threatening eviction. The Hannons simply stopped answering the door. Finally on November 29, Catherine and Peter received a notice informing them Walters had applied to the rent board for a "certificate of eviction." Peter contacted a friend who happened to be a lawyer, although he no longer practiced. He immediately requested a hearing before the board to present their case, although he bluntly told Peter they didn't stand a chance.

On December 3 their hearing was held. The lawyer described the events mentioned above in legal terms, while Walters' lawyer produced evidence that the Hannons had no paid rent for what was now three months. The board seemed somewhat sympathetic, but in the end determined that Walters had "just cause" for eviction proceedings, and the certificate was granted.

At this point Peter began to realize he had little hope of winning in court, and he certainly had no intention of paying the back rent. As the Hannons' lawyer pointed out, from a strictly legal standpoint, their actions were clearly illegal. Peter, not wishing to have their possessions confiscated by Walters or the court, began moving them in clandestine fashion to the home of Catherine's older sister in New Hampshire.

On December 7, the Hannons received a fourteen-day notice to vacate their home. This was followed by an eviction writ issued by the court. Peter immediately turned this over to his lawyer. I asked Peter what he was feeling at this time. "I felt remarkably calm, but a little angry. I'd pretty well resigned myself to the outcome, and was just anxious to get it over with—that's why we didn't want a continuation or an appeal, but the indifference of the Judge to the situation, I mean, his callousness towards throwing people out of their homes, that really got to me. He didn't even want to hear why we stopped paying rent."

On January 6 the Hannons went to court for their hearing. The proceedings went about as expected, with the exception of one more ugly twist added by Walters' lawyer. As I was forbidden to carry my notebook into the courtroom, I can only report its essence. After a good deal of talking by both lawyers at the Judge's bench, Walters' attorney raised his voice to a level for all to hear, saying that although Mr. Walters did not wish to pursue this line on legal grounds, a certain piece of information might be relevant to the case. Somehow, he had managed to discover that Peter and Catherine were not married at the time they signed the lease, a fact which might render the lease invalid. It was a cruel, and totally unnecessary, addition to an already unfair proceeding. The remark left the

Hannons' lawyer speechless, as they had not even considered the matter.

Both Peter and Catherine were visibly shaken by the dis-. closure, Peter red with rage and Catherine near tears, not because of any shame but because of the senselessness of this vicious attempt to publicly discredit them. To make matters worse, the Judge continued this bitter farce by looking oh! so righteous and asking each, in his gravest tone, if it were true, and then lecturing them on their "sins." Finally the Hannons' lawyer managed to put an end to this inquisition. The remainder of the hearing might be reduced to three questions. How much was the rent? Was it paid? And did you follow the legal procedures for withholding rent? Needless to say, Judgment was given, and the Execution papers were issued.

Five: WORK

Injustice at Work

The law is a jungle, inside of which there are traps for law breakers. Anyone who ventures into those traps is caught and punished. He is presumed to have done an injustice to someone; this is sometimes true and sometimes the opposite of the truth. But all around those traps there are the thickets of law itself, in which anything is permitted, and is legal, if sustained by power and privilege. Within this jungle, safe from the traps, are the factories, offices, and other places where people expend so much of their time and life-force: the job.

The injustice of the job is so accepted—so deep within the law, so long-rooted in our culture and lives, so often subtle, so elusive to correction—that we tend to overlook it in the quest for more dramatic problems. But it is there, whether we are women secretaries, black or white factory workers, or schoolteachers. It is there in the boredom of jobs undertaken not by choice but by desperation or in the indignities suffered at the hands of bureaucrats, bosses, and underlings.

The workplace is a world of its own, with its own rules, its own habits, its own culture. Like other such closed worlds—the military, the schools, the prisons—it is mostly ignored by the law, because it does its jobs of control well, relieving the law and the larger forces of government so they can concentrate on more gross problems. Anyone inside this world of

217

work who feels injustice and looks around desperately for help from the law will rarely find it.

In this way, the feudal system, with its myriad tiny fiefdoms of servitude and lordship, has been carried over into the institutions of modern society. Who owns the enterprise, how its fruits are distributed, who makes decisions, how long people work and under what conditions, who is fired and who is taken on—all this is decided by the rules of the jungle, but all soothed and smoothed by coffee breaks, Christmas parties, and tiny gifts hanging from the giant trees.

The problems seem small, almost petty. But put together in one life they are damaging; put together in one society they poison a whole culture.

In Boston, a young delivery man, Bill M., tells how the company expects him, though he gets no more pay than the ordinary truck drivers, to do more than deliver goods. They want him to be "a goodwill man who is calm and courteous to the customers, a public relations man who must sell the customer on the service of the company, an extension of the company's image." He says (his choice of emphasis):

"The clean-cut appearance of the worker is important, because beards are *not* allowed nor is long hair. Black drivers are *allowed* to wear an Afro-American hair style as long as it is moderate and follows the contour of the head. Moustaches are now *allowed;* however, they must be neatly trimmed. Sideburns must also be neatly trimmed and cannot fall below the lowest part of the ear. When I first applied for employment some sixteen months ago, I had a moustache, and it was strongly suggested to me that I would be hired if the moustache came off. It did! Whenever a supervisor feels that your hair is too long, he will tell you to get a haircut before you report for work the next time."

The same grooming rules, he says, apply to the workers whose jobs are inside the terminal facility—loaders, sorters, unloaders—although they never see the customers. This was explained by a company official who said that "if you allowed the inside men to grow a beard or long hair, then the drivers would demand the same rights." Wouldn't that be terrible, Bill M. comments.

The delivery man has to be sure he makes his normal number of stops, and does not return from them too early (which causes suspicion that he should really have a bigger load), or too late (which leads to the idea he is loafing). In either case, the supervisor may decide to accompany him on his next day or two. And so, Bill M. says, "Nobody wants a supervisor hanging on his neck for a whole day or two so we literally run during the course of the day."

He adds, "A supervisor can tell you to stop talking to another worker whenever he feels like it! It makes no difference whatsoever that you can perform your tasks as well as you always do. If he doesn't like it, he will order you to stop, and failure to do so may result in your dismissal."

Another thing that vexes Bill M. is the requirement that employees show I.D. cards upon both entering and leaving each day:

"The building is surrounded by a wire cyclone fence and access is controlled at two points. These points are manned by hired security guards. You can imagine the hassle that one must go through in the winter time to take off his gloves and dig through his wallet to produce this card. I can understand why they have you show it when you enter, but I will never understand why you have to show it when you leave. Perhaps they are afraid I may have parachuted in or pole vaulted over the fence.

"Unfortunately, an employee does not receive his permanent I.D. card until about two months after he has been working there. Until that time, you are required to sign in and out at the guard shack. During the winter or during a rainstorm, I have seen as many as twenty men standing there in a line, completely drenched or half-freezing, just waiting to sign out. This situation is absolutely ridiculous, but the company adheres to it. Apparently the company has more respect for its security system than it does for its workers, who are the backbone of its very life."

A secret-police atmosphere of reporting and surveillance is common in work situations. Bill tells about the company installing a series of overhead catwalks, which get people from one area to another efficiently but which also serve as an observation platform. He says: "This Orwellian device causes a great deal of distress to many workers. You can imagine what it is like trying to perform your job fully knowing that either a security guard or a supervisor is standing directly over you watching your every action. This goes on night after night, and certainly has an intimidating effect upon the workers."

There is cruelty in the world of work, so accustomed is that world to the race for profit, for promotion, for personal advancement, so deep are the frustrations of unsatisfying work. Its victims seek other victims. This cruelty is infectious, found not only in the corporate bureaucracy but in the trade union and in the personal relations of the job. When a new employee is both black and foreign-born, there is a special possibility for hurt. This is what Charles Ramsey, a Jamaica-born Negro, found when he came to the United States, and took a job with a large trucking company in Boston.

Robert Dannin, a student interviewer, talked with Ramsey many times and recorded their conversations. Other workers made Ramsey conscious of his race, and when he complained to management it was treated as a joke. "One day a young worker, Walter, told me that I shouldn't be working there, but rather sweeping on the docks. I complained and the next moment I saw Walter and Eddie, the office manager, laughing and joking."

Some fellow employees put a picture of a monkey up on the office wall. "I knew that it was meant for me. A girl

named Karen would look at the picture and then turn to me."
She would mimic a monkey's motions. Ramsey pointed out
that management was not directly responsible for his problems
on the job. It was other workers. "They made things hard for
me. They are the ones who called me a nigger." But the pas-
sivity of management suggested acquiescence.

One fellow employee told Ramsey she would get someone
to beat him up. Ramsey replied that if she were the least bit
interested in that man she should not put him up to that, because he would not live long. "Of course, I have never been
violent. I have been very happy since arriving in this country.
I have been at peace with everyone. Not even on the streets
with all that has been happening has anyone ever come to
fight me—not even any sharp quarrels. I walk away if a person attempts to provoke me.

"But in the office where you are working, you begin to
realize that one must retaliate, because you spend more time
per day in the office than perhaps at home. During that long
dreary day, you can justify that sort of retaliation. Conrad
[an office manager] once told me that this was because people
in the office are tired all day long. They become frustrated and
flare up. But I wondered why they never flared up at each
other—why all this aggression directed toward me, and why
then do they call me 'ole nigger.' All that can't be right."

Things got worse. "That morning Ralph [another employee]
promised to shoot me—and 'all niggers' in fact—that cleared
everything up. That was the end. I could see that management
wanted to get rid of me too." The office manager told Ramsey,
when he complained about the threat of shooting, that he took
the matter "too personally." Ramsey replied: "If you say that
what Ralph said wasn't personal, then you are saying that I
am not a person."

Ramsey told Robert Dunnin, his student interviewer, "It's
sad. I don't know. I always grew up with a hope. Even though
some things instill fear in me, I want to hope. Deep down I

have even tried to give allowances for the way those people treated me, for the fact that they weren't accustomed to sitting at a desk with a black man. Maybe they were kind of frightened—I don't know! I had been there days, weeks, months, a year, and if they were intelligent or sensitive humans, they should have become accustomed to me. I'm not a monkey or a gorilla—they know I'm a person, but they just hated and wanted to make me feel embarrassed.

"I would go home and reflect, 'My God, to think that one has to go through this in order to earn a living.'"

Ramsey needed to support his family. "I have two boys. One goes to Boston College and the other to Cambridge High and Latin. So I am responsible for them. The rest of my family is still in Jamaica. On Saturday I go to the market and must keep house for myself. I try to keep it as tidy as possible. On Sundays I go to church. . . . That's how I live. I usually find enough to do to pass the days."

Could the law help Ramsey in a situation like this? He heard about the Massachusetts Commission Against Discrimination, and went to them, told them about his situation. They began an investigation. Immediately, he was fired by the company. The Commission ordered him reinstated. But it had no machinery for enforcing this ruling. The company refused to rehire him. Ramsey was told he would need a lawyer. In the meantime he had to pay rent, $125 a month, and other expenses.

He began to apply for other jobs, but everyone asked him for a reference from his last employer. He was without a job, and had to go on welfare.

For Charles Ramsey, neither the United States Constitution, the civil rights laws, nor the Massachusetts Commission Against Discrimination could secure for him the most basic element of justice, the right to be considered a person.

"Meaninglessness and mindlessness" is how Richard Convicer describes his part-time evening job. He had two tasks: filing accounts, and looking for accounts in the files. This drab job was ennobled by an introductory speech given to the file clerks the first week by the assistant manager: "You are now a member of this Company and I should like to convey to you my personal welcome. We are glad to have you with us to share in the opportunities afforded by our large and growing organization and trust that the relationship now established will be a long and happy one."

Apparently, a relationship between the employee and the filing cabinet was seen as important. Relationships among the employees were discouraged. "While one is in the filing section, he is not permitted to talk. . . . If one is caught talking, he is immediately told to be quiet."

Women were not hired for this job. The reason given was that it was too dangerous for them to leave the job at 8 P.M. and walk to the subway. Convicer comments: "Strangely, however, they didn't consider that these girls would be accompanied by the male employees and so their safety seems not to have been the real concern. . . . The company feared that the workers might partake in sexual activities instead of keeping their minds on the files."

The atmosphere of what Convicer calls "depersonalization" was strengthened by the absence of channels for complaints or suggestions. There seemed to be no one at hand to receive them. Instead, decision making seemed to emanate from distant, mysterious, and unreachable sources. Workers were told to do things in a certain way because "New York wants it that way."

While workers were not encouraged to communicate with one another, the company communicated with them, largely through a company newspaper. Its main purpose, Convicer says, "is to propagandize the company's goals." He could not find any "letters to the editor" criticizing the company. Instead there were stories on people observing their anniversaries (not with their wives or husbands, but with the company), items on who was retiring, and "stories concerning tragedies in which the company comes to the rescue to pay the claim."

The company newspaper did not hesitate to give its employees the only political material they got on the job. An Election Day editorial read: "Election time is here again and it's time . . . to cast that precious ballot. Not only is this a privilege—it is an obligation. It is an obligation to those hundreds of thousands of Americans who have died or are dying on battlefields throughout the world in order to protect your freedom."

Indoctrination was low key but tied to basic necessities. A sign at the coffee machine shows a woman calling the police to preserve order. A sign in the snackroom says: "Our employees are patriotically and for their own security investing in U.S. Savings Bonds. . . ." Convicer comments: "For enduring the brainwashing, oppression, and meaninglessness of the company, the average worker in the filing department receives ninety dollars gross per week."

Convicer, as an evening worker, had access to the office of the vice-president, and concluded that "the revolution against the aristocracy they tell about in history books has never really taken place." In the vice-president's office, he found a setting totally different from the conditions under which the workers did their jobs. "He had wall-to-wall carpeting, a sofa, three easy chairs, drapes, a liquor cabinet, a refrigerator, and a private bathroom. On his mahogany desk lay a stack of *Harvard Business Reviews,* and a pamphlet of the Algonquin Club of Boston. Four pictures showing the old aristocratic Boston hung on his walls, and behind his desk were pictures of him and his family dressed regally while riding thoroughbreds."

All this is not likely to make any of us raise an eyebrow.

Is that not because the enormous disparity between working conditions of ordinary workers and executives is so deeply a part of our culture that we never dream of questioning it? Then we are a bit startled when someone notices it.

Convicer ends his brief account of the workday tersely: "One is only too glad to leave at 4:30 P.M. The people move quickly to the elevators, then downstairs past the American flag, finally to be free—until tomorrow."

A woman factory worker, Marie Pat Pierce, gives another view of justice at work. She worked for seven years in a factory in New Bedford, run by a typically middle-sized corporation with plants in Arizona, Pennsylvania, Texas, and California. Its president owns 35 percent of its stock, and in 1970, when $936,000 in dividends were distributed, his share came to $325,000. This was in addition to his salary, expenses, and bonuses.

Marie Pat Pierce points out that although 95 percent of the workers in the Final Inspection Division are women, all the supervisors are men. "If you ask why, you are told very shortly there will be a woman supervisor—and that ends the conversation. Many of the older women working in my department have forgotten more than the supervisors know, but that doesn't make any difference."

It was her personal experience that made Marie Pat Pierce conscious of the company's treatment of women. "A few years ago I was suspended for three days from work because my children were still young and I had to take time off when they were sick. . . . But I refused to let this get me down and stayed with the company."

She concludes: "They want people who keep quiet, squeal on one another, and are very good little robots. The fact that many have to take nerve pills before starting their day, and a week doesn't go by that there aren't two or three people who break down and cry, doesn't mean a thing to them. But times are changing, and from now on, more people will speak out and demand from their so-called bosses that they be treated the way the bosses themselves would like to be treated."

The Boston area is crowded with colleges and universities, and great numbers of women work there as secretaries or as administrators or teachers. But their experiences show a pattern not too different from that of the woman factory worker. Human consideration is lacking. Promotions are very hard to get. In 1970, a congressional committee issued a report, "Discrimination Against Women," in which it said: "Of all the 411 tenured professors at the Graduate School of Arts and Sciences at Harvard University, the number of women is zero."

Also in 1970, a group of women in the New University Conference put out a booklet called "How Harvard Rules Women": "The relation of Harvard to its women is similar to that of the missionary to his heathen. And your feelings, if you're a woman who has made it to America's loftiest and oldest bastion of intellect and the ruling class, are often similar to those of the heathen imported for cultural development to imperialist shores—a mixture of gratitude, awe, doubt that you're worth the honor, and sometimes, dimly or blazingly, resentment that you're considered inferior."

"How Harvard Rules Women" deserves quoting at length:

"Everywhere around you, whether you're a student or an employee, are subtle testimonies to your biological obtrusiveness. Those sober-suited gentlemen who, with scholarly purpose and carefully averted eyes, sidestep you in the shadowy corridors of the Widener stacks, those men younger and older who, as you enter the Widener reading room, inspect your legs as you pass to your seat; or who, in Holyoke offices, inspect your legs as you pass to your desk; all of the masculine worthies on the conglomerate Harvard faculties, with their mild manners, their green bookbags, their after-dinner-sherry gentility and their government affiliations, overwhelm you with the sense that your womanhood is never neutral, but always provocative—of intellectual opprobrium, of patronage humorous or curt, of sexual appraisal, of sexual advance. So that your sexuality at Harvard, as in society at large, is made for you an ever-present, a gnawing thing, to be dealt with in whatever way you can.

"To work at Harvard—as a file clerk or as a student—is to work for the Man. Departments and administrative offices, chaired and headed by men, and staffed by men at the higher levels of command are nearly universally staffed by women at the lower levels of obedience and service. So that within the onerous relationship of wage-labor personnel to management there enters the additional burden of sexism, which demands a pleasing appearance (and often enough encourages a sexually provocative one; puts a little pzazz into the routine . . .); the willingness to serve cheerfully as the woman behind the Man—or, to use the common term, the 'girl' behind the Man (as in: 'I'll send my girl down with coffee.').

"Sexism in the Harvard bureaucracy has its subtle permutations. A widely acknowledged rumor, for example, is that your pay goes up in accordance with the status of the Man you're working for. Professor X, with his joint-departmental appointment and his spinoff think-tank work in Washington, can, for example, command a higher salary for his pretty menial than, say Assistant Professor Y can, or lower-level administrator Mr. Z. . . .

"Never were the economics of *all* women's oppression so succinctly put as when a Harvard Dean commented on the role of Radcliffe women in the Harvard strike, 1969: 'They were so insolent, the worst of the bunch. At least you have to respect the boys just a little since they have something real riding on this. The thing is Vietnam for many of them, and if they get chucked out for this their chances of being sent are far greater. But if the girls get heaved, they'll just go off to secretarial school' (Boston *Sunday Globe,* October 12, 1969).

"In fact, a 'girl' with a Radcliffe B.A. can, often enough, get only a secretarial or a lower-level technical job. In this the kinship of 'educated women' with 'uneducated' ones is clear—they are all included in the basic definition of women's role in the political economy; they serve as unpaid household labor, that is, as 'wives and mothers.' Any other job you take, if you're a woman, is culturally, insofar as the world judges you; psychologically, insofar as you judge yourself; and economically, inasmuch as you're paid less, relative to that primary role-definition.

"This holds as true for a Radcliffe woman as it does for her sister at North Shore Community College, not to mention her sister with no college education at all. Malcolm X said to the black professor: 'You know what you call a black man with a Ph.D.? You call him nigger.' And a woman with an education is still a chick, a broad, a skirt, a piece of ass, a 'girl'. . . ."

What can women do about this? The writers in "How Harvard Rules Women" concluded that change would take a revolution, and the revolution would have to begin immediately:

"First of all, we must make our present lives more bearable, and to that end, institute some immediate changes. Second, we must reeducate ourselves—a process that involves developing the self-confidence, the trust in each other, and the collective force our social conditioning has hitherto prevented us from developing. Such a process . . . can be effected, we feel, only through the actual doing of collective work on real projects. Third, we realize that Socialist revolutions in other countries, with the possible exception of China—and, to a lesser extent, Cuba—haven't really altered the psychological and cultural statuses of women. It isn't at the point that revolution takes place that one ensures such profound change; one must begin long before."

These conclusions for women workers might well be applied to the problems of male workers—whether blue- or white-collar, clerks or laborers or teachers. It will take revolutionary changes, begun now under the most difficult of circumstances, to diminish or eliminate the gross injustice of the workplace.

H.Z.

Six: **HEALTH**

Two-Class Health Care in the Boston Ghetto

by Jonathan Kozol

Justice must begin with one's body, one's mind. If we all do not have an equal chance to stay healthy, to be cured if we become sick, then injustice exists at the most fundamental level of human existence. And if a country has great resources for health, and those resources are available according to one's wealth, if lack of money means that you and your children will die sooner, get sicker quicker, get cured later or never, then we cannot talk of justice at all. In the city hospitals of the country, where the poor come, desperate and in ill health, we see this most clearly, most shamefully.

Jonathan Kozol, who wrote about the problems of poor children in Boston's schools in his book *Death at an Early Age,* here writes about Boston City Hospital. Since he wrote this article, there have been reforms: certain doctors have been dismissed, certain practices have been changed. But the fundamental fact about city hospitals and the medical treatment of the poor remains: it is inferior and humiliating; money still determines the most basic biological facts about people's lives. With this in mind, his essay remains an instruction and a warning. . . . (H.Z.)

On the morning of Thursday, January 8, 1970, the city of Boston woke up to discover that the century-old and long-respected medical training center of its three prestigious schools of medicine, Boston City Hospital, had been denied accreditation for the first time in 104 years.

"CITY HOSPITAL LOSES ACCREDITATION" was the front-page headline in the Boston *Herald-Traveler*. "REPORT CITES 52 DEFICIENCIES. [Includes] HOUSE-KEEPING, FIRE SET-UP . . ."

The storm that broke loose on that day in 1970 has not yet quieted, even though the hospital was reaccredited in December, 1972. It is the same storm that has also started to engulf such institutions as Harlem Hospital and Lincoln Hospital in New York City, Cook County Hospital in Chicago, and a dozen other ghetto hospitals in a dozen other major cities.

The issue is not a matter of "technical" failures in administration or personnel. The issue is not the old and almost comfortable issue of archaic plant or antiquated apparatus. The issue is not one of "allocation of available resources." The issue is black people. The issue is white medicine. The issue is poor people, in a society dominated by the rich. The issue is colonial health care in its worst, most blatant, and most devastating form. The issue is two-class medicine in a racist and divided social order. Yet these are the words nobody wants to use.

"There's shenanigans going on here." John Knowles seemed to see the loss of accreditation as a direct insult both to him and his coworkers: "It's like being hit in the face with a cold codfish." He proceeded to promise: "Six months from now, this hospital will be fully accredited."

But six months later the hospital was still not accredited. Instead for much of the next eighteen months the house officers (residents and interns) of the BCH began to bombard Boston's press and public with a number of disturbing revelations:

ITEM: Incompetent administration, near total chaos in the patient record files, possible contamination of the pediatric wards, and worse—all of this had led to a massive emigration of the nursing staff. Two hundred and seventy-six nurses walked out of BCH in less than one year.

Statistics tabulated by the residents and interns for June–July, 1971, demonstrated the results: Wards were left uncovered for as long as eight or sixteen hours in one day. Eight to sixteen hours of nonsupervision, according to a statement given to the press September 2, was "a rule rather than . . . an exception."

ITEM: On ten occasions, during one week of observation, "an entire ward was . . . without a nurse for an eight-hour shift." Over the weekend of August 27 to August 29, according to the press release made public on September 2, "there were fifteen such occasions."

ITEM: According to an additional press release (October 29, 1971), wards were still being left uncovered: this over a period lasting often "up to, and beyond, eight hours." Said the house officers: "The patient suffers from this situation." The situation, they added—in wording which could not fail to terrify large numbers of prospective patients of BCH—has reached the point at which it has begun to cause *"unnecessary morbidity and mortality. . . ."* *

ITEM: Medical records, said the doctors, were in total disarray. The medical records library, upon which a physician must rely in order to make judgments in regard to diagnosis, surgery or medication, "currently has a backlog dating back to 1969." Four thousand, five hundred records, according to the doctors, "are not complete and on the shelf. . . ." There are approximately thirty-nine letter-file drawers packed with loose reports not filed in patients' records. . . . "The medical record retrieval rate for the clinics is approximately eighty percent. . . ."

Since BCH clinics handle about one thousand appointments in an average day, this means that two hundred patients every day were being seen without their medical records.

* Italics added.

ITEM: The report which had withdrawn accreditation from BCH placed special emphasis on possible contamination of obstetric wards. In one of the items put forth to the public by a member of the pediatric staff of BCH, the additional point was made that chaos in the area of pediatric record keeping was causing danger to the health of children. Said Dr. Patricia Moffat, in a statement that constituted the clearest possible warning to those people who had entrusted newborn infants to the care of BCH: *"We are having difficulty practicing good pediatrics in the present situation. . . ."* *

The house officers did not limit their condemnations to abstract polemics. In a series of documented narratives released to the press and public on September 13, 1971, the residents and interns gave the Boston public a number of detailed instances of sickness, death, and degradation in the wards of BCH:

ITEM: The nursing office supplied a first-year nursing student to care for an elderly man suffering extensive burns. "Burns are extremely complicated, requiring a registered nurse, sterile-gowned and masked, to change dressings, apply medications, closely follow the vital signs, and give intravenous fluids. It was against hospital regulations for a first-year student even to take blood pressures."

The man died shortly after.

ITEM: "A sixty-five-year-old woman four months after a heart attack was paralyzed by a severe stroke and admitted to a ward which housed two different medical services because of ward closings due to the nursing shortage. As she got better, she had to be moved to another ward which did not have continuous nursing coverage. Unable to call anyone to help her with a bedpan, she fell trying to get on a bedside commode unassisted and suffered a painful, nonhealing fracture of the hip."

ITEM: "A man with lung disease stopped breathing and

* Italics added.

was put on a respirator in a ward covered only by a licensed practical nurse who is not qualified to give the intensive care such a problem requires. . . . The third day the patient was transferred to another ward where two registered nurses cared for twenty-four patients, ten on the danger list. He would have gone to the intensive care unit if it was not operating at half-capacity due to lack of nurses. He died after five days in the hospital."

ITEM: Another patient was expected to die after having a massive brain hemorrhage: "His family was told, but they still harbored hope. He was moved out of an intensive care unit which was half empty due to the nursing shortage and the same day died when his respirator was accidentally disconnected on a large ward with only one nurse."

ITEM: "Mr. C. was naked in the middle of the hall, being weighed on a bed scale that looked like a fork-lift truck; after his weight had been recorded he was noted to have died and was put back to bed. . . . Mrs. D. was found dead in bed and a rectal temperature on the bedside chart showed she had previously been well on her way to room temperature. When the nursing student who took it was asked her condition she said she was better behaved than usual. . . ."

There are these words in a statement of the Executive Committee of the House Officers Association of BCH: "The professional staff of Boston City Hospital is well attuned to crisis since all of us have lived in a somewhat varying, but always critical situation relative to patient care. Invariably, each crisis has been met with a response which has been barely adequate. . . . At this point in the 104-year history of Boston City Hospital, the always critical situation has become catastrophic. . . . The professional staff cannot provide levels of patient care which are even minimally acceptable."

How is it that this kind of situation—once documented, once examined, once revealed—was nonetheless allowed to go on for so long unabated, uninterrupted, untransformed?

The answer, as provided in the words of certain limited numbers of courageous doctors, is one which will be startling to many of the trusting citizens of Boston:

Boston's three prestigious schools of medicine—Harvard, Tufts, and Boston University—possess a vested interest of a rather dramatic and unexpected character in *perpetuation of the two-class apparatus.* If it were not for institutions such as BCH, it is not clear where medical researchers, students, and professors could find the varied, plentiful, and unprotesting "materials" they need, whether for education or for research purposes. This does not mean that schools of medicine, their research teams and teaching faculties want poor hospital conditions, physical debilitation or administrative breakdown. It does, however, indicate that universities and deans of medicine, for reasons of political self-interest, do not intend to interrupt an amicable and nonprovocative liaison with the trustees and directors of the hospitals that serve the ghetto population. Ethics might call for protest; plain good sense might call for transformation of the physical conditions; yet short-term politics and short-term calculation call for diplomatic silence, acquiescence, and collusion.

This point—the connection between the ghetto hospital and school of medicine—has been articulated in the most unyielding terms by a doctor in the Boston–Cambridge complex whose academic status renders statements of this kind almost irrefutable.

John C. Norman is a cardiovascular surgeon on the staff of Harvard Medical School and BCH. He is an Associate Professor at Harvard; operates the Sears Surgical Research Laboratories, Harvard Unit, Boston City Hospital; commutes to Houston, where he works with Denton Cooley, and to Washington, D.C., where he serves on a number of government commissions. He is widely recognized as one of the most distinguished research surgeons in the nation.

In an article which drew considerable attention here when

it was published in *The New England Journal of Medicine* (December, 1969), Dr. Norman wrote these words: "To raise the question . . . of racism in consideration of . . . the problems of the ghetto is naive. . . . The ghetto resident offers, in the depersonalized language of the medical profession, excellent teaching 'material'. . . . What better way to perpetuate the system of exploitation than to learn basic clinical medicine from ghetto residents and subsequently deliver that expertise to suburban patients?" Cynically, Dr. Norman added, one could argue that the ghetto is "best suited" for such exploitation.

In a personal interview last April, Dr. Norman made specific reference to the situation here within BCH: "We lost a patient last week. . . . What can I say? The situation is obvious to all who work here. The atmosphere is antediluvian. . . . The hospital functions on the brink of disaster."

In reply to a question bearing on the quality of clinic service, Dr. Norman answered in these terms: "If my own daughter were treated the way that I see people treated in this place, I'd tear the hospital apart."

Grim evidence of the debilitated character of clinic service at BCH was brought to light in Boston during April, 1972. A confidential survey, compiled by students at the Boston University School of Medicine, each of whom had served in the gynecological-obstetrics ward, and released to the public in a front-page story in the Boston *Globe,* made allegations of criminal malpractice, racism, and discrimination.

The statements, published in the *Globe* of April 20, 1972, included these extraordinary charges:

(1) Excessive and unnecessary surgery is performed—not for the benefit of the patients, often, indeed against their medical best interest, but because the interns and the residents have need of one particular operation for their training purposes.

(2) Too often, when there are several possible alternatives,

the more radical and more dangerous option is selected, not to benefit patients, but again to give the interns and the residents useful "experience."

(3) Records of patients are left incomplete, and do not give correct descriptions of the operations that have been performed. That is: *They do not accurately record unnecessary surgery.*

(4) Coercion is applied to patients to put signatures on surgical consent forms; permission is obtained, especially from those who do not speak English, without a prior explanation of the actual operation they are legally inviting by their signature.

(5) In one of the most shocking items listed, but presented with painstaking caution in the choice of words—even in the choice of verb forms—the medical students expressed concern over "the possibility" that black and Spanish-speaking women might "more often be sterilized by hysterectomy," while white women are more likely to be sterilized by "less radical" procedures, e.g., having their tubes tied off.

The medical students, observed the *Globe*'s reporter, "recognize" that this final allegation is "highly inflammatory." They emphasize, he said, their observations only raise "the possibility" of such extraordinary practice.

In confirmation of these allegations, the *Globe* extracted several individual case histories. These were selected by the *Globe* out of the twenty-five to thirty which the medical students had compiled.

CASE ONE: A seventeen-year-old woman was admitted to BCH twelve weeks into a normal pregnancy for an abortion. The medical students charge that the three procedures available for abortion were not explained to her. The three options were (1) suction evacuation, (2) saline induction, (3) hysterotomy.

"The patient was told it was too late for her to have suction evacuation." Instead, she was told that a hysterotomy was necessary. She was never told of the possibility of saline induction.

The students charge that the choice of a hysterotomy was made exclusively for teaching reasons, not out of consideration for the woman's welfare. In support of this charge, they quoted the following exchange:

STUDENT: Why didn't you do a suction evacuation?

RESIDENT: Fifteen weeks pregnant requires saline induction or hysterotomy. (*The patient was only twelve weeks pregnant.*)

STUDENT: Why wasn't a saline done?

RESIDENT: Dr. X wanted a hysterotomy done for the experience.

In accord with the determination of Dr. X, the woman received a hysterotomy. If she ever intends to have children, she will have to have them by caesarean.

CASE TWO: A thirty-six-year-old black Portuguese woman was admitted for sterilization. According to the medical students, there was discussion on teaching rounds with a senior resident "as to whether they could 'get' a vaginal hysterectomy 'out' of this case."

The students allege that a resident outlined the following options in declining preference: (1) vaginal hysterectomy, (2) total abdominal hysterectomy, (3) bilateral tubal ligation (i.e., tying off of the tubes).

STUDENT: Why is tubal ligation the last choice?

RESIDENT: We want the teaching experience. She's thirty-six and doesn't need her uterus.

The students' report included these remarks:

"The patient wanted a sterilization.

"The patient believed she was to have her tubes tied.

"The patient did not realize or understand the papers she signed authorized a hysterectomy.

"The patient was adamant in not wanting a hysterectomy."

The report states that the woman hastily signed herself out

of Boston City Hospital—to the probable frustration of those interns, residents, and doctors who saw in her another opportunity to "get" a hysterectomy.

CASE THREE: A thirty-year-old Spanish-speaking woman was admitted for sterilization by tubal ligation. The students quote a medical report, which "indicates both ovaries are completely normal."

The surgical report does not make any mention of a removal of one ovary.

Despite this lack of surgical record, however, a "pathology report" exists in which a lab examination states that the right ovary—having been removed and studied—had been proven to be normal. According to the students, the lab report gives evidence that "a normal right ovary" *had been removed.* The unnecessary operation was not entered in the patient's record, nor was it entered in the surgical report.

CASE FOUR: A teen-age girl was admitted for an infection of the external genitalia. The infection was determined to be herpes genitalis.

The resident, according to the students' allegations, told the intern to perform the surgical procedure which is known as a "biopsy" (i.e., to cut away a piece of tissue). He recommended only mild sedation (Demerol), despite the fact that the lesions were described to be "exquisitely painful."

The students' report continues with this charge: The senior physician advised the resident that a biopsy would not yield significant data of any therapeutic use—i.e., of benefit to the patient. The senior physician observed, in addition, "that a biopsy without general anesthesia in the operating room would be unforgivably painful. . . ."

The resident, however, proceeded against the explicit counsel of the senior doctor: "Despite this advice, the patient is taken into a treatment room. . . ." The unnecessary—and "exquisitely painful"—surgery is carried out, "while the patient screams in pain."

The four cases, here extracted, give damaging confirmation of the charge of racist exploitation of poor women for the sake of student preparation: "training-purposes." We do not need to speculate for very long upon the kinds of repercussions and reactions that we might expect if allegations such as these were ever lodged against Beth Israel or Doctors Hospital.*

Medical school reaction, in this situation, is well worth examination:

The officials in charge of gynecology and obstetrics at Boston University were immediately brought forward to give answers. Initial defense was offered by the chairman of the Department of Obstetrics, Dr. David Charles: "Look," he began, "I was gone from the country for nearly three months."

Having established that he was not present during the entire period in question, and therefore had no means by which to make informed replies, he then proceeded to attack the students for both credibility and motives: "These students are trying to spread the blame around to some fine men."

In the event that there might be some truth in what the students said, it still would be wrong (Dr. Charles replied) to condemn the entire service "because of one bad apple."

The second-in-command of gynecology and obstetrics at Boston University, Dr. Joel Rankin, offered a more serious refutation: These students, said Dr. Rankin, are not in a position to "evaluate" what they perceive or hear. Words, for example, spoken "in jest or in bravado by a resident" could be easily "misinterpreted."

The most serious response, however, was provided by the Dean of Medicine at BU: Ephraim Freedman. Dr. Freedman stated first that he had spoken with some of these students and

---

* The case histories here extracted have been quoted from the Boston *Globe*, not from the written documents. These documents are now in the possession of this author. In certain instances, the *Globe*'s reporter paraphrases, alters, or corrects details. The differences, however, between the *Globe*'s report and the original documents are not substantial. In no case do they overstate the impact of the allegations.

had no reason to cast doubt upon their accuracy. This, how-ever, he said, was not the real point. The issue, he said, is not what has been done: it is the level of patient service that can be offered from the present moment onward. This—the service at the present time—he said, "is above question or reproach."

In regard to the past, he said, he saw no reason to go "hunting" on the basis of "some allegations."

In the opinion of several dozen black and Spanish-speaking women who had been mistreated in the previous twelve months within the BU service, there was, on the contrary, excellent reason to go "hunting" into "allegations": especially when those allegations raised some highly damaging questions in regard to the ethics of the very men who sought to neutralize their import.

The *Globe,* unlike most other major U.S. dailies, employs a number of first-rate medical reporters. In spite of their efforts, and even in face of the most detailed and careful documentation, the paper has remained in an ambiguous position in regard to Boston City Hospital. The editorial bias tends, if anything, to be apologetic. In a lead editorial, published in the days immediately after BCH had lost accreditation, the *Globe* headline read:

"BCH is alive and well." It went on: "The public need not doubt the quality of medical care available at City Hospital. The unanimous endorsement of the current administration and of its future plans by the deans of Boston's three great medical schools should remove any doubt on this score."

The deans, the doctors, and the owners of newspapers send their wives and children to the prestige hospitals. The ghetto mothers and their children go into BCH. The perpetuation of the two-class system assures the rich their wives and children will have first-class service only by virtue of denying it to others.

Is it implied, in allegations such as these, that doctors, deans and owners of newspapers *wish poor people ill?* Is there the implication here that good and earnest liberals can seriously be callous to the sickness of poor people?

Arguments like these are misleading: the problem is not *personal malice*. It is *institutional exploitation*. The decent and enlightened young director of Beth Israel, Mitchell Rabkin, can argue, with persuasiveness and truth, that neither malice, bigotry, nor law excludes poor people from his door, nor excellent service, *once they get there*. He refuses to recognize, however, as do nine-tenths of his close colleagues, that all of their decencies, good intentions, and real acts of kindness, put together, never can change the basic evil which exists in two distinct and separate forms of service: one *primarily* for the upper class, the other *exclusively* for its maids and menials. This is the issue that none of these deans and doctors dares to face; yet this is the issue that we need to force—and deal with.

Even the extraordinarily conservative and back-bending figures provided by statisticians constitute alarming commentaries on the two-class medical system that still prevails in the U.S. Paul Parker, top-ranking statistician in the Massachusetts Department of Health and Hospitals, spoke to me in his office at the Lemuel Shattuck Hospital in Boston during November, 1971. Dr. Parker was reluctant, at the start, to recognize significant differences between his white and nonwhite infant-death statistics. When at last, however, he sat down to spread before me sheets of statistical data which his office had prepared, two notable—and disturbing—items were immediately apparent:

(1) Figures for "neonatal death"—death within the first four weeks of life—broken down by hospitals, reveal that the rate of death at Boston City Hospital during 1969 (the latest year for which reliable statistics were then available to Parker) was 20.1 per thousand. Figures for the same year at the two prestigious hospitals which serve primarily white and well-to-do Bostonians presented a disturbing contrast: Figures for Beth Israel, were 9.7 per thousand; those for Boston Lying-In

almost the same. Figures for Boston's two important Catholic hospitals—those that offer pediatric and obstetric care—St. Margaret's and St. Elizabeth's—were, for the former, 14.3 per thousand and, for the latter, 16 per thousand.

These figures reflect in microcosm the classic breakdown of health service as it now is offered to poor people in this nation: In terms of infant death and early childhood survival, our chances are best if we are white and well-to-do; they diminish somewhat if we are white, but not so well-to-do; they diminish most of all if we are black or Spanish-speaking. Few statistics that are available to us today in the United States speak with greater power, or with more disheartening arithmetic, to the price that is paid in life and death, and in distorted growth, by the ongoing situation of race bias and class exploitation according to which essential services are offered to sick people.

(2) In my interview with Dr. Parker last November, I was also shown comparative statistics for infant malformation. These figures, which contrasted white to nonwhite infant malformation in the state of Massachusetts, were sufficiently disturbing that Dr. Parker asked me not to quote them without caution. He specifically asked me to be certain that I made quite clear that figures of this kind do not imply genetic differences: "There is danger, otherwise, that figures such as these might be misunderstood." They do *not* indicate genetic differences. They indicate, rather, that institutional discrimination in health services now purveyed to poor black people in the state of Massachusetts—including, among them prenatal, gynecological, and obstetric care—do presently lead to an alarming increment of infant malformation, including retardation, consequent from brain damage, among nonwhite children.

Dr. Parker had begun our interview in a rather cautious, apologetic, and defensive state of mind. He concluded it, however, in a mood which was disturbed and sober: "In terms of neonatal death and of congenital malformation," he observed, "the figures for black children born in the United States are at least 50 percent greater, and often two to three times greater than the rate for whites."

"The rate for blacks," he concluded, with the sight of a man who, in the last event, cannot refute his own statistics, *"is just not coming down."*

The figures quoted here, from Parker's records, do not of course suggest that Boston—or the state of Massachusetts—is in a position which is inferior to that of other states or cities. Black children, nationwide, die within the first twelve months of life between two and three times as frequently as white children born in private hospitals. For children born in predominantly white and middle-class hospitals, the rate is in the range of ten to fifteen infant deaths per thousand. For those, however, who are born in ghetto neighborhoods, or in their counterparts in rural slums, the figures start at twenty-five or thirty, and go up sometimes as high as sixty. In Boston City Hospital, to take one obvious example, during 1971, the rate for infant death during the first twelve months of life—according to figures supplied by the hospital director—was twenty-nine per thousand: 50 percent greater than the national (i.e., total, black-white) figure: twice as high as the rate for whites alone.

If we look not just at total ghetto areas, but at specific census tracts within these population areas, we find entire blocks in which the infant death rate is a good deal higher even than these figures indicate. Dr. H. Jack Geiger, Tufts New England Medical Center, Boston, reported in his well-known Lowell Lecture, "Health and Social Change," that there are "a number of Northern ghetto census tracts in which the infant death rate now exceeds one hundred deaths for every thousand live births." This is close to ten times the rate in Scarsdale.

National figures are available also for the death rate among adults. The risk of dying prior to age thirty-five, for those both black and poor, is four times the average for the nation as a whole. Ghetto hospitals like Boston City Hospital, Cook County, and Harlem Hospital do not assume, and *never* have assumed, a comparable level of prenatal supervision. It is one of several grim, yet casual, means by which the two-class health-care apparatus of this nation and this social order function to degrade and brutalize those who must bear the burden of black skin, low income, or the lack of power, access, and connections.

I sat one evening, during the past winter, and spoke of the situation at Boston City Hospital with one of the older doctors that I know: one of the elder statesmen of the medical power structure of this city.

"Who can deny it?" he said to me at length, in speaking of the sharp decline in patient care: "The total collapse in patient services at BCH follows the direct line of change in race and ethnic character. BCH was once a noble, world-renowned and even brilliant medical institution; those were the days when it served mostly those of Yankee, Irish, Jewish, and Italian origin. In the past twenty years, the ethnic character has shifted. There are less Irish, fewer Italians, almost no Jews at all. It has become a hospital for the untouchables—and it has become third-rate.

"There is still some excellent research going on. There are still large numbers of distinguished men and women working there in every field; but BCH is a ghetto dumping ground today. If racism in medicine means anything at all in 1973, then it means Boston City Hospital."

It can be expected, in the months ahead, that we shall be informed by those in power at the BCH, that the very problems we have here described are, *just at this moment,* in the process of correction. It is axiomatic, in a dangerous confrontation of this kind, that protest is absorbed into "ongoing processes" of simulated self-correction.

If the spotlight falls on insufficient supervision of poor patients in the larger wards, the hospital goes out and hires several hundred nurses to be present for the next arrival of the TV cameras. If the gynecological and obstetric areas come under condemnation, the hospital puts out several million dollars to obtain new technological devices, rebuild contaminated areas, repaint the corridors. If the charge is made that BCH does not reflect the wishes, voices, power of its client population, the Mayor goes out and finds another willing black or Puerto Rican to sit without protest, or in helpless protest, on the trustee board.

Each issue, protest, item of indignation—so long as it bears violence potential—brings pacification equal to the danger. The larger issue of a two-class medical apparatus serving rich men and rich women in one setting, poor men and poor women in another, goes on unaltered.

Life and death, relief from pain, removal of tumors or removal of a womb, remain "consumer items." Some of us buy the best: at Massachusetts General Hospital, Beth Israel, Doctors Hospital, or the Mayo Clinic. Others get cheaper stuff right off the racks: at Lincoln Hospital, Cook County, BCH.

Short-run strategies in Boston, as in other cities, call for emergency shuttle runs from BCH to several of the most exclusive private clinics, hospitals, and doctors' offices. They call, as well, for massive efforts at consumer education, above all to do battle with the intimidation factors (psychological, cultural, and ideological): factors which have power so often to hold back the ghetto poor from utilization of the services of first-class hospitals, even in situations where there is no legal or financial barrier. In situations where these legal and financial barriers exist, militant tactics call as well for direct action at the rich suburban homes of powerful white doctors, for neighborhood control and consumer supervision of the staff, the finances, and training practices of the ghetto hospitals.

Long-range protest must, however, raise more radical and comprehensive issues: How much longer can this nation label itself a democratic social order, as long as life and death re-

main consumer items? What do such words as "equal opportunity" conceivably imply to thousands of kids who do not
have an equal chance to see the fifth week of their lives? It is
no exaggeration to state that those who die by consequence
of two-class medicine in the United States are victims of institutional murder. Nothing can change until the men and
women who now acquiesce in practices of this barbaric character can be compelled to be accountable for what they now
endow, empower, and attempt to whitewash.

Eighteen blocks—and the uncertain ethics of the American
medical profession—mark off the distance between the wealthy
Boston Lying-In and the poor BCH. The one cannot exist without the other.

The distance between them never will be spanned without
a medical revolution that transforms them both.

Mental Institutions for the Poor

What happens when someone is labeled "mentally ill"? We know that people become so troubled that they need help. But do institutions help? Can we trust the judgments made by those in power (doctors, judges, parents) on sending people into mental institutions? The law in Massachusetts permits putting a person into such an institution against his or her will if that person is a danger to other people or to "valuable property," or "is likely to conduct himself in a manner which clearly violates the established laws, ordinances, conventions, or morals of the community."

That last part is frightening. One thinks of those committed to mental institutions in the Soviet Union because they didn't go along with the prevailing ideas. According to the Massachusetts statute, radicals, anarchists, unconventional people, anyone who is likely to commit civil disobedience, anyone who is ready to defy the existing moral codes, could be committed. It would take two doctors, one judge, and a hearing to do it.

Here is what happened to Morris Margolis, who was abandoned in 1912 by his immigrant parents in Boston when he was three. At the age of seven he became a ward of the state and was sent to a state school for the retarded, where he spent ten years. At seventeen, he escaped, fled to Cleveland, sold newspapers to support himself until he was apprehended by police and returned to Massachusetts.

He was mentally retarded. But he was uneducated, illiterate, barely able to speak and understand English. He was committed to Bridgewater State Hospital, and there he spent twenty-one years. During that time, he lost his once-good health—he had multiple nose fractures and lost most of his teeth as a result of beatings in Bridgewater. "I didn't think I'd ever get out," he told UPI reporter Richard Gaines in the spring of 1973. "I tried to hang myself once, but I didn't die. I just turned yellow. I guess God didn't want me."

Morris told Boston University student Sheri Rak: "I screamed for them to listen to me—that I wasn't supposed to be there—but they packed me in ice until I was too cold to holler anymore. But then someone listened one day, and looked me and my file up. They found I was right. They said they were sorry."

In 1946 a fellow inmate who could write wrote a letter to a rabbi, asking for help. The rabbi contacted a dentist, who visited Margolis and then spoke to a state parole officer, who petitioned for Margolis' freedom. Margolis was pardoned and freed. He became an elevator operator at a hotel, then worked at a bar, saved some money, traveled to Reno, to California, Mexico, Chicago, Jamaica. "I wanted to see the world before I died."

When he developed heart trouble and leg trouble and couldn't work anymore, Margolis went on welfare. He became a constant attendant at the Suffolk County Courthouse, where long ago he had been committed to Brdgewater. Richard Gaines describes him: "Morris is a small man with stumps where teeth used to be. His over-sized coat hangs on hunched shoulders. A fine old bowler covers a baldish head. . . . Margolis passes winter days watching the administration of justice in Boston's busy courtrooms and summer days walking and talking on Boston Common. At night he returns to a cluttered five-by-ten room in the South End where he lives on $134 a month from welfare."

Morris Margolis comments on his own life, and on a decade of court watching. "I believe I understand that there's no justice at all. If you got no money, you go to jail."

There were 103 men like Morris Margolis in Bridgewater, who were "discovered" to have been wrongly confined. Now old, they were released not long ago.

But what if you are really mentally ill, and also poor, and you are therefore confined to a state hospital, "rightfully"? There may be no such thing as *rightful* confinement to a state mental institution, if it is a house of horrors that torments but does not really help its patients.

Boston State Hospital is a mental institution, one of Boston's oldest. Constance Paige investigated it in February, 1973, for the Boston *Phoenix:*

"At night, Boston State has only one doctor on call for seven hundred patients, and that doctor is responsible for both medical and psychiatric emergencies. During the day, most of the wards are understaffed as well, with one or two nurses and maybe five attendants covering thirty to forty students. . . .

"Emergency equipment also is often lacking. . . . no intravenous fluids or apparatus, no emergency drugs, no electrocardiographs, no laryngoscopes (to help a patient breathe). . . . Too often, vital medical information never gets reported." A nurse had made note three times of bleeding in an old woman, but no one ever did anything about it until a doctor discovered the woman in a state of shock. "The roster of medical neglect is chilling."

Reporter Paige interviewed Dr. George Fishman, a psychiatric resident, who was finishing his six-month training period at the hospital. Fishman told her:

"The raison d'être of the state hospital is the function of a garbage pail, a place to take somebody who's noxious to somebody else . . . not to treat somebody who is upset in himself. The state is happy to have a place to dump somebody who is a pain in the ass on the street.

"After that, it doesn't make a damn bit of difference what happens. If he leaves the hospital totally psychotic, if his life is still a wreck and his character has disintegrated and within himself there's no future, that doesn't matter, as long as he can keep his mouth shut.

"The state only mans the hospital with enough staff to do caretaking. The therapy is something we do over and above, and really, that's where the struggle comes in. What we spend our time doing is to make sure that the patient is fed, bedded, and drugged."

Drugs like Thorazine are used in heavy doses to keep the patients passive. And there is a seclusion room into which patients are put more to punish them than to help them, a tiny, smelly room, either too hot or too cold, with just a bare mattress.

Dr. Fishman said: "The psychotic person wants to prove to himself that he's not crud. So an awful lot comes out. All kinds of yelling, screaming, destructiveness. And it's got to be staged somewhere. That's the purpose of the hospital. The trouble is if somebody's disturbed, he gets labeled a pain in the neck. He's treated almost as if he were malevolent. Not because the staff here are mean or cruel, but because they're incredibly overworked.

"What in essence happens is that the patient is nonvalidated. He was bold enough to engage in your world and register a complaint. He cared enough about the world to tell you that it rots. That is real interaction. But he gets told, go back and play. . . .

"This place is a vacuum. There are no constructive activities, nothing to foster a patient's healthy interests. . . . When you finally break down the walls and say 'Ah! Here's the world,' the patient says, 'What the fuck.' "

Constance Paige reports: "The environment is not just brutal but barren, without even the barest necessities. There are no toilet seats, for instance, and often no towels. . . . Wards are sometimes so overcrowded that patients have to sleep in the halls." And things will get worse, she reports, because funds have been cut by the federal government, and by the state.

The chief administrator at Boston State, she says, "seems to maintain a certain prestige and popularity by sheer force of charm. A large and friendly man, he laces his conversation with dulcet chuckles and breathless belly laughs that disarm even his most vehement detractors. But charm cannot help the patients, patients who come to the hospital year after year, patients who have nowhere else to go."

Where are the mentally retarded children of the poor sent? To Belchertown State School for the mentally retarded, "a place where outrage is the norm," says Joe Klein, who did a study of Belchertown for *The Real Paper* in December, 1972. He was prompted by the fact that in the past month, four children at Belchertown had died: one by choking on his dinner, another by swallowing an open safety pin, another by eating so much her stomach burst, another because she wandered off on her way back from church.

Klein contacted a mother of one of the dead children, who said to him:

"I don't know why I should talk to you. You're just a journalist and I'm just a private citizen, and neither of us can do anything to move the bureaucracy. Even if I gave you my side of the story, it would just be my word against theirs. And they'd say I was just a hysterical mother. It's my fault anyway. I signed my child into that place. I had to say that my child was a menace to society. That's what you have to do to put someone in Belchertown. So I'm responsible too. And all I can say is that between us, me and the state did a great job of murdering my child."

Klein looked into the deaths and concluded: "At least one life certainly was lost due to negligence, and the others might have been saved had it not been for the overcrowding, understaffing, inadequate medical services, and generally oppressive atmosphere that encourages rebellion even among those with IQs of less than 60."

Belchertown was established in 1922, and when, in 1972, someone suggested commemorating its fiftieth anniversary, a father of one of the boys there, Benjamin Ricci, president of the Belchertown Friends Association, said: "The only way to commemorate Belchertown is to get those children out and then blow the damn place up."

Joe Klein describes his visit to one of the dayrooms in Belchertown: "The attendent unlocked the door to the dayroom in K building and a lot of things began happening at once: There was a general movement toward us, but at the same time there were men posed in corners of the room, like twisted sculptures, who didn't even turn their heads. The others were drifting closer, though, and a part of me, frightened, curled back inside myself. A man held his wrist out, showing the terrible scar on it. He walked around the room like that, continually showing his scar to everyone, forever. Another wanted to shake hands. The hand was limp and cold, but polite as if it belonged to a minister. All around there were twitchers and moaners and screamers. About sixty men in this one room, barren except for plastic chairs and a television in a cage. A man was banging the lock on the television cage, back and forth. Another, with his pants down and shirt up over his face, was immobile against the wall. Another was flat on his back with his feet against the wall, locked into a position reminiscent of a rebellious teen-ager, but meekly compliant when the attendant told him to get up. The smell in this chamber was overwhelming."

Parents began to organize and act. One mother found her child bruised and scarred on every visit. She said: "For a long time I was so ashamed, I was afraid to speak up. Now I'm just angry. If the government came into my house and found me treating my son the way he's been treated at Belchertown, I'd be arrested for child abuse."

That mother, along with Ben Ricci and twenty-five other parents of patients, filed suit in early 1972 in Federal District Court on behalf of their children, saying the state was denying the children's constitutional right to adequate living conditions and treatment. They cited instances in their brief:

"Plaintiff Cheryl Dumas is deaf and has been at Belchertown State School for twenty-four years. She has not received education or training on how to communicate or otherwise handle her deafness. . . .

"Plaintiff Timothy Packard is said to have emotional problems. Despite repeated promises to his parents, he was not given meaningful programming. Timothy can speak fluently but is unable to read or write. He has not attended school. The official reasons given were his behavior problems. Belchertown State School never gave the plaintiff any psychological or psychiatric help. . . .

"Plaintiff Kevin O'Neill developed permanent and incurable contractures (shrinkage of muscles) of both legs at Belchertown State School due to lack of physical therapy and orthopedic services."

The state's Attorney General responded to the suit by arguing that since the retarded are "voluntarily" admitted to Belchertown (that is, their parents sign them in) they don't have the constitutional right to demand anything.

Belchertown is an excellent example of how a liberal society perpetuates its horrors. It has been studied and investigated again and again, in 1964, in 1968, in 1969, twice in 1970, twice in 1971, three times in 1972. Many plans have been submitted. The superintendent is sympathetic. He agrees that he must move toward closing the place down. The Governor visits it and is appalled. It is still there.

H.Z.

Mental Institutions for the Well-Off

by *Margaret Kiphuth*

The mentally disturbed poor in Boston go to Bridgewater or Boston State. The mentally disturbed rich go to McLean's, where a year's stay may cost $15,000 or more. For the poor it is far, far worse. But rich or poor, the mentally troubled cannot find justice in a society intolerant of those who do not fit quietly into its madness.

What follows is a remarkable discussion of the treatment of mental illness in our society, by Margaret Kiphuth, a young woman who spent three years in McLean Hospital. (H.Z.)

A medical authority wrote in the seventeenth century:

Discipline, threats, fetters, and blows are needed as much as medical treatment. Truly nothing is more necessary and more effective for the recovery of these people than forcing them to respect and fear intimidation. By this method, the mind, held back by restraint, is induced to give up its arrogance and wild ideas and it soon becomes meek and orderly. This is why maniacs often recover much sooner if they are treated with torture and torments in a hovel instead of with medicants.

Today much has genuinely changed. Psychiatry has become a recognized and accepted branch of medical science and people dedicated to the rehabilitation of the mentally ill are trained professionally in techniques that reject the use of physical torture and mental torment. Public attitudes have also improved. The disturbed person is more frequently seen as needing concerned and sympathetic help. Community mental health programs and child guidance centers have been established all over the country.

But it is my contention that although the blatantly brutish attitudes have improved, the ancient traditions of dehumanization, punishment, coercion to conformity, and repression still prevail. Couched in psychiatric jargon and shielded by professional status, these traditions are subtly perpetuated and permeate our mental hospitals and community mental health programs. I do not question the goodwill or dedication of the majority of the people engaged in social work, psychiatry, psychology, and so on. I believe that most of them *are* trying to help the disturbed person, are trying to alleviate his confusion and unhappiness and help him to feel at one with himself, help him to achieve a satisfying life experience in his relations with himself and his work and friends. But these intentions, which emphasize the individual, become distorted because there is a general assumption that the alleviation of anxiety is effected by a reduction of conflict with the prevailing society, and that the achievement of happiness is effected by a comfortable reintegration of the patient into the prevailing society.

Today that society is middle class, with all the values, aspirations, and concepts of happiness that class entails. As professional people, the psychiatrists, psychologists, and social workers are a part of the middle class, or at least are trained in the bourgeois psychoanalytic concepts of one-to-one treatment. Treatment of the emotionally disturbed becomes resocialization rather than reindividualization. To try to help patients to find a workable relationship with society is not repressive or coercive in itself; but the workable relationship is based on society's terms, not those of the individual, and that is coercive.

Granted, many patients are from the middle class and do wish to return to it, but many, whether from the middle class or not, are in hospitals or clinics just because they are unhappy in the middle class or their values are in conflict with the middle-class prescription for life. It is in this situation that the responsibility of the hospital or clinic is to help the patient accept rather than deny himself, to help the patient strengthen his values rather than compromise them, and to help him establish a healthy, valid relationship with society in terms of himself rather than conform and adjust in terms of a value system that denies him. To do otherwise is to destroy the patient and, further, to quell any forces which might constructively question, even transform the prevailing society whose own general health needs examination.

My fear is that psychiatric programs today are forgetting to appraise the prevailing bourgeois society and that as a result hospitalization treatment plans are programs of subtle repression, and community mental health work, particularly in lower socioeconomic areas, is also programmed repression or at "best" mere pacification. The grounds upon which I base this fear are first the experiences I had as a mental patient for two and one half years at McLean Hospital. Second I have impressions from several years of posthospitalization therapy and four years of work with disturbed and/or "deprived" children in an infantile autism research center, a child guidance center, a camp for schizophrenic children, and in a day-care center.

The primary experience from which I am generalizing is of course my own hospitalization. I entered McLean in 1962. The hospital had just formed an "Intensive Individualized Treatment Program" for adolescents.

Discussion of treatment and its effects is confined to the

adolescent population mainly because I cannot presume to know what effects treatment had on the adult population and because adolescents pose a particularly difficult problem in the area of treatment (and management!). Highly influenced and constricted in perception by their family and experiential background, they are yet free technically to truly examine alternatives of action and values that will determine or set the direction of the rest of their lives.

In 1962 the basic rate for room and board at McLean (excluding the cost of medication, psychotherapy, or special nursing) was $48 a day. Obviously the general population was from the middle or upper classes financially, in spite of insurance plans and the availability of some aid. McLean thus represents a rather rarefied hospital experience. But just because of their exceptional facilities, psychiatric training programs, and large professional staff membership, their obligation is increased to truly concern themselves with each patient as a separate individual.

Several factors inhibited the hospital in fulfilling this obligation. One such factor was an overriding concern for society's judgment of the hospital's success. Another factor was the staff's own assumptions about happiness. It is a rare family that wants a psychiatrist returning to them a child who rejects their way of life, their values, their hopes for his happiness, and who has adopted a way of life that is frightening or immoral or irresponsible in their eyes. The family's criterion for success is, yes, that the child be happy, but in a way that the parent can at least half understand or identify with. I do not wish to be unfair. The hospital did a great deal in this area. Their concern was with the patient first. They supported the patient's needs, not the family's, in this struggle, and where necessary they worked earnestly to help the family understand and accept the child's needs for a different life. But the hospital itself, no matter how flexible it tried to be, had trouble seeing "success" in happy carpenters, motorcycle mechanics, or jazz musicians.

For example, there was a boy whose only form of communication, whose only means of self-expression and release from tension, was to play the piano. No matter how much the hospital tried they were unable to change this, and I don't think they had the right to demand that this change. What they did have a responsibility to do, however, was to strengthen and build upon this core, to make it a viable basis for a meaningful life. But this same boy was heavily involved in the use of drugs, and so the hospital, equating the jazz world entirely with drugs, would not let him even think in terms of becoming a jazz musician. He was directed toward college and other work. He was denied what meaning his life had, what little sense of himself that he had. He died of an overdose in his family's suburban home.

Another boy wanted to play the drums. He was told he would never be allowed to take anything but a nine-to-five job. Nine-to-five, no matter what the job, no matter whether it made him happy or not. Another boy who had a beard was told one day that he would be discharged from the hospital as soon as he shaved. During the month that followed until he finally acquiesced there was nothing else demanded from him. His beard was not related to anything; it simply symbolized something that was not consistent with the current middle-class standards. The hospital's demand exemplified the staff's refusal to accept the validity or health of any society but their own.

The hospital's assumptions thus paralleled those of the parents, that happiness and security could only be obtained through the established order. As I said, many of the adolescents, oriented to the established order, did feel most comfortable thinking in terms of going to college or getting a nine-to-five job. Those who wanted to live differently were forced back to this way of life. Perhaps the main problem was that the hospital was afraid to support any ways of feeling or acting that might justify or openly express the patient's conflict with his family and/or middle-class society. This defensive fear of conflict, underlying every treatment plan, was what distorted every good intention of the hospital as well.

This suppression of conflict led to a demand for conformity that was essentially a denial of the patient. It is not that the hospital did not allow happiness, it is that they wanted one to be happy their way. Sometimes it is sort of difficult to work up enthusiasm over making a pair of moccasins or a tile table in occupational therapy; sometimes it is even annoying; most often it is just plain insulting. But the hospital staff was in a position of immense power—it held the keys, it had been deemed professionally qualified to enforce its judgments of what was healthy and what was sick. Hence, any form of anger, resistance, or dissent could be called hostility, sickness, or a discipline problem and dealt with accordingly.

It is hardly overstatement to call their suggestions or demands a coercion to conformity because the hospital program also entailed an intricate system of reward and punishment called privileges and restrictions. If one did not go to group therapy, one might not be allowed to go to the coffee shop in the evening. If one were not out of bed by eight, one might not be allowed to leave the ward during the day. An even more devastating use of punishment was evident when a patient said he felt lousy one day and was then restricted to the ward or not let out without a staff escort. Even depression was met with reprisal. Apparently depression was equated with a total inability to function. And the patient, being restricted, was without the opportunity to exercise whatever abilities or self-control he might have left with which he might combat his depression. The chance to make decisions and maintain some self-respect was wrested from him.

Although the hospital supported the patient by decrying

the pain that parents had sometimes caused their children and seemed to be liberating them from the ordeal of coping with punitive treatment, they were in fact only substituting their own form of the same thing. And somehow the hospital experience of this was even worse than at home, for the only justification one can find for parental actions is that they are utilizing any and all tactics out of love, unthinking and misdirected perhaps, but at least love. The hospital on the other hand was working out of a framework of detached, scientific, objective aloofness which made their judgments even more dictatorial and cruel. A parent might regiment his child because his child's actions made him angry or fearful, but the hospital protected and sanctified its policies on the basis that the child's actions were sick or hostile. The patient was thereby rendered even more helpless in his attempts to support or judge himself and his rebellion.

There were hideous results of this system of reprisal. The patient had to learn to assume the façade that the doctors wanted to see. He had to learn to manipulate and appease the staff before he could gain the freedom to exercise his own judgment. He came to believe in what Harlan Ellison calls a "crap game culture—where only the coolest, hippest, most inventive and cunning win." It is a remarkable person who, having come to the hospital for help, can maintain his self-confidence in the face of such apparently irrefutable psychiatric judgments. And even if this is possible, how can he maintain his self-respect while living out such a compromising double life? It is also most difficult to free oneself of the hate and fear and sense of alienation that go into being sick when one has to deal with people in this way. One ends up simulating acquiescence and in the process one either gives up and lets the judgments of others determine one's life, or else one's covert feelings of revolt and hate deepen and become more destructive.

Perhaps this is why nearly all the adolescents, while at the hospital or after being discharged, became involved in drugs. Drugs were a means of avoiding decisions and action, a means of dulling confusion, a means of glossing over the conflict which one had not been taught to cope with at the hospital.

Anger, doubt, and rebellion could not be expressed in discussion or in a refusal to obey; anger could not be directed at the staff or it would be punished. But anger has to have an outlet and the only means of expression left was to hurt oneself. Young people learned the arts of cutting their wrists, swallowing any bleach, tacks, or glass they could get their hands on. One was never taught to cope with anger, to assess one's anger. One was never taught to believe in one's own dissent or to channel its expression constructively. One was never taught to use anger against a person, an object, a system as a force for persuading that person, transforming that object, or recreating that system. One could only explode and destroy the object or destroy himself.

It must be reiterated that the hospital was not motivated by a desire to hurt or cripple their patients. But, constricted by their own assumptions of what happiness was, blind to any forms of security and satisfaction other than those offered by the established order of society, and fearful of any conflict or dissent that questioned these assumptions, their intentions were distorted. As a result all their therapeutic methods were perverted.

Thus, even individualized psychotherapy was brought into the service of a treatment program that ultimately dehumanized the patient. To suppress conflict was not enough; that would be mere treatment of a symptom. To exorcise the basis of the conflict, to modify or destroy the emotional substance that created and supported it was their goal. From their point of view this was justifiable. Conflict causes anxiety; anxiety and unbearable unhappiness were the reasons we were in the hospital; and therefore the roots of the conflict must be eliminated or resolved for us to feel at one with ourselves and happy and safe. But the resolution of conflict within oneself, the assessment of one's confusion and the eventual acceptance and unification of one's emotions into an internal value system does not necessarily mean that one will thereby reduce one's conflict with the external middle-class society and its value system. What the doctors assumed was that the resolution of conflict meant acceptance of and reintegration into the prevailing order.

To resolve conflict by repressing or eliminating the emotional substance of which it is an expression is to violate and negate the very core and integrity of a person. That wellspring of ideas and dreams and feelings constitutes the "vital I" of each separate person, the distinct unique soul of every human being. Each man must reach into his soul, confront it, and accept it in full before he can work to formalize it into a value system upon which he bases his relationship with society. A psychiatrist can help his patient to reach and experience and examine his soul. But if the psychiatrist brings with him middle-class value judgments that direct the examination, if he brings middle-class expectations as to the final expression one's soul will take, he can only end in demanding that his patient reject or disavow some part of his soul that has been considered "inappropriate," essentially that he reject or disavow some part of himself.

In its least destructive aspect psychotherapy can be simply rude and intrusive. As Antonin Artaud, the great French dramatist, wrote in a letter to a psychiatrist friend:

"Had I told you that the psychoanalysis to which I finally consented left an unforgettable impression on me? You know well enough what a distaste, essentially neural and instinctive, I revealed for this kind of treatment when I met you. You were able to change my mind; if not from an intellectual point of view—for there is in this inquisitiveness, in this penetration of my consciousness by a foreign intellect, a kind of 'prostitution,' a shamelessness I shall always repulse—still from an experimental view I was able to assess the benefits I had derived from it and if need be I would consent again to a similar venture; but from the very depths of my being I am determined to avoid it, like any other attempt to enclose my consciousness in precept or formula, or any verbal systematization."

Artaud was incarcerated in mental hospitals for nine years. His story epitomizes in the extreme the way in which an emphasis on society rather than the individual can lead to psychiatric brutality and a dehumanization of the patient.

To prevent Artaud from "slipping into insanity," an "intellectual weakening and stagnation," he was administered shock therapy. In the process he lost all his teeth, suffered damage to a vertebra, and experienced excruciating pain. Even worse are his doctor, Ferdière's, comments: "He gave up washing, and I had to insist he go with the nurses to the bathroom before he came round to *obeying* me." (Emphasis added.)

When asked if Artaud had been cured at Rodez, the last hospital in which he was confined, Ferdière responded: "What does curing a madness like Artaud's amount to? Simply this. To make it possible for him to live in society. Artaud, when he left Rodez, was a gentleman who had learned to behave properly, that is to say, without seizing by the throat the first man he met, or insulting a passing woman because she was wearing a blouse that displeased him." And so the object of four years at Rodez, of shock therapy, and of a curious kind of poetic brainwashing, was to transform the rebel poet into a "gentleman." In Rodez the "Orderly and Unimaginative trampled the spirit of anarchy and rebellion." Artaud wrote virtually nothing after his release from Rodez.

This then is my horror of the modern psychiatric treatment programs—that the majority of present-day psychiatrists are so rigidly professional that they are no longer human, that they are devoid of humor, and that they no longer see the disturbed as human beings but as patients who must be re-socialized. And that the majority of psychiatrists are so bour-geois-oriented and so need to avoid conflict themselves that they truly have become the "Orderly and Unimaginative." They are unable to cope with anarchy and rebellion, and they use their professional power to divest their patients of any belief in their spontaneous gut response to present-day society. The spirit of anarchy and rebellion stems from the vital core, the vital basis of the individuality of each person. To excise this spirit, to repress it, to devalue it, is to ask the patient to hate, to disavow himself. It is to empty the patient of his energy and selfhood, to castrate him, to annihilate him.

What I mean is that the hospital stole our dreams. Dreams were called fantasies, they were made clinical crimes. We were indoctrinated with values that denied our dreams, the values of practicality, doing the acceptable, avoiding conflict and pain. And in the end we were empty. I cannot explain what I mean by dreams except by citing a letter of Antonin Artaud's.

"Once upon a time there was a blazing fire inside me. The cold could do nothing against it, a usefulness, a spring no autumn could touch; a source of light, glowing wells of joy that seemed inexhaustible. Not happiness, I mean joy, felicity, which made it possible for me to live. . . . there was an enormous energy there. . . . a force . . . it must have been the life force, mustn't it? And then it grew weaker and all dies away. . . .

"There is around me a tendency which you particularly share to believe me *cured,* to think I have attained a normal life. Which is not true. . . . There is in me something rotten; there is in my psyche a kind of intrinsic corruption which prevents me from enjoying what destiny offers. My inner ef-fervescence is dead. Listlessness wholly possesses my mind.

The images, the ideas I find, I come upon as if by chance; they are as a forced remembering with but the appearance of new life—the quality is *effected*. This is not a fantasy, an imagination. It is the fact that I am no longer myself, that my authentic self sleeps. I must go to my images. I gather them in slow handfuls; they do not come to me, no longer force themselves on me. In such conditions I am without criteria. These images, whose value is their authenticity, are no longer valuable, being but effigies, reflections of thoughts previously ruminated, or ruminated by others, not now and personally *thought*. . . . It's a matter of flashing *vigorousness*, of truth, of reality. There is no longer life. Life does not join, does not inspire what I think. I say LIFE. I do not say one tint of life. I say life whole, essentially the inspiration: the initial spark from which all thought ignites—this core. I feel myself dead at the core."

This is what I mean by empty and dehumanized. This is the danger of psychiatry when it is middle-class oriented, bent on maintaining the status quo, bent on repressing and avoiding conflict. No person, no institution, has the right to do this to anyone. The hospital's responsibility is to recognize that there are a variety of possible achievements and fulfillments in life, a variety of forms which "mental health" can take. They must be able to cope with and respond to a multivalue and multipersonality type structure of life. If a person, in full conjunction with his soul, himself, is still in conflict with society, then it is the hospital's responsibility to support and strengthen the person so that he can live with conflict. They must instill what David Riesman calls the courage to face aloneness and the possibility of defeat in one's personal life or one's work without being morally destroyed. They must instill the nerve to be oneself even when that self is not approved by the dominant ethics, values, or mere trends of a society.

A Postscript
by
Douglas Segal

Conditions may have changed at McLean's in the decade since Meg Kiphuth was there. But certain fundamental features apparently remain, according to Douglas Segal, who got out of McLean's in mid-1972. He arrived there deeply depressed, fearful, sometimes self-destructive, and was immediately given high dosages of Thorazine and other drugs. Even after he had calmed down, he was kept on high dosages for eight and a half months. This completely immobilized him, gave him continuous constipation, prevented him from concentrating aurally or visually. The medication made it "incredibly difficult for me to express myself emotionally. I was, literally, in a stupor." His original prognosis, for five to six months in the hospital, was revised to one year. "I bitterly resented being kept behind locked doors, and my feelings of being caged, coupled with my feelings of hopelessness about my situation, led me to make frequent escape attempts.

"Although I often got off the hospital grounds, I was always persuaded to return, and was always punished by at least a week's restriction to the hall. I also was punished every time I refused to attend hall meeting by being restricted for a day, and by being denied visitors and the right to make or receive calls. I found being cut off from the outside world a terrifying and dehumanizing experience. I feel such action on the part of a supposedly enlightened hospital staff something short of barbaric. I also feel that such forms of 'treatment' as wet packs and being locked in isolation should have been abandoned one hundred years ago. Also, the practice of 'supervising' a patient's mail is not befitting a penal institution, let alone a hospital of McLean's standing.

"My situation at the hospital grew steadily worse. My therapist and I never established a working relationship. After my last escape attempt, during which I was caught and returned to the hall, I tried to commit suicide by hanging myself with the cord to my electric guitar. I was inspired by a patient who had successfully accomplished that in Cadman House just a few weeks before. I didn't have in me whatever is necessary to carry out such an endeavor, and the staff found me with the cord still around my neck."

Finally, a new psychiatric social worker turned up who helped Segal. After a while he visited the man's home and family and began making his way toward good health. He got out of McLean's. "I am returning to school to dedicate my life to improving the methods of treatment of people with emotional problems and the care that they receive while hospitalized. I think locked wards for any but the violently disturbed are unconscionable. A person can have no dignity in a cage, nor if he or she has to please the keeper to be allowed the privilege of taking a walk in the fresh air." He found encouraging signs of change at McLean's but deplored the drugs as "chemical straitjackets."

"I also believe that hospitalization for longer than six months is self-defeating. The longer a person is hospitalized, the harder it is for him to reenter the world. My life will be dedicated to finding alternatives for these conditions. To believe they do not exist is to give up hope."

Seven: **SCHOOLS**

All Schools Are Prep Schools

All schools *prepare* us for what is to come later—that is, for us to take our place in a certain kind of society, and to fit well into that society. And since the larger society divides people into certain groups (successful and unsuccessful, rich and poor, men and women, black and white) it makes sense that schools should prepare us for this by starting those divisions early.

And how does the school *know* how to divide us? Well, sex and race are easy to figure out. (See "A Black Student Sits in the Assembly" later in this section.) But what about *class*—that is, whether we will end up as executives or politicians or college professors on the one hand, or mechanics and clerks and secretaries on the other? The school is helped in making those divisions by what we already are when we come into school—what kind of neighborhood we live in, who our parents are, how we dress, how we speak. With those starting clues, the system makes its judgments early: it puts us into certain kinds of schools, then into certain kinds of classes, then into certain groups within each class.

A French economist and social critic, André Gorz, wrote in early 1971 (in a magazine called *Upstart*):

"In fact, workers are selected by an educational system which, from the outset, dooms the children of the so-called lower classes to fail at school and thereby to have no other choice but to accept the most ungratifying and oppressive jobs. All available studies, whether of the United States or France, prove that a child's success or failure in school is in fact decided by his social and family background well before he enters grammar school. Furthermore, the studies show that the present educational system does not function to equalize the opportunities for education but, on the contrary, performs a function of social selection and discrimination."

In March, 1971, a newspaper put out by a group of Boston schoolteachers, called *The Red Pencil*, devoted to a radical critique of the school system and constructive suggestions for change, published a special issue on "tracking." By *tracking*, they meant the way schools put children into different tracks, some of which head for college and better jobs, others of which head for trade school and lower positions in society. They wrote:

"The myth that schools are the pathway to mobility within a democratic classless society is contradicted by statistics as well as common sense observation. Schools serve to perpetuate the inequalities in our stratified society. An 'education' is one of the major forms of inheritance passed on to the children of the rich. The poor continue to get poor education. Tracking is one mechanism that insures that all kids will not be given an equal education.

"Our schools prepare certain kids—usually the children of the rich and usually white—for technical and professional jobs and others for the production line or poorly paid service occupations. Also, rather than training all students for the labor force, the school functions to keep some of them unemployed and channels them into the army or housework."

The Red Pencil carried an article based on a study by Ray C. Rist, which appeared in 1970 in the *Harvard Educational Review*. What this study showed was that even after children are segregated (by class and by race) into neighborhood schools that reflect their parents' color and economic standing, the process of selection, of tracking, still goes on inside each classroom. And it starts right at the beginning, in kindergarten.

Rist found that a kindergarten teacher put youngsters at different tables according to his estimate of whether they were "good" students. And it seemed that the children at Table 1, who wore better clothes and had more substantial family backgrounds, would be physically closer to the middle-class teacher and have a lot of verbal interaction with her. None of the Table 1 children's families would be on welfare. But many at Table 2 and Table 3 would be.

It was not conscious discrimination on the part of the teacher. It seemed built into his or her consciousness, into the system of education. In one classroom, when the teacher, the day after Halloween, invited the students to come to the front of the class and tell about their experiences, she called on five from Table 1 and one from Table 2.

The *Red Pencil* authors, Becky Pierce and Joan Green, tell more about Rist's study:

"Another example quoted was a skit, arranged by the teacher and acted out by the students, on how a family should come together to eat supper. The mother, father, and daughter were played by Table 1 kids; only the son was played by a boy from Table 2. As the skit progressed the Table 2 boy made very few contributions to the conversation. (In real life he had no father and his mother was supported by ADC [Aid to Dependent Children] funds.) The teacher, dissatisfied with the boy's performance, asked him to take his seat and replaced him with a boy from Table 1."

Similarly, when the teacher wrote on the blackboard, it was so arranged that Table 1 children could see it much better than anyone else. It was not surprising that in class discussion,

Table 2 children spoke up much less than Table 1 children. Indeed, what happened was a gradual withdrawal of the Table 2 and Table 3 children.

"How did the children respond to each other? The children at Table 1 often ridiculed and belittled the children at the other two tables. . . . The lower-class children . . . very often made hostile and belittling remarks to one another, having internalized the teacher's attitudes toward them."

Pierce and Green say: "The responses of all the students showed that they had learned well the teacher's lesson that it is acceptable to treat lower-status people badly, and that higher-status people must be treated with respect." What the study also showed was not that children are naturally cruel and hostile, but that they *learned* to be, and learned the pattern: who was vulnerable and who was not.

When Dr. Rist followed up these kindergarten children he found that, in the next grades, the status they had become accustomed to was perpetuated. And so, the reinforcement of "better" and "worse," "smarter" and "dumber" became powerful.

All of this may be misleading; it may suggest that schools are the chief sources of the channeling of children into predetermined ranks. But, also in *Red Pencil,* Constance Lorman wrote about what happened when tracking was done away with in her suburban school; that is, the formal separation of children into college-bound and noncollege-bound stopped, and students were mixed up in each class. She found that "students have continued to group themselves in ways that are more insidious, more rigid and more durable than any mere rearranging of classroom assignments appears to modify. In other words, a culture that is grouped according to class, race, and sex has done its stratifying work long before kids arrive in school."

With this warning—that the tracking in schools is only part of a larger process of tracking which has already begun and which it is very hard for schools to undo even with "reforms" —we might look at another kind of tracking. This is the reinforcement of sex inequality in the schools. It was discussed by Adria Reich, a Newton High School teacher, in *The Red Pencil*. (Her essay follows this one.)

There is another kind of preparation that schools give children, besides that which prepares them to take a certain place, a certain rank in society. Schools get them ready to behave, in whatever situation they find themselves in. And students learn this not from what they read in schoolbooks, nor from what the teachers give in their lessons. They learn this behavior preparation from the most powerful kind of teaching there is, which is not telling, but *showing*. School *shows* children that there are people with power (the principal, the teacher) who should be obeyed, who are wiser, who can give rewards and punishments. School *shows* people that they will be more successful if they act as the authorities tell them to act, that they will be treated badly if they speak up critically, if they rebel, especially if they try to organize their fellow students in such rebellion.

Herb Gintis, a Harvard economist who did studies of education, was quoted as follows in *The Red Pencil*:

"Educational institutions, by being as authoritarian, as autocratic, as bureaucratic and as undemocratic as the productive units, help create people that will fit. The purpose of schooling is to produce certain types of workers—workers who submit to authority, who don't question standards of discipline, who don't know how to cooperate with fellow workers, who take orders rather than use their own initiative, who are competitive and who don't expect to do creative work."

And so, there is an almost military regimentation in most schools in our society, especially at the lower levels, where children are lined up, seated, moved here and there. They learn to stay in line, and that they may talk or go to the bathroom only at the will of the teacher. When they get into high school, the situation doesn't change that much. If they should get into school athletics, they face the authoritarianism of the coach-player system, and the "rules," off the field as well as on. If they get onto the school newspaper, they learn about censorship. They learn, indeed, to censor themselves in advance, so they won't get into trouble.

The Red Pencil published a poem written by a public school student, Jeff McIntyre, called "School Day."

the teacher's face
flexed contortions
or an irate father
& a prison guard
his voice a
flaming cannon
from hell echoing
down the hall
　"shut-up
　& get a pass"
as the child
melted into
the floor
baked in
an oven
of hot breath
knowing he had
nowhere to turn
no excuses accepted
in this menagerie
of madness
called school

What of the "progressive" schools, and what of the numbers of public schools with new liberal rules, enlightened principals and young, "with it" teachers? In general, these are not in the lower-class neighborhoods, where the obedience of the production line or the army is the rule; they are in the "better" neighborhoods, where the children of professional and business people study. And here too, the preparation is appropriate; because young people who are going to be scientists or college professors or business executives or lawyers or doctors or government officials must have more leeway, must be leaders, not followers, may have to *give* orders as well as take them.

Yet, this is deceptive. Because even with the freer atmosphere of the new, enlightened schools, there are boundaries beyond which that freedom cannot be exercised. This can be seen most clearly in colleges and universities, which are not training people for assembly-line jobs, but to be persons of standing in the society, professionals who will have a great degree of freedom, who will fill the middle and upper positions in society. Colleges and universities give more leeway to the student than elementary schools and high schools. Dress is unregulated, students can choose their programs of study and their electives within those programs. There are daring courses, critical of the existing social structure, and greater ranges of controversial discussion in the classroom. There is much talk of "academic freedom." And yet, the power in the university is still concentrated at the top, in the hands of the president and the board of trustees, the students are still at the bottom of this hierarchy of power, and at crucial moments the hand of government or the hand of corporate business may intrude.

The university may *teach* Locke and Jefferson, even Marx and Kropotkin. But it *shows* that ultimately, in this microcosm of our social structure, there is very little democracy, that money and power rule. Students are thus well prepared for a society where, as educated professionals, they will have more freedom and more resources than the kids who were tracked into blue-collar jobs or the armed forces, but must still play the game according to the rules made by those with more freedom, more resources, more power.

Boston University might serve as an illustration. It has had a reputation as a fairly good school academically, and a relatively liberal one. But students and faculty learned the limits of this liberalism after demonstrations against military recruiters on campus in 1972 led the Department of Defense to threaten to cut off some research contracts. Although the faculty had voted to suspend military recruiting until both faculty and students could decide, and although students did decide, in a referendum, that they did not want military recruiting on campus, the president restored recruitment. There were two important lessons to *show* students: democracy had to give way when money was involved; and the government, especially the military, could not be defied.

Then more lessons came. In the spring of 1973, faculty and students came to campus one day to find a "provisional code" in operation, which made certain activities by students and faculty subject to penalties. For instance, if students or faculty members did not produce an identification card for a campus police officer, they might be ordered off campus, and if they refused to leave, might be suspended from the campus. For infractions of the code faculty and students were to be tried by a court where the prosecutor was appointed by the president of the university. The judge was also appointed by the president, and the three-person jury was selected by a committee appointed by the president, with all appeals from the court to go to the president.

It was a time when in the country at large, despite voting, a three-part government of checks and balances, and a Bill of Rights, the President was carrying on a war on his own. In the United States, democracy seemed to exist more on paper than in reality. The situation at Boston University was a good preparation for students going out into this world.

H.Z.

Sexual Tracking—
and Other School Tricks

by Adria Reich

I guess I complain a lot about my job because people are always asking me, "Why do you stay in teaching?" The answer I've finally come to is that—as hard as the work is—every year of teaching I have become more convinced of the crucial function the schools serve in molding and preparing us for our roles in society.

In my first year of teaching, I was shocked by the content I was given to present. As a social studies teacher, my job consisted basically of justifying our present system and building cynicism about the possibilities of any real change. The second year I realized with a start that I could teach all the radical content I wanted and still be socializing my students to be obedient, unquestioning, competitive wage earners. I became aware of the extent to which behavior patterns are taught and reinforced in school.

Returning to school this year with an expanded women's consciousness, I realize that my discoveries of the last two years have particular applicability to women, that there are crucial differences in both academic and behavioral training according to sex. In our educational system women are tracked into special schools and courses, fed curriculum that presents us as adjuncts to men, taught to act like "young ladies" and expected to participate in activities that subordinate us to men.

1. *Sexual tracking:* Sexual tracking exists both between schools and within schools. Most school systems include technical high schools devoted to math and science, that are exclusively or predominantly male. Vocational or trade schools are segregated by sex—with most of the funds going to job-training programs for males. Programs for females are minuscule by comparison and usually include only training for such careers as dental hygienist or industrial cook. A female student desiring vocational education in any other field is out of luck.

The same pattern exists within so-called academic schools. If a male is judged "nonacademic," he has a choice between shop or "mechanical arts" classes and business courses such as bookkeeping and accounting. Somehow, when a female is "nonacademic," she finds herself automatically in the business track, with a full load of bookkeeping, typing, and shorthand. The reasoning seems to be that if she's not good at verbal abstractions, she will certainly love these courses. I find this assumption incorrect for many of my business-track female students. Some are miserable enough to quit school, figuring (rightly) that they are not learning anything anyway. The truth is that they receive no training in any skills, but plenty of training in feeling worthless, acting stupid and finding escape and "success" through their men. They leave school anxious to get married and have babies, and prepared to accept jobs as marginal, semiskilled workers.

2. *Curriculum:* As part of a unit on education in American society this year, my students and I looked at some children's readers. We found story after story presenting little girls as adjuncts to the adventures and pranks of active little boys, and presenting women only as housewives and mothers, or occasionally as nurses, teachers, or secretaries. All of these books serve as good background for the history texts children will get later that focus on the decisions and actions of famous men. The history of women's oppression and women's struggles is never presented. We arise out of nowhere to win the vote and

are as quickly disposed of. Women are given no one with whom to identify, no past to call their own.

3. *Hidden Curriculum:* In every classroom, behavior as well as content information is taught. The first-grade teacher asks, "Which of my big strong boys will help me put the chairs away?" "Which one of my little mothers will help clean up the room?" The teacher accepts and expects aggressive behavior on the part of the males, but expects only the most ladylike behavior from the females. One ironic result of this is that even when females initiate aggressive action such as spitballs, invariably a male in the class gets blamed.

By high school, behavior reinforcement has become more subtle; much has already been internalized. I have found when I need help with the projector or other equipment, males are the ones to volunteer. When a bulletin board needs lettering, a female volunteers. More important, this role differentiation even extends into class discussion. By high school, teachers and students have come to expect that males will be better at political discussions. Many females will clam up as soon as an important societal issue is raised. If they can be persuaded to participate at all it is usually in a discussion on the "human side of things." For instance, I have been able to draw female students into discussions on the effects of the war on the Vietnamese people or on our own soldiers, but almost never into discussions of the various peace plans or political lineup of forces. As a teacher, it is difficult to avoid feeling a preference for a predominantly male class, because discussion goes so much better. Teachers, both female and male, can be heard complaining about that class "that is mostly girls!"

4. *Social Climate:* The school reflects the social climate of the society and also does its share to promote the type of social relationships sanctioned by the society. Sometime during adolescence most of us are taught that the important thing in life for women is to please men—which often means being pretty, silly, passive, and patient, well-dressed and well-groomed. We

learn to submerge our real personalities and feelings. We are never encouraged to think of work as more than something to do until marriage; all other women are our competitors in the search for dates.

The school is more than an arena where these social-sexual relationships approved and produced by the society are played out. Through its rule and activity structure, the school contributes significantly to the development of these relationships.

For years, dress codes have kept female students looking and feeling like teen-age date bait. While males could wear the same pair of pants day after day, females are learning to be consumers and put together many different "outfits." The effect of this has been not only psychological but also physical. Wearing a skirt restricts movement and actions; looking like a lady makes you act more like one. ("Don't get it dirty," Mother says.) While this rule is loosening up, many schools still expect good grooming on the part of the females. Girls are informally lectured on how they let themselves go or don't seem to care about themselves anymore.

One favorite way of handling females who present behavior problems is to remind them of their proper role—cajole them into behaving, with encouraging words like "You could be an attractive girl."

The activity structure also contributes to the social climate. In many schools the athletic teams are still the most important extracurricular activity. But sports programs for female students are peripheral at best, sometimes even a target for derision. The place for the female who wants to share in the excitement of the athletic program is the cheerleading squad, not the basketball team. Females with real athletic ability are thus faced with the choice of becoming isolated as "girls sports types" or participating vicariously through their men in the real sports program. And most women are not encouraged to be physical—to know anything about their bodies—except as sexual objects.

Besides athletics for both male and female students, there is only a limited range of activities in which to participate and excel. If your talents and inclinations lie in other directions you are deemed unworthy or stupid. And for the women, the range is even narrower than for the men. The clubs in which females play an active role, the offices to which we are elected have to do with service—tutoring, scholarship funds, hospital volunteer work, etc. The more public the position, the more the person holding it is considered a spokesman, the more likely it will be filled by a male. Student council president, head of the debate club, representative of the school at a statewide conference will generally be a male.

Although much of this role differentiation is informal, it is formally sanctioned by the school in the awarding of special honors. At the end of every year awards are given to the most successful male student and the most successful female student. Although the image of the successful student varies somewhat according to the class background of the students, there are basic similarities in all schools—especially in the difference between the criteria for successful females and males. The successful male student is usually athletic, aggressive, a leader in many school activities—often he has done something deemed courageous. The successful female, on the other hand, is pretty, well-groomed, polite, has done outstanding service to the school and usually "added enthusiasm" to one project or another. Although not all students compete for these awards, all students are affected by the criteria, and judged by adults in the school by the extent of their conforming to them.

There are, of course, exceptions to this role delineation. In almost every school there is an elite group of females whose intelligence and verbal abilities enable them to compete effectively with the males. Their rejection of the roles defined for them, however, is not necessarily a rejection of the whole role system. They simply consider themselves to be "like boys" and therefore worthy of rising above the traditional positions reserved for the girls. They are highly critical of the other girls in the school, seeing them as giggly, silly, overly madeup nonentities. This is one example of how we learn to turn against each other instead of the system that is oppressing us all.

Sexual tracking is only one aspect of the function schools serve in our society. If schools are to prepare students for life in America, schools must be as stratified as life itself. They serve to legitimize and maintain the inequalities in the society. The interlocking mechanisms discussed above—through which women are taught their roles—also play an important part in channeling students along socioeconomic and racial lines. Tracking, ideological training, behavioral training, rules, and activities obviously serve to perpetuate inequalities of race and class, as well as sex.

Faced with this channeling process, what can a teacher do?

We can try to adjust our own teaching to compensate for the textbooks and readings—by leaving out the most objectionable passages, adding small units on women, Vietnam, racism, dissent. We can try to change the nature of the teacher-student relationships in our classrooms—by dressing more casually, sending fewer cut slips, giving fewer tests, grading easier, seeing students outside of class. But it is obvious that one teacher cannot fight channeling; it is a process that goes way beyond the classroom.

We can't stop the type of sexual channeling that goes on until we make changes in the society into which women are being channeled, but we can create a "breathing space" for young women by interfering with the ability of the educational system to fulfill its function of socialization. We can develop programs that will expose the nature of sexual channeling. The basis exists for powerful local alliances—with women in the community or in local colleges joining together with students and teachers.

The existence of a growing women's movement, both inside

and outside the schools, gives me confidence that an effective strategy can be developed around the specific forms of channeling reserved for women.

Following are some suggestions of how these alliances might operate:

1. Women outside schools (neither teachers nor students) can:
   a. Make available birth-control information and sex information to females in secondary schools.
   b. Offer training in self-defense.
   c. Offer skills in mechanical arts, shop, etc.

We can do this with the help of a sympathetic teacher in the school who sends students to us, or by setting up a storefront or information center near the school and leafleting the school about it. As students take advantage of our services they should be encouraged to work out a strategy for demanding that such information and skills be provided in school.

2. Women who teach education courses or those who are teachers can form work collectives to develop lists of elementary-school-level books in which females are not as role stereotyped as in most, and they can write new stories—demanding credit from their universities or release time for curriculum development from the school where they teach. This work should be coordinated with efforts by other collectives to organize women in the community around the elementary school to demand an end to sexist readers and education.

3. Women in education schools or in teaching can form work collectives to develop history and literature curriculum relevant to women. They should demand credit from their college or release time from their school. Female students in high schools can demand this information be included in their courses or that special courses for credit be given by teachers of their choosing.

4. Women teachers and students can form grievance com-

mittees within the school to look into cases of discrimination and sexism—either formal or informal—against women students or teachers. They can also demand control over at least one issue of the school newspaper to discuss women's position in the school.

The Wellesley Incident

by Joan M. Carrigan

Wellesley, Massachusetts, is described by the Massachusetts Department of Commerce as "a highly desirable suburb of Boston." It is a refuge from the stinking ratholes of Roxbury, west on the Turnpike twelve miles down the paved corridor.

There are many who own Boston but live in Wellesley. The town boasts leaders of industry, real estate magnates, a university president, sports notables, and professionals of international reputation.

These 10.5 square miles of trees, lawns, and "estates" which elsewhere would be known as neighborhoods, have a population of 29,829. Of these, 37 are black, 66 individuals with potential identity crises are classified as "other." There are 56 horses.

At least 80.5 percent of the town's citizens have completed high school. The average income is twice that of the metropolitan Boston area; at least half the Wellesley breadwinners earn more than $10,000 a year.

Wellesley not only respects and cherishes the channels, system, and values of the American dream, it is the culmination of that dream. Moreover, it is an escape from the American nightmare. Recently, when a Wellesley mother wrote to the high school protesting the use of the book *Manchild in the Promised Land*, the matter was discussed by a member of the English department, and a member of the administration. The teacher noted with dismay that the mother expressed disapproval at exposing children to such unpleasant worlds. "But don't you see," the administrator replied, "that's why she moved here."

In 1965 it was suggested that perhaps Wellesley might benefit from bringing black students from Roxbury to the high school. This was the signal for the right wing, of which Wellesley has a vociferous number, to fan fears that the blacks from the city Wellesley sought to own but disown "were coming" and would, as one of the black students put it, "corrupt all their innocent kids."

On May 31, 1968, nearly alone among the schools of the commonwealth, Wellesley Senior High remained open to compensate for one of the "snow days" of the harsh winter. With the authorization of the school committee and the administration, a group of teachers sought help from the community in organizing a program to reflect the realities of a nation shocked at the murder of Martin Luther King and passive in the face of the ominous conclusions of the Kerner Report.

The Wellesley Committee Against Racism was formed after the death of Dr. King by a very small, liberal segment of the community. At a meeting of this group, a representative of the teachers said that some of her colleagues felt that the proposed program should be more than just intellectual and theoretical. They wanted a feeling about racism transmitted to the kids—an emotionally affecting experience which could begin to express what it was like to be poor and black.

Mrs. Kay Cottle, a young English teacher at the high school, had been very impressed with a performance earlier in the year given under the auspices of the dramatic club by the Theatre Company of Boston. She suggested that the company be invited to participate. The cost was expected to be $100, and the school authorized the teachers to request financial assistance from the Committee Against Racism. Pemberton Minster, chairman of the educational subcommittee, said that his group would be responsible for raising the necessary funds.

Panel members were also selected by the coordinating group, which consisted of members of the English and history faculties. One of the panelists was Mrs. Cottle's husband Tom, an assistant professor of social relations at Harvard.

Mrs. Cottle contacted the Theatre Company and asked them to put together the program. They agreed. However, all her later attempts to contact them to determine what they had planned were unsuccessful.

The entire presentation of May 31 was entitled Black History Day. As NET television station WGBH evaluated it in a special program entitled "The Wellesley Incident," "Black History Day in Wellesley High School was supposed to help create an awareness of black aspirations and black frustrations. Black History Day was supposed to bridge the misunderstanding between the have-nots and the haves, a bridge between the open suburbs and the closed cities." On the appointed day, there were two sessions of the assembly scheduled so that the whole school could be accommodated. Programs were printed which included the names of two teachers assigned to introduce the Theatre Company to the audience. One was Thomas Fitzsimmons, an English teacher and long-time Wellesley resident, who was to provide the introduction at one assembly. Mrs. Cottle was to provide the other. They were never called upon, however, as the group began its presentation without an introduction.

Mr. Wilbur Crockett, a Wellesley institution and the chairman of the English department, described his impression of the presentation and the reaction of the audience.

"It was most artistically conceived and nicely done. A very professional group. As I sat there, I thought, 'This is marvelous.' The black experience can't be told of prettily. This was genuine theater of protest. It was a play of consequence, and it had the ring of authority."

The list of readings included excerpts from Genet's *The Blacks, Native Son, Marat-Sade*, a poem by Langston Hughes and several other dramatic selections. None of these was even referred to in the ensuing furor. After a presentation of excerpts from LeRoi Jones' *The Slave,* the entire day took its identity from that. All else was forgotten and " 'The Slave' Controversy" or "The Wellesley Incident" raged on, literally turning school, town, and family into bitter factions.

In an article written for *Saturday Review,* Tom Cottle described what he observed during that presentation. "Throughout the performance the faces of the students told the real story. They were utterly involved and swept in the fire of black and white dramatists, poets, and actors. They laughed at times and literally squealed with excitement at other times. They were angry and frightened, perplexed and relieved. School was good. And I thought that if it takes a Kerner Report and the assassination of a great man, well then, that's what it takes."

While Mr. Cottle was observing the students, another drama was going on. Upon hearing a line from *The Slave,* "Sit the fuck down," and after watching a black man lean over the chair on which his white ex-wife was sitting and kiss her on the neck (according to the actor who did it and numerous interviews with members of the audience), some teachers and several janitors actually ran from the gymnasium—a few with their hands over their ears. One teacher, an older woman, fell in her anxious struggle to escape the bleachers. Another fled to her confessor. The boys' gym teacher was wringing his hands in agony. A young woman on the faculty cried, "If my Mummy had known I'd listened to this, she'd disown me."

The offending tableau became known as "the rape scene," the "obscenity" became known as "The Word," and the tranquil days of the tweedy, well-heeled town of Wellesley became known as the past.

As Mr. Crockett, a kindly, judicious, and rather frail man with a heart condition, left the gymnasium, another teacher quite a bit younger and twice his size cornered and grabbed him, shook him and demanded, "Do you approve of this?"

Crockett replied, "Heartily." The teacher, George Kerivan, warned, "I'm going to call every household in Wellesley and tell them that you approve of this." In his view, the presentation was "smut."

A statement by Chief of Police Robert MacBey: "I was first made aware on Friday afternoon of the program held during the morning at the Senior High School. As told to me by a parent of two high school students who had not himself been a witness, I found it inconceivable that anything as indecent would be held before a 'captive' audience in a public school. On Saturday and Sunday I received many calls from Wellesley parents, none of them witnesses. I then felt it my duty to further investigate. It was determined that the offensive part of the program was excerpts from a play *The Slave* by LeRoi Jones. I obtained this play at the Wellesley Public Library.

"After reading *The Slave* I then contacted some persons that I had been informed were present and invited them to my office on Wednesday to question them as to what they had seen and heard. As a result, in my opinion, a violation of law had been committed and I cite Chapter No. 272— Section 28 of the Massachusetts General Laws."

This law refers to the introduction of lewd and obscene material tending to corrupt the morals of minors and carries a penalty of not more than five years in prison and/or a fine of $100 to $500.

Monday, June 10, 1968, several days after the assassination of Robert F. Kennedy, the people of Wellesley jammed the high school auditorium to discuss obscenity. According to *The Wellesley Townsman* of June 13, 1968, "The front of the hall was filled with students who by their applause appeared to approve of the controversial play, but the larger part of the audience appeared to be critical."

Principal Samuel Graves spoke first. Among his comments, "I go on record that the type of language used in that portion of *The Slave* should not be used before an audience of high school students. [Applause.] I have no desire to stifle free, public discussion of the day's most pressing issues. . . . But these problems do not have to be voiced with four-letter words."

Graves promised that there would be no repetition of this type of performance. He stressed that a high school shouldn't run away from problems of the outside world, but that all sides of the issue should be presented. Given all the alternatives, he concluded, the children could reach their own conclusions "free from any attempt at indoctrination." [Wild applause.]

A letter was then read from some twenty teachers proposing that "rather than allowing mutual bitterness and recriminations between opposing members of the faculty to predominate, we use our energies to devise ways of having school programs on urgent issues of concern to us all that would be mutually satisfactory but still come to grips with the realities of the world around us."

Some teachers rose to "seriously question the propriety of those who arranged the program." Others bemoaned the current situation in the high school, saying they were "shocked at the decline in moral strength."

One student introduced a petition with, by his count, 364 student signatures endorsing the program and recommending more of the same.

A woman took the floor to say that she was not an American and she thought perhaps the practice of her native land should be followed here—that those teachers who gave too much freedom to students be "investigated." According to Tom Cottle, "Like the principal's, her words were all well received."

A parent chided the gathering, and said that in his opinion as a psychiatrist, the young people would not be forever corrupted, since four-letter words are not known to inflict permanent damage. He reminded the group of the real obscenity of a murder of yet another great American.

Another speaker, a housewife and parent, said, "To quote the words 'embarrassed, disgusted, and shamed' used by a teacher to describe how he felt at seeing the play, I feel embarrassed that our Wellesley children, our Boston neighbors, and the world around us, watch while Wellesley, whose very affluence should dictate its leadership in resolving the racial crisis, gets hung up on a few ugly words, and even threatens some of its most honorable, courageous, generous, and concerned teachers and citizens who are struggling to wake up our complacent suburbs to the issues ahead of us."

While she was speaking, groups of men scattered in twos and threes all over the hall, rose and began chanting dementedly, "Say the Word, Say the Word, Say the Word."

At this point, the chair continued to ignore the flock of long-haired students directly in front of the speaker's rostrum, who had been seeking recognition. Instead, Ed Bryant, a shorn ex-football player and outstanding student who had graduated the previous week, was recognized. He made his way to the front of the auditorium from the left side. He struggled to be heard over the chanting, and began:

"May 31 I was a student at Wellesley High School. Now I'm a graduate which puts me out into the real world. We're all here tonight because some of you were offended by some language, in a play by LeRoi Jones, *The Slave*, which was presented to your children. I'd like to tell you something about your children, 'cause I don't think you know an awful lot about them. I'd first like to quote to you one particular line that was followed by the walkout of a teacher, so I assume that was an offensive line. The Negro, who I am told is a poet, told his ex-wife and her husband, and I quote him, 'Sit the fuck down.' Now this offended an awful lot of people, I would gather, because this is going to corrupt our youth and it presents a distorted picture of morality, and it gives us the idea that this is socially acceptable. I know this is horrid, but I'd like to point a few things out to you first. First time I ever heard the word 'fuck' I was five years old and it was in Wellesley, Massachusetts. There are students in Wellesley High School who go to church, and their parents go to church too, and they can't say a sentence without 'fuck.' "

Before he could conclude, many adults ran, literally screaming, from the hall. Others, mainly the men who had been chanting, began to charge the stage. Screams of, "Kill him." "Get him." "Stop him." "Suffocate him." filled the room. Tom Cottle reported: "In grief, women placed their hands over their mouths. Men shook their fists. . . . The walls of Wellesley were totally destroyed now, and the very foundations had given way. Screaming, yelling, dismayed, angered, crying, they piled out of the auditorium."

One parent said, "I never saw anything like it. Women and men teachers stood up and waved their arms in the air. They were screaming, 'Get out. Let's get him.' The Word took on a reality. These people were being fucked! They ran for the doors. It was a near riot."

A policeman ran to the front of the auditorium, spoke for an instant with the chairman, and grabbed the student in a half nelson and hustled him out of the building. Bryant repeatedly screamed for help. An American Civil Liberties Union lawyer ran after the policeman, who was twisting the boy's arm severely, identified himself, and said, "I wouldn't hurt that boy if I were you." Ed later said, "I don't know if he would have broken my arm or not, but after the lawyer arrived he did lessen the pressure." The policeman then handcuffed the boy, who was not resisting arrest, brought him to the station, and charged him with disturbing the peace. When asked why he was handcuffed, Bryant remarked, "Because I was such a dangerous criminal." The policeman continued to treat him in a manner he described as "rather contemptuous."

Meanwhile, in the auditorium a black parent told the

gathering that whites in the audience had turned on her when she protested the tone of the meeting and screamed, "If you don't like it, go back to Africa." The next day this woman's son was "flattened" outside the high school.

At the close of the meeting, the town was far from satisfied. The teachers even less so. No one came forward to protest the treatment of Ed Bryant. Many were frightened and shaken. Others said it was the most violent and hateful display that they had ever witnessed. One woman said the people seemed "truly to have gone mad." Students were incredulous at seeing parents and teachers turn on each other with shouts and threats, curses and waving fists. Some students said the whole ugly incident reminded them of *The Crucible.*

Nevertheless, those forces within the town and especially within the high school which maintained that "this time they had gone too far" furiously demanded revenge. This cry for retribution came to settle on two teachers, Kay Cottle and Tom Fitzsimmons, as well as Pemberton Minster, a Wellesley parent and father of seven, and two members of the Theatre Company.

These five individuals were summoned to show cause why a complaint should not be issued against them under Section 28 of Chapter 272 of the General Laws, for tending to "corrupt the morals of youth" by introducing lewd and obscene material to minors which "is utterly without redeeming social importance for such minors."

The summons was served to Mr. Fitzsimmons by a plainclothesman who came to his classroom during the school day. Some of the students present found this quite amusing.

The majority faction of the faculty was particularly anxious for punishment of Mrs. Cottle up to and including imprisonment despite the fact that she was eight months pregnant.

She and Mr. Minster, Ed Bryant, and the school administration received hate mail, some threatening violence and much of it using obscenity. Among the more respectable charges were that the school was harboring Communists, that it was a cesspool and den of inquity. Ed Bryant was called a nigger lover.

Mr. Crockett, very concerned because two members of his department were being charged, determined not to fold beneath the pressure. Like many others in the town he was concerned that the "history department had pretty much folded its tent," as many teachers in that former bastion of liberalism, some who were already leaning toward departure, either left or were weeded out.

As he remembers it, "Nobody came to Mr. Fitzsimmons' rescue. And he of course had nothing to do with it. Nothing, not even sympathy. Teachers were delighted that he and Mrs. Cottle were involved. One member of the administration said, 'Tom, this will learn ya'.' Others testified against them. Mrs. Cottle was stunning and had every virtue and talent. Other women on the faculty hated her, and wanted punishment. Eddie was a very interesting boy. A brilliant student without a thread of insincerity in his body."

Pemberton Minster was also very upset. He was aware that the children of citizens who were tutoring black students were being beaten. The chairman of the Committee Against Racism had been stoned in view of the police, and his landlord had refused to renew his lease.

Many newspapers were quoting Minster without ever having contacted him. One of his children finally obtained a retraction from one. He said, "The most terrifying thing of all was not for me but for my children. They were reading and hearing things about me that were totally unfounded, and they knew it.

"My role was totally distorted. The school committee and administration approved the program and authorized several teachers to ask our committee to raise the one hundred dollars it would cost for the Theatre Company. I raised the money.

"We had no say over the program. All I knew was that it was a biracial company which did repertory and reportedly was excellent. There was dishonesty and lack of moral courage on the part of the police and school administration. They had authorized the performance. Mr. Fitzsimmons had nothing to do with it. The Police Chief and Sam Graves [the principal] and the school committee knew that for a fact. I talked at length with them about it, but they wouldn't do anything. There was criminal mistreatment of this man. It was sickening and disheartening. The police were given our names by Sam Graves who had received a written program forty-eight hours before it was put on and approved it. The Theatre Company of Boston told me the Wellesley performance was unusual because there were no requests for donations."

The five individuals who had been summoned, and Ed Bryant, appeared in court the day after the open meeting, Tuesday, June 11, 1968. The case was continued until September 12, 1968, because of the imminent birth of Mrs. Cottle's baby.

Ed Bryant was permitted to write an apology to the town and escape further punishment. This was no easy thing for him to do, but he said, "It might have destroyed my parents. I wouldn't have been able to live here ever again. It just wasn't worth it. But if I'd been able to take it through the courts, I would have won eventually."

On this same day the Committee Against Racism obtained permission to gather at the conference room in the town library to read *The Slave,* which few were acquainted with although many were passing vehement judgment upon it. According to *The Townsman,* the library trustees saw no reason to forbid the gathering since the audience was not "captive," and the committee had a "clear purpose" in reading the play.

The Board of Selectmen, however, ruled that "in the interests of public safety and welfare," no building of the town was to be used to "exhibit" LeRoi Jones' *The Slave*. Permission to assemble was thus denied.

By a vote of 2 to 1, this same board voted against taking criminal action against the five individuals summoned. One of the Selectmen, David Sargent, called the citing of two teachers out of two hundred "a terrible thing." He went on to say that new teachers would be fearful of coming into a community where they had to answer to every group in town. He continued, "I think this is an incursion of book burning. . . . I'm for academic freedom."

Mr. Rhome, another Selectman, agreed with Mr. Sargent, saying, "I think that it is a shocking thing to bring these criminal proceedings against these teachers. To me, these people are not being prosecuted, they are being persecuted."

Mr. Wilder, the third member, dissented saying, "I don't think the Town of Wellesley should sponsor such programs." In spite of the 2 to 1 decision, the charges were continued, since the courts were not bound by a Board of Selectmen decision.

On September 12, 1968, in the Dedham District Court a closed hearing was held on "The Slave Incident." Two teachers representing the majority opinion of the high school faculty were called to testify. According to Mr. Minster both denied that the play was sexually stimulating although they protested its lewd and obscene nature and particularly the "rape and chase scene."

Mr. Minster felt that although there was no such scene, these people actually believed that they had seen rape. "In this country, that's rape—for a white woman to be kissed by a black man. In these people's minds it couldn't be voluntary."

The Judge asked Mr. Kerivan, one of the teachers protesting the showing of *The Slave* (the same man who had accosted Mr. Crockett the day of the performance), "How wide is your experience in the theater?" Mr. Kerivan admitted it was not extensive.

Although no one reportedly testified that the play was sexually stimulating, Judge Rider ruled the play obscene and said that a crime had been committed. However, he dismissed the charges against the teachers, the Theatre Company, and Mr. Minster because of a lack of evidence that these people were connected with the presentation on May 31, 1968.

Mr. Minster claims that "the police intentionally presented no evidence because they clearly didn't want a trial. They knew the truth would come out. The only guilty party, if anyone were, was the school administration. The Judge conveniently ruled the play obscene but said there wasn't enough evidence for probable cause.

"At this point, they wanted to cool it because Wellesley had become the laughingstock of the whole East Coast. Even beforehand the police told me not to worry. I wanted to force a trial. If I had done something wrong—put me in jail. If they believed I had, then they were derelict in their duty not to put me in jail. The police refused to submit evidence linking me to the play although there was written evidence that I raised the money and the party to whom I gave it refused even to say he took the money.

"My attorney told me that it would probably take two years before the case was settled. He expected guilty verdicts until it got to the State Supreme Court. But the Theatre Company asked me not to. Their main income was from performances such as they gave in Wellesley. After two years of this, they thought they'd be out of business."

In other words, Minster was asked, you feel that the obscene ruling and the hearing was just to satisfy the sensibilities of the town that someone had suffered? He replied, "Exactly."

He added that the behavior of the citizens and officials came as no surprise. "There is very little moral courage in

Wellesley. The only support I got was from the Jewish community. I hate to classify that way, but it's the truth. None from anyplace else. They were the people who showed us kindness and a willingness to continue their association with us. They also volunteered financial help."

Minster concluded, "You know, those same teachers who stood against us laughed in open amusement at the party they gave for the graduates when the kids were all getting drunk on liquor supplied by one of the members of the school committee—openly breaking the law."

Unlike Mr. Minster, Tom Fitzsimmons was not prepared for the hypocrisy and viciousness in some parts of the Wellesley community. He is a mild-mannered, uncontroversial veteran teacher who had resided in Wellesley with his wife and children for many years. His experience defies the Wellesley *Booster*'s claim that "Teaching in Wellesley is not just a job. It is a highly desirable and satisfying way of life."

As he relates his story, "I am very—well—embittered. I'll never feel the same about Wellesley. Especially about the police. The way they handled it was so dumb. Now I can really imagine an innocent man can be taken from his home by the police, and charged, and brought up before the bar of justice and convicted, and still be perfectly innocent. Because it happened to me. Of course we were not convicted in the end. But I've never been exonerated. Never. I was an innocent bystander. But I've never had my name cleared by the administration or the school committee. Never even a letter or an apology, let alone support.

"And the attitude of some of the teachers. Two in particular who wanted—well—revenge. They wanted Mrs. Cottle to go to prison. Really, they wanted punishment. Jail. One was simply a reactionary. The other saw political advantage.

"It was a nightmare. A witch hunt. I was an idealist. That's why I'm here. But my sense of the goodness of people is sadly shaken . . . about American life, the American community, and American ideals. It's a greedy, grab kind of world. My concept of every person being his brother's keeper—well. I could count on the fingers of one hand the phone calls of support I got in all this time. Even at my church, some people thought it was funny. There was no sense of the anguish it caused. It's a cold, apathetic world. And the students are as apathetic as the rest. There's no new love generation. There are very few, even among us teachers, who are concerned.

"Not very hopeful. I suppose education is the only answer. But if Wellesley is what we've got, if this is what we've been aiming for, well it just hasn't worked."

Exactly where the responsibility rests for what happened in Wellesley is something no one can say with certainty. Today, few people believe The Word was anything more than an excuse for the explosion of long-fostering conflicts. For instance:

1. There was great division among the high school faculty between liberals in the history and English departments who wanted a more flexible, relaxed school atmosphere and conservatives in language, sciences and math, who required daily, regimented study and who championed discipline.

2. In one short year there had been a furor because of a dress code, a drug inquisition in which students had their lockers searched and were quizzed without counsel and according to some parents tricked by the administration into confessions and naming of names upon being falsely told that others had "talked." Janitors had been deputized. Students with long hair had been beaten and spat upon, and although drug use was widespread, only what the Police Chief referred to as "the hippie element" were exposed.

3. Mrs. Cottle had won the enmity of many when she championed the unshorn students who were being harassed. Whether or not her pregnancy further unconsciously incited the people outraged by The Word, who sought to indict her, can never be determined.

4. The introduction of METCO [a program for busing

black children into suburban schools] in 1966 had galvanized the right. The Old Guard had been outraged with the influx of Irish, Italians, Jews, and others who had "made it" and invaded the sacrosanct town. METCO for many was the ultimate insult. Townspeople who previously held that the ghettos were not in need of massive funding or rehabilitation now feared that the black students would bring lice and disease as well as moral decay to their children. One resident noted, "The same people who were worried that the METCO kids would come out here and write dirty words on the bathroom walls were outraged at *The Slave*."

There was also the very acute lack of information within the town. The local paper is tightly run, Republican, and very conservative. One housewife noted, "There is no real communication of facts. We haven't a paper. This is the biggest problem in terms of community life and civil liberties. There is no reporting and there are no facts. If you can't get to people—get the facts to them—there's no way to know where they stand."

The acting editor of the local paper affirmed his close connection with the police and his intimate knowledge of them and stated that they "were anything but brutal." The arresting officer he asserted was "one of the gentlest persons you ever saw. He wouldn't hurt a fly."

The Slave has left lasting scars. Families were literally turned against one another. Many students were appalled at the vindictive tactics of the teachers, administration, and parents. One participant on the WGBH program said, "It was a chance for us to see what our parents are really like."

Unlike Pemberton Minster, many were unprepared for the depth of Wellesley's hypocrisy. One young girl said, "Where was the school committee meeting when the kids with long hair were beaten up? Where was the horror and righteous indignation then? What about threatening Mr. Crockett, who'd been a sick man? People really showed their values. It's all right to be violent and hurt people, but it's not all right to say *fuck*."

Another participant in the WGBH program, an older woman, asked, "Are the parents the problem? A lot of grown-up, educated people, who did go to college, who did go to good schools, don't seem to know about the world."

The existence of the Constitution, of their elected representatives, of their local police, and even of their churches proved in the final analysis and in the rage of passion and prejudice to be of very meager comfort.

Most insiduous of all is the close cooperation between the town officials, the police, and town's only newspapers. In this very closed and powerful town there are few impartial voices, and there is the very real concern that the vast majority of the citizens will never be told of the treatment or punishment accorded to those who trample on the sensibilities of the town, or those who are wrongly accused of doing so.

The most disturbing fact of all is that this entire affair was not a carefully orchestrated vendetta. To a great extent the injustice was unconscious and unrecognized. There was no outcry, no protest, no sense of a need to reexamine the process or its result. All the events of the Wellesley Incident seemed to nearly all those who witnessed it or heard of it, perfectly within the framework of the American system. And in the narrowest meaning of that system, they were right.

Ed Bryant is still confident that he would have won his case even if it took the Supreme Court to do it, although he now is aware of some of the extrajudicial pressures which can force a person who is convinced of his innocence to retreat.

Pemberton Minster found that it is not simple to wage a protracted legal battle for many reasons, including the harsh fact that some individuals cannot afford to exonerate themselves in court and buy food for their family at the same time.

The question remains, if these people and others like them

who have prestige in our society, who can read, who know their rights, who can afford a good lawyer—if they can be accorded such shabby treatment at the bar of justice, then what hope have the poor, ignorant, or illiterate of this culture?

This travesty is rather a small one. No one was murdered. No one was maimed. No bombs were dropped. Nevertheless, it poses very real questions for a people complacent with the values of American life. The Wellesley Incident did not take place in the fetid ignorance of the Mississippi backwater. It took place in the affluent ignorance of one of the most privileged ten square miles in the world.

The citizens screaming, "Kill him!" at a five-foot-five boy of seventeen whom they had cheered a few months before on the football field were not poverty-stricken or starving, over-crowded or illiterate. Many had enjoyed the best education and care this society has to offer, and they believed that they had reaped more generously than most the fruits of the American experiment. They were the most civilized of men. If the Wellesley *Booster* is correct in thinking that the town enfolds "all that is best and most desirable in the climate of modern progress," then it clearly is not enough.

A Black Student Sits in the Assembly While the Mayor Speaks ("If You're Black, There's No Explanation")

by Richard Wornum

In the school I go to there is so much racial tension. One day the Mayor came to speak, and they had all the seniors down there, white and black. Everybody. And all the black students sat together. The issue was just there. Everybody knew it was on the other guy's mind. The white-black thing. And, well, when a black student got up to ask Mayor White a question all the white students looked at him; and they looked at him and said—(I don't know what they had on their minds, you could tell it wasn't hate, it wasn't fear, I don't know what it was, something that exists, something that exists today, they just looked at him, as if to say)—"What the hell is he doing here?" He asked a question. The Mayor gave him a political answer.

Then a white boy got up and asked the Mayor a question that pertained to back in September when a bunch of black students over at English High School caused a big ruckus over not being able to wear African garb or African clothing to school. He said his question: "Why wasn't there more reparations taken against those students over at English who caused that whole ruckus, those colored kids at English, when they caused that trouble?" He, he had a hate in his voice, and yet I don't know why he asked it; he was sort of like asking it to say to us in the back, "Who the hell do you think you are?" ('Cause that's where all the black kids were sitting.) "Who the hell do you think you are? Why don't you do something about these black kids? Why are you letting them get away with all this?" When he said this, there was thunderous applause from all the white students. Everybody applauded. "Yeahhhh," you know, and the Mayor, the answer the Mayor gave him doesn't even have anything to do with what I am trying to say here. What I am trying to say is this: that kid didn't know what had gone on, he was so—I don't know how to put it—he really didn't know what had gone on. He thought we had caused so much trouble. The black people, you know, the black students had caused so much trouble, and nothing had been done against them.

All of them . . . the attitude in the school. They look at you and they say, "I know you hate me. You're a trouble-maker, you, you want to mess up things. I want to fuck you up because you think like that." And, I just pictured in my mind what had gone on when they had all that trouble at English. At English a whole bunch of students, black students, sat outside the school. All the city, the whole city was behind this thing that they couldn't wear African dress to school. So everybody black, all the black students, went up to English and sat outside the school. I don't know, it was a little over-drawn-out in the sense that they went to all other schools and broke windows and assaulted white people, but we paid, *we did pay*.

After school in Dudley Street Station, when the white students were coming home, there were crowds of black people. Not there to break up or damage things. There were people who were there to do that, but they were so few. Most people were curious, and they were there to see what had happened, what was going to go on. And there were police, hundreds of police, there to restore "law and order." American law and order. The police didn't know what was going on. They saw a race riot coming, the whole thing. All the police could see was that another race riot was going to break out there. They didn't see what was going on. They didn't see the issue. These people weren't here to tear up, they were asking for something, and this was their way of asking for it, by being out there. Most people were out there for curiosity's sake. The police were out there in their riot-clad uniforms, guns, mostly night sticks. Ready to repel anything that came over.

I recall one incident—a bus full of white students from a school pulled in. Everybody ran into the station to see what was going to happen. The police headed the white students into vans and took them to another station to go home. Well, it's, it's like a circus. There were a million police there, they had the police academy there. They were all lined up. You got a chance to see the new equipment.

I myself went up for curiosity's sake, to see what was going on. And then it happened—one person in the crowd threw a bottle at a group of police officers. Everybody there felt what I felt the minute they saw the bottle going from the crowd. The police are going to come at us. I can't stand there and say, "I didn't do it." I'm black. If I stay there, I'm going to get fucked up. So everybody ran. I said to myself, I said, "Calm down, don't run." I ran, I was running. Everybody was running. There were hundreds of people running down the street. The policeman who got hit really got mad. He threw off his helmet, he chased the crowd, he drew his gun from his holster, and then, in the final second raised it in the air, and shot in the air. I heard that shot, I fled. I just ran my ass off: I was scared. The police lined up and drove the crowd back. If you just, there was—it's hard to explain—there was no room for the innocent person. The person doing his everyday thing, coming home from work. They didn't know he was coming home from work, they didn't know he didn't have a brick in his pocket, getting ready to throw it. He was black, so he couldn't, he couldn't go to Dudley Street Station. It went on like this for the rest of the day.

This white boy in the assembly, he didn't know this. This

white boy, he doesn't know what it is to have this happen to him. If something happens in that situation and you're around, you're black, you can't stand there and say, "Listen, officer, I didn't do this, I didn't do that." You're black, you're there. He's not going to listen to you; something happens.

The fear, the fear is something that this white boy would probably never understand, and yet he gets up and asks a question, "Why wasn't there any reparations against those black students at English." There are reparations against black people every day of the week. It didn't end that afternoon. I was scared, I didn't want to stay down there. Every time I saw a police car I was frightened. Someone could throw something off a rooftop—I'd just be walking down the street. They'd jump out and they'd just get me because I was there and I was black. No explanation. No explanation possible. It's like you're all one faith, you're all evil. All out to kill.

And the white boy talks about reparations. He thinks I hate him, he thinks I want to cut him, to kill him. But this is what I'm going through.

We stood on the regular corner, a bunch of us, watching what was going on, talking about it, and then, as it got night, about nine o'clock, there seemed to be double the amount of police in the area. There were cars cruising, like it was a combat zone, like you see on TV when an escaped prisoner is behind enemy lines and you got a million cars out looking for him. And if they see him they're going to shoot him. They're going to shoot him. So they were driving around. And they were all over the place. Patrolling like it was a combat zone. A car went by at least every three seconds. We were just watching. Six in a car, lights out, cruising slow. The way the projects is built, too, it's like a prison camp. There's just all these buildings and about four streets around them, and one or two that go through. And they were just cruising around and through.

We were standing there, and then a car pulled up; it was

dark; it was a police car. There were six officers in it. It was cruising really slow. It was about a hundred yards up, it pulled close to the curb. They came at us, I thought it was going to be the usual thing. "Come on, boys, move on. Move on." But I had forgotten this was like war. They didn't need an excuse. We just had to be there. Pulled up slow, real slow. I was leaning on the light pole, and they pulled up right next to me. There was fifteen of us standing there, only six officers in the car. Everybody started to run. I said, "Don't run, don't run."

After the first one started running, the officer jumped out of the car, and he ran after him, real quick. When we saw this, we all started to run. He pulled out his night stick and grabbed one of my friends. I heard the night stick, I heard it. I just heard it, mahogany across his head. Poop, poop. I looked at him. Three more jumped out of the car. They all jumped out of the car. Everybody was running. It was like mice. We were running. I looked back. Everybody said, "Come on, Rick." I started running. I ran across the street, up the street, I just kept running, I was running. All I could see was he was behind me. He had his gun out, I just ran straight up. People said, we could of jumped 'em, we could of killed them. Did you ever think of that? Yeah, jump 'em and kill 'em. One stays in on the radio and calls for help. There were thirty cars out in the area.

Two-block area. They were patrolling. I was frightened. They had dispersed the crowd. We ran up into the project, into a building. I was really frightened. Some guys like the excitement, but it was scaring the hell out of me. I knew what was going on. It was like war. We didn't do anything. We just had on the other uniform, and they shot at us. The hard part was getting back to the other side of the projects to get home without getting shot because I had the uniform on. It was like I was a spy, and I had infiltrated into enemy territory and I had to get back. It all sounds farfetched, but this is how it was. It was like war. White against black. They were up there to kill us, to get us out of there. And there was nothing we could do.

The whole issue was overdrawn. And the white boy sits in the assembly hall and talks about reparations. He doesn't know, he doesn't understand. And when I tell him, he thinks I'm trying to get him to sympathize with me. The whole idea, if he were black, I, I don't know, if he were black, and it happened to him, what would he do, how would he feel? I don't know, I just know how I feel. And when he says something like this, I want to kill him. Because he doesn't understand, he doesn't know what's going on in me. And it would never happen to him.

Well, anyway, I was on the other side of the projects. I had to get home. I was at a friend's house. And now that they had us running, we were really afraid. They just got out there in their riot helmets. When we saw them I was afraid, like they were aliens from another planet. They were so far superior to us. I was afraid that I couldn't even stand to explain myself. They'd just turn the ray gun, and Zap, I was gone. So I had to try and get home, to the safety of my home, what little shelter it offered—off the street, before it happened to me. I saw Johnny go down. When they hit him with a night stick, I was really frightened. So I left the building. Two police cars coming down the street. Adams Street. Everyone is looking out their windows. "Run Rickie. Run, run," they say. "Run, Mike. Run."

I got all scared. I yelled out, "I didn't do anything, why should I run?" They didn't know. Cops didn't know. They cruised down, three cars on the street. One drives down into the park; there are kids running. They say, "It's fun, it's fun; we just throw a rock at 'em. It's fun. Come on. Run, you guys."

I didn't do anything, but I knew I had to run. I ran; I got into the next building. I went from building to building. Anyway, I was scared as hell, but I made it. I went over four friends' houses trying to get in, that's how scared I was. It wasn't like I could just walk home; I wanted to stay at someone's house all night. I saw Johnny go down. I didn't want a night stick coming across my head. For not doing anything, just for being black. But I had the other uniform on, and our army didn't have any weapons. Our army didn't have any weapons at all. They were annihilating us. Now it wasn't like this all over the city—no, no, just down here in the projects.

Reparations . . . we were paying. Oh, we could have shot a cop. Shoot a cop, yeah. You'll get away with it, but eight of your people will get killed for it. They'll have to shoot someone black. They got to. All they can see in their minds is that you're trying to get them. They don't understand that you're not. You're just black, you're out there. They can't understand, I mean, they can't see. So, I made it to the other side of the projects. And I had a long walk down a long stretch. Mike went into his house. I was going to go in with him, but I thought I could make it. I don't know, I got my composure back. Man, this was the projects, this was where I was supposed to be cool. Supposed to be the hangout, man—I lay down there all the time. I walk, I feel proud because I know no one can touch me. But tonight, oh, I lose my cool—because they're fucking me up. Not me, my people. I see all around me.

So I walk down. And then a wagon comes by me. I turn around; I'm frightened. They're cruising slow, the lights are off. All I can see is someone jumping out of the back and coming out and messing me up. I just keep walking. I get in the parking lot, the parking lot for my house. I come up the stairs. I get into the hallway. All I can see is a police officer running in the other side of the hallway and grabbing me for something someone else has done. I walk up the stairs, I get in the house. I look out, I don't want to show my parents I'm scared; I don't want to show my brothers I'm scared. I got to be cool, I play it cool, I come in my room. I lay down on my bed and think. I say damn, God, why does this happen? What's going on? Why are they fucking us up, I say. I sat in the window the rest of the night. The cars were cruising through. There wasn't one or two—there were twenty police cars. Six officers in each car, six officers in a car. And he says reparations.

Most of the people out there were out there looking. They were out there to see. To see what was going on, to see the new riot equipment, to see what was going on. One person would do something, everybody pays. Everybody pays. All this over wanting to wear a dashiki to school. A member of the school committee wants to call up the National Guard, because those blacks are coming up, the blacks are all getting drunk, and they're going to come out and tear the city up. It's not like that. It's not like that. Those white boys at school look at me, and we joke about it. But I know deep down in their minds how they feel. They don't understand. I could see me now, coming in with a patch on my head, seventeen stitches where I had gotten clobbered, going up on the stage and looking at them and pleading with them to understand. I know they wouldn't understand. I just know they wouldn't.

What could I say to the Mayor? What could I do? The next day I saw Johnny. Four stitches, a big patch cut out of that Afro of his. Barry Campbell, served in the army, ex-marine. He wouldn't throw a bottle. Twenty-four years old, a man, walking home, going across the street. They came at him; there was nothing he could say, they just came down on him with a stick. It all sounds like a story, but it's true, it happened. It happened in the United States of America. The cops were restoring Law and Order. There was no one white down here. Getting the niggers off the street. And boy did we pay. Now, back in the assembly hall, the white boy talks about reparations. Why weren't there any? They cheer. The Mayor gives a political answer.

Well, the assembly before this one with the Mayor, they saluted the flag, and the black students did not stand; we sat, and all put up clenched fists. So now the students jump up, "Why didn't we pledge allegiance to the flag?"

The Mayor says, "I don't know."

They stand up and say the pledge. They all look back at us. "What are you going to do, you blackies? What do you want?"

I wonder, I wonder what we want. I'm frightened. If it happens down here, and I'm black, there's nothing anybody black, there's nothing you can do. I figured this would be something I could do to make them understand. To make the white world understand how black people feel. We don't hate whites. We resent what they've done to us. They hate us. I don't know, maybe they're afraid. I don't know. I don't understand it. I can't explain what this feeling is they have against us. All I know is, this is what it's like for me.

This is what goes on in my mind when he says something like that. There's no way I can express it to him, to change his mind. I can understand his side of the story, partially, partially. But when I plead with him, "How would you like to be black?" he thinks I'm crying poormouth, police brutality—blacks always cry police brutality. Jesus, if they only knew. If they really only knew. This is what it's like to live down in here. It was like war. Mike turns to me, and he says, "Rick," he says, "They aren't jiving around, man. It's war." They're down here to kill us, and we don't have any weapons. It's like the North and the South are fighting, and we're in the North and we got a Confederate uniform; and they don't come off, because these uniforms are made of skin. Black skin. What can I do? I really wish there was something I could do. They just don't understand. The whites just don't understand.

Eight: **FIGHTING BACK**

"The People First" versus Judge Troy

by Shamus Glynn

We saw earlier in this book that a judge in a district court is king of the courtroom and can remove anyone from it he pleases. In the working-class district of Dorchester in 1972, something historic happened: a group of ordinary people organized a campaign against a powerful judge who had mistreated countless people in his courtroom, and succeeded in removing that judge from his bench and from the courtroom. The judge was Jerome P. Troy, the group was called *TPF*—The People First, and the story is told here by a member of that group, Shamus Glynn. (H.Z.)

First, we need to understand why so many people in Dorchester ended up in court.

Dorchester is the largest working-class community in Boston. Its three-decker apartment buildings date from the turn of the century, when the Irish were still pouring in, fleeing Ireland's rural poverty to work in the factories and construction sites of industrial New England for the lowest wages. Over the years, some moved up the social scale, but most have remained in Dorchester, working in the factories and offices, driving the buses, digging the ditches.

Trapped in a job he will probably have for the rest of his life, a Dorchester man tries to find a small amount of enjoyment at home, and in the tavern. On Sundays, when the taverns close, the churches take over. The men don't often ask much for themselves—usually a car, a TV, a comfortable home, a brighter future for their children.

But in these times of breakdown and crisis, the family is under tremendous pressure. The material goods that a family has worked so hard for do very little to ease the strain. With every small setback, hope for the children is shaken. The increased pressure leads to heavier drinking, fights at home, barroom brawls, car accidents, loss of jobs, welfare problems, and perhaps the breakup of the family. Police come into the picture; people are brought into court.

How about the children? Whether in public or parochial school, the educational experience is poor. In school youngsters begin to relate to each other independent of their families. Groups band together and find a park or corner in their neighborhood where they can hang around. To have fun they play sports, cards, dice, pitch nickels, and smoke cigarettes. When these activities become boring it's on to other more exciting things: alcohol, drugs, sex, stealing cars.

Under great pressure to plan their own futures, and yet seeing the almost nonexistent rewards that their families have received for all their sacrifices and hardships, the kids become discouraged. They rebel against the alienation and frustrations of their parents' lives; they refuse to accept their fate. They instinctively and unconsciously seek a meaningful life. Failing to find it, some will submit and accept the present structure of society.

Most, however, will resist the pressure and live day to day, seeking excitement, adventure, love, friendship, and happiness. To avoid falling into their parents' shoes, they will try get-rich-quick schemes, they will try to live somehow, even on very little money, without a regular job. In complete opposition to their parents' living for a brighter future, they want now the so-called good things in life, which they see reserved for the middle and upper classes. The tension between what they want and what they get causes a chronic crisis. In this crisis, the use of drugs and alcohol has spread throughout Dorchester.

Riding through Dorchester, you can see groups of kids clustered on every corner and in every park. In smaller numbers but just as visible are the police, who are continually stopping, breaking up, and shaking down the groups. If no one has any grass or beer with them the cops will give the order: Get off the corner, take off! The group usually begins to move, not out of respect for authority, but out of feelings of powerlessness. The cops get back into their car while threatening: "If we see any of you kids again tonight we're going to pull you in." The kids start walking away slowly and defiantly as the cops drive off. As soon as the police car is a block away, the gang can be seen back on their corner. In a short time the cops are back. The cops use their power to arrest and beat some people.

The police are one of the social institutions which must concentrate their energy on containing the reaction to a social crisis. If you were to follow around any cop's car for a night you would realize that the police are at war with the young people of Dorchester. There are a few patrols of cops who are known throughout Dorchester who stop at every corner and park, and usually provoke an incident which will almost always end in their favor. The majority of the police patrols leave the dirty work to these young cops. When an incident breaks out, they support them with whatever is necessary: clearing the area, using violence, covering up for each other.

People with money seem to settle a lot of their problems privately—at home, or in a psychiatrist's office. Or they go away to Europe. They have time, space, wealth, to take care of things without getting involved with the law. In Dorchester, men, women, and their children, find themselves in court. By 1972, of all the district courts in Massachusetts, Dorchester had the largest case load of criminal and juvenile complaints, and the second largest load of civil complaints. In that year, without counting drunks and minor traffic offenses, the load in Dorchester District Court reached the astounding total of twenty thousand cases.

This meant that the court was deeply involved in the everyday personal lives of the people of Dorchester. It had become the most powerful institution in the community. And the most powerful figure in that court was Judge Jerome P. Troy.

For ten years, Judge Troy, with his cronies, treated the Dorchester District Court as his private preserve. They ran the court, and through it, the community, as a feudal lord run his estate. With the power of the court at his disposal, Troy was able to give favors. In return, he received favors: from businessmen he got a share of their profits or their services; from bakers, free pastry; from landlords, investment opportunities; from lawyers, free legal services; from politicians, political favors. The Judge could give out jobs in the court, lucrative assignments to lawyers, favorable decisions in cases. If someone did not go along with the Judge, there were consequences: The Judge could issue complaints, he could fine, he could jail.

Thus, a small group of men used their public power for private gain to make decisions that would affect the lives of thousands of Dorchester families. Here is how it worked, as we in Dorchester observed it.

The public business of the court usually began at 10 A.M., when Judge Troy came out of his chambers with a smile and the court was called to order. Troy, and his clerk for the regular session, James Buckley, took a quiet look around the court —from the dock holding the defendants, to the lawyer's section, to the spectators (mostly family and friends of the defendants), to the long line of police—and then business began.

Buckley would call out the name of the defendant, who, just brought from jail, then stood in the dock on the Judge's right, or, if bail had been made, walked to the witness stand on the left of the Judge. The defendant's name was reread along with the charges. Buckley would ask for a plea of "guilty or not guilty," and sometimes the defendant would be advised of his right to be represented by a lawyer. The defendant might be asked if he would like the court to appoint a lawyer or whether he would obtain private counsel. Buckley would do this with such great speed that generally it would be inaudible to the defendant, about ten feet away.

Then Buckley would turn to Troy and discuss the matter of bail. Troy often questioned or attacked the defendant. With an air of contempt, he would ask: "Haven't you been arrested for this crime before?" "Don't you understand we have to protect the community from people like you?" "How can we be sure you won't break the law while you're out on bail?"

If the defendant was a woman, he would ask: "Are you on welfare?" If the answer was yes, he would proceed with: "Do you live with your husband now?" If the answer was no, he would ask: "Whom do you live with?"

Troy would then ask the woman if she was willing to take out a warrant for her husband's arrest. He would tell her of the tremendous burden she was to the taxpayers, finishing with: "You can't expect taxpayers to support you; you must take out a warrant on your husband." Sometimes he would tell the woman if she did not want to take out a warrant he would have her thrown off the welfare rolls.

Troy and Buckley would use the bail system to coerce defendants. The bails Troy imposed on defendants were exceptionally high—38 percent of them were over ten thousand dollars, a percentage from double to ten times that of any of the other seventy-eight district courts in Massachusetts. This meant tremendous profits for bondsmen, including two, Santion and Maher, who were Troy appointees.

In many cases, Troy appointed private counsel instead of a Massachusetts Defenders Committee lawyer. In 1968, this cost the state $37,500, of which at least $20,000 went to Troy's ex-partner, his secretary's son and brother, and other lawyers connected with Troy. In 1969, the figure rose to $70,000, and in 1970 it reached $120,000.

Troy might criticize and interrupt the testimony of the defendant or disrupt the defendant's counsel or read his own mail during defense arguments. Guilt, in his court, seemed to have much to do with the defendant's age, race, or financial status. To avoid a guilty finding and a stiff sentence, it seemed to help to have a lawyer who was a friend of Troy's, or to know a politician or a courthouse worker.

Arraignments and imposition of bail were done at great speed, and then the court would take up the cases that had been continued to that day. Again, Troy and Buckley would maintain a speedy pace, allowing no lengthy defense arguments. A typical day at Dorchester court would end sometime between noon and 1 P.M., after a remarkable number of arraignments and trials had been disposed of. Troy and Buckley would leave immediately, for Troy had an active business life. The prisoners who couldn't make bail or those who were sentenced would wait in the lockup downstairs to be transported to the Youth Service Board, or Concord, or Deer Island, or the Charles Street Jail.

In the fall of 1970, TPF—The People First—decided to take on Judge Troy. TPF was a community organization, new to Dorchester, made up of mostly young people. Some were ex-students who had moved into the community, others were local people—veterans returned from Vietnam, young mothers. What bound them together was a belief that there was a social crisis in America caused by a small group which held power and profited from the institutions of the society. TPF wanted to change the institutions in Dorchester to benefit the community instead of a few. The group soon became aware that the district court was the seat of power, and that Judge Troy had profited from this power.

TPF began putting out a newspaper which attacked Judge Troy, the Dorchester court, the big landlords, and other people in powerful positions. The newspaper was passed out by TPF members at corners, parks, shopping centers, and churches, and it was received with enthusiasm. TPF was saying what people in the community had wanted for a long time to say. But these people were very skeptical about anybody being able to get Troy out of Dorchester court.

TPF was determined to try. They talked to some lawyers from the Massachusetts Law Reform Institute who had filed a suit against Troy which was dismissed by the court. In February, 1971, the members of TPF decided to involve the community in a campaign against Troy by circulating petitions for his removal.

The petition demanded Troy's removal on the ground that he had constantly violated the constitutional rights of defendants appearing before him. He had done this by: 1) setting excessively high bails, 2) failing to advise defendants of their rights to appeal bail, 3) imposing sentences and fines that were cruel and unusual punishment for relatively minor infractions, 4) discriminating against defendants on the basis of age, appearance, race, and financial status, and 5) refusing to allow lawyers, in many instances, to conduct a full and adequate defense.

Also cited in the petition were Troy's involvement in the Tenean Beach Marina project, from which he profited, as well as in the Tri-State Realty Corporation, and his wasting of public funds by the appointment of lawyers with whom he had business deals, in place of public defenders.

TPF decided on a goal of ten thousand signatures on the petition. Every day, members would go to street corners, barrooms, subway stations, bus stops, churches, shopping centers, beaches, and parks to talk to people about Troy and to collect signatures. "WANTED" posters were printed up and posted throughout Dorchester. After five months of collecting signatures on petitions and talking with many people, TPF decided to hold a public trial of Jerome P. Troy.

The trial was held at a park located in the center of Dorchester and was attended by over five hundred Dorchester residents. TPF presented its case against Troy and talked about the progress of the campaign to stop him. A statement was read by a member of the Dorchester Tenants Action Council in support of TPF's efforts against Troy. After that, many people from the community, and lawyers who had defended clients in front of Troy, came to the stand. This is what they told:

The mother of a family on welfare talked about the time her husband was accused of and arrested for kidnapping a teen-age girl (a policeman's daughter). The mother said that her husband was placed on $35,000 bail, which Troy refused to believe the defendant could not afford. After spending time in Charles Street Jail, the defendant was convicted in a trial during which Troy refused to listen to his defense. The woman said that when her husband appealed, Troy once again placed $35,000 bail on him. The case was dismissed in Superior Court, but only after the woman's husband had spent several months in Charles Street Jail.

A Boston lawyer, Jerry Katz, told the people at the trial of an experience he had had when he defended two blacks who had been arrested for assaulting two police officers. One man asked a cop why he had given him a ticket when there were other cars parked illegally. The cops knocked that man to the ground. They arrested him and a bystander who protested the actions of the two policemen. Although the incident happened at 5 P.M., the two men were not booked at the police station until 7 P.M. and were hospitalized as a result of the police beating. When the case went to trial, Attorney Katz had ten witnesses ready to testify for the defendants. During one of these witnesses' testimony, Troy had a discussion with the clerk. He then interrupted the witness, saying, "I find the defendants guilty and sentence them to six months in jail." When the lawyer protested that he had a right to finish his defense, Troy told him to shut up or he would be locked up too.

After the scheduled testimony at the public trial, many other people spontaneously came up to the stand and told stories which corroborated what the earlier witnesses had said. The public trial of Judge Troy was an exciting experience for the five hundred people there. It was, finally, their day in court, their chance to testify, uninterrupted and unthreatened, against Troy.

After that, support for the campaign increased tremendously. The circulation of the TPF newspaper increased to twenty thousand. "Troy Wanted" posters and "Stop Troy" posters and buttons were seen all over Dorchester.

As the public trial of Troy ended, TPF was nearing its goal of ten thousand signatures on the petition. For the next month and a half, TPF was everywhere in the community collecting signatures. In September, when the goal of ten thousand signatures was reached, TPF organized a march through Dorchester, past the courthouse to a nearby park. About three hundred people marched to the park, and from there a group of about thirty went by car to the Newton Courthouse, to visit the Chief Justice of the District Courts. There, Chief Justice Flaschner was presented with the petition. Accepting it, he said that he must have definite proof of Troy's misdeeds before he could do anything.

In the next month TPF contacted many people who had gone to court in front of Troy and talked to them about writing affidavits about their experiences. From them, thirty-eight affidavits were selected. These were the clearest examples of Troy's unconstitutional practices: setting high bails, violations of defendants' rights, using bail to coerce defendants. The affidavits were sworn out with the help of a lawyer from Boston Legal Assistance Project, Mike Feldman, who became TPF's lawyer on the Troy case.

TPF then again went to Newton, this time with the affidavits, and presented them to Judge Flaschner. Flaschner simply said he would take the matter into consideration and if there was reason to do so he would investigate. TPF wanted Flaschner to suspend Troy pending the outcome of the investigation, but he said he did not have the power to do it. TPF continued to put pressure on Troy and the courts, printing and distributing news of Troy and of the campaign against him.

After Judge Flaschner reviewed the affidavits, he decided that an investigation was needed. A grievance committee of three judges—Garvey of Westfield District Court, Bacigalup of Lawrence District Court, and Faschner himself, would hear testimony and make a decision on the matter.

TPF called for that hearing to be open, and asked that Troy be suspended pending the outcome. It continued to talk to people in Dorchester, to print leaflets and distribute its newspaper with the latest information. By now the campaign had such widespread support that the Boston *Globe* joined in. However, Flaschner refused to open the hearing and continued to say that he did not have the power to suspend Troy. Flaschner then appointed Mike Feldman, TPF's lawyer, and Robert Spangenberg, director of the Boston Legal Assistance Project, to present evidence on the affidavits.

The hearings began on February 8, 1972, and in the next fifteen days, sixty-nine witnesses testified. Troy was present. He and his attorney, J. J. Sullivan, called twenty-six witnesses: twelve of them police officers, three court officers, and seven lawyers. Feldman presented forty-three witnesses: fifteen defendants, two mothers of defendants, five attorneys, and twenty-one court observers who had witnessed Troy's practices. The transcript of the hearing came to 2,395 pages.

At the end of April, the grievance committee completed and released to the public a 43-page report. It found that the TPF charges were true, that Troy was guilty of: 1) denial of bail, 2) abusive use of bail, 3) noncompliance with the laws regulating bail practices, and 4) noncompliance with the laws providing right to counsel and defendants' rights during trial.

However, the report cleared Troy of discrimination against the young, poor, and black as a group. "No showing was made that Judge Troy discriminated against any class or kind of persons appearing before him, with the possible exception of defendants in nonsupport and illegitimacy cases, particularly where the complainants or the families of the defendants were on public assistance." The report did say that "Judge Troy's lack of concern for the defendants as individual human beings is demonstrated in the examination of these cases."

The judicial committee condemned the practice by Troy and Buckley of racing through arraignments and trials. "Therefore, when Judge Troy and Mr. Buckley handled Dorchester Court Criminal session . . . the court was likely to be open for about two hours. . . . Its significance is highlighted by the fact that the adult criminal case load in Dorchester court is one of the largest among the district courts in the commonwealth."

The report, and transcripts of the hearings, were given to the Supreme Judicial Court and the Boston Bar Association for their consideration. Although the report left much to be desired, it supported most of the allegations against Troy. TPF again called for his immediate suspension, with enthusiastic support from the Dorchester community.

The Supreme Judicial Council of Massachusetts sent the report back to Flaschner and told him to take action to rectify the situation. Flaschner replied that he did not have sufficient power to change the conditions in Dorchester District Court. Flaschner said that, as Chief Justice of the District Courts, he had the power to investigate, but not to discipline judges. The Supreme Judicial Court again sent the report back, stating that Flaschner had the necessary power. Public pressure continued to build, and as the summer of 1972 approached, Flaschner acted. He suspended Troy from sitting on any criminal cases, and confined him to civil cases outside of Dorchester for the summer.

That summer, the Boston Bar Association, of which Troy was a member, undertook an investigation into the case. The investigation was the result of the petition signed by ten thousand Dorchester residents, which TPF had filed with the Bar Association at the same time it was presented to Flaschner.

When Troy returned to Dorchester court after Labor Day, 1972, he was presented with a basket of flowers by the police from Station Eleven. The Bar Association was then completing what is called an "information," a petition for action by the Supreme Judicial Court. Based on the transcript of the testimony before Flaschner, the petition reiterated all the TPF charges that had been supported by Flaschner's investigation, and charged Troy with "gross judicial misconduct."

The Supreme Judicial Court of Massachusetts was now compelled to take up the Troy question itself. With TPF repeating its demand for Troy's suspension, the Supreme Judicial Court decided that a trial was necessary. But, on the basis of its pretrial investigation, it suspended Troy from all judicial duties pending the outcome of the trial. It was a major victory for TPF and Dorchester.

At the S.J.C. trial, Troy's practices of denying bail, setting high bails, not appointing counsel, and other violations of defendants' rights, were brought out. There was evidence that Troy had ignored the instructions of the Chief Justice on bail. There was also evidence that Troy had given false testimony under oath and had altered court records. Testimony was given of Troy's misuse of courthouse personnel, and he was accused of judicial misconduct. His fund-raising activities and questionable business deals were also brought out.

Troy could not refute effectively any of these charges in the course of the trial. In the summer and fall of 1973, his case moved to its end. The Supreme Judicial Court found him guilty of six serious charges of misconduct; it disbarred him as a lawyer, and enjoined him from sitting as a judge. When he refused to resign, so that he could keep receiving his salary even without occupying the bench, the Massachusetts Legislature approved a special petition for his removal, to be presented to the Governor's Executive Council, The Council voted for it, the Governor signed it, and that was the end of Judge Troy's reign in Dorchester.

As for TPF, it found itself hard-put to maintain its pace. It had originated as a combination of students wanting to know about Dorchester, and Dorchester people eager to discuss all sorts of social problems with the students. Together, they had put out a newspaper, launched the campaign against Troy, and developed other programs. A food coop grew quickly, a welfare group was formed, a housing committee tackled the problem of Dorchester being invaded by the University of Massachusetts. People got together to fight the high rates of the gas company and its practice of shutting off gas for non-payment of bills, even where this endangered people's health. The TPF newspaper carried articles about the elections, prisons, cops, the war, women, the economy, drugs, working conditions.

But TPF itself began to fall apart, while some of its programs (food coop, tenants group, newspaper) continued. It was still not clear how a successful campaign on one issue could be used to build a permanent grass-roots organization to defend the rights of people in a community. The removal of Troy was only a beginning.

Tenants Organizing

by Mark Stern and Joseph Cirincione

Having discovered that they could not depend on the courts to stop rent increases ("Review would discourage the increased involvement of the private sector ————" *Hahn v. Gottlieb*), the tenants in one housing development decided to organize. Mark Stern, who provides the material for this story, put it this way. (H.Z.)

"The courts had dealt the tenants a stunning blow. There was only one game left. The game was power politics in a special form—tenants unions. They had learned and are still learning that the only people they can depend on are themselves, and the only way they can stop a rent hike is to confront the landlord, and any federal or judicial agency that comes to his aid, with their collective economic power."

Max and William Kargman, father and son, were general partners of a complex of realty companies (at least twenty-seven companies and thirteen corporations and trusts). Max Kargman was quoted in the Boston *Globe* on his use of the 221-d3 federal program (described earlier in this book in the essay on housing): "Isn't it great to be in a business where you render a public service and you make a profit at the same time?" As for his use of the tax shelter provided by the federal

334

government, he said: "That's what makes the whole deal work. It's what makes it profitable for the builder. Otherwise why should he put in all this time and effort, with all the risks and struggle? For what?"

Kargman's First Realty Company prints handbooks for its tenants which help in understanding why they might want to organize. The handbook says:

"You are about to become a resident of one of the finest housing complexes in Massachusetts. To enable you to get the maximum satisfaction and trouble-free enjoyment of your home, the following rules, regulations, and instructions were prepared for your use.

"The management and maintenance of ———— Village is being handled by the ———— Company, an affiliate of the First Realty Company of Boston, 151 Tremont Street (Penthouse), Boston.

"If any problems arise within your apartment or if you have any questions of a minor nature, *Please call the code-a-phone . . . Leave your name, address, and nature of trouble. A permanent record will be made of your problem and action will be taken on the following day. In order to have your problem taken care of, you must call this number. Under no circumstances are you to call the main office, the superintendent's office or apartment, or go to his apartment or any maintenance man's apartment . . .*

"Because this is a limited dividend housing complex, tardiness in rents cannot be permitted. A $4 service fee for additional computer and bookkeeping time is automatically added to all accounts not paid in full by the first of the month. A $5 service charge is added to all those tenants' accounts whose rent check is returned for lack of funds. As soon as an account shows a two-month lapse in rental payment and late fees, a fourteen-day eviction notice is served. The tenant is responsible for all court costs, legal fees, or charges incurred with the processing of his eviction. . . .

"Individual dishwashers, clothes washers, or other washing machines are not permitted within an apartment. . . .

"All costs for repairs which are not due to normal usage are incurred by the tenant. . . .

"The tenant is required to pay for broken windows in his apartment regardless of who breaks the window. . . .

"No window boxes, flower boxes, or pots or any other articles are permitted on the sill of any window. . . ."

Mark Stern writes:

"These are not all the rules, nor are they the harshest. Furthermore, they are not wholly accurate. The Code-A-Phone, even First Realty would admit, is a failure. Eviction notices have gone out whenever rent was a few days late and residents, at times, were accustomed to getting at least two or three notices a year.

"The fee for late rent has a small history all its own. First it was a $4 late fee. When late fees were outlawed by Massachusetts General Laws, it was converted into a $10 legal fee payable to the law firm of Kargman and Kargman. When this practice was questioned by the tenants before the FHA it was converted into a $25 legal fee to a firm that moved into the Penthouse of 151 Tremont Street, with the First Realty offices."

What follows is a description by Stern and Cirincione of how the tenants organized:

The first union in a Kargman development was formed at Brandywyne Village after a series of meetings of tenants following rent increases of $16. Two large meetings were held at a local church hall, but both resulted only in confusion and disappointment. And the rent increases went virtually unopposed.

A few months later, one tenant, Fred, was fined $4 for putting his garbage out on the wrong day following a change in garbage pickup days about which he had received no notice.

He refused to pay the fine, was sent a lawyer's letter and a bill for $50, which he ignored, and then was sent a court summons and a bill for $100. He felt he had no choice but to pay up at that point or get evicted. But he did more than pay up. He brought a few of his neighbors to a meeting of tenants from the black community projects with whom I (then an administrative assistant in the City of Boston Mayor's Office of Human Rights) was working.

Over the next few months, this small group of tenants, and I, and a few student volunteers circulated questionnaires by going door to door to about one-third of the apartments in this 410-unit complex. We documented the existence of numerous violations of municipal and state ordinances, abuses of FHA regulations, and blatantly deceptive accounting practices. We found that the regulatory agencies—the city and the FHA—had never taken any action to enforce these codes and eliminate the violations and deceptive practices of the landlord. And they seemed to have no intention of doing much more than paying lip service to the tenants' complaints.

The surveys disclosed that the rent-increase issue was too far in the past to rally the tenants around it. However, certain issues provided a core of dissatisfaction around which tenants could organize. Chief among these were the fines and the physical conditions of the development.

The development had been built on a swamp, and the land beneath the homes sank a few inches each year. The homes themselves were built on piles that did not sink, but the steps leading to them were not so constructed and were in many cases wholly disconnected. Furthermore, in the open spaces created underneath the homes, now only a few years old, rats and skunks were nesting, and water pipes were exposed. The pipes froze in the winter and frequently erupted.

Nothing was done about these problems by the owner because the development's constructor was a Kargman-related company—Jefferson Construction. Thus the landlord chose to shift the costs of the above troubles to the tenants, in rent, rather than bring action against the construction company.

The tenants called for election of a tenants council in the early part of the winter. Very few tenants, even among those who expressed anger at the conditions, came. Apparently they felt that this union would be no more effective than the meetings of large numbers of tenants had been four months before.

However, by chance as much as anything else, this proved not to be true. First Realty was in the process of constructing a high-rise housing development in the same community and the community leaders were unhappy about the plans, the lack of recreational facilities, and the lack of prior consultation with them. They invited the newly elected tenants council to meet with them to discuss fighting this second development. And after hearing the documentation that resulted from the surveys, they resolved to work to stop the development and to assist the tenants council in getting their grievances heard and satisfactorily resolved.

Legal action and political pressure were brought to bear against the city and a loophole was found in First Realty's obtaining of a building permit. Construction was halted and First Realty found that they were at a standstill while construction costs were increasing.

Because of these high costs, First Realty agreed to meet with the tenants council to discuss grievances. At the first meeting the membership of the council tripled, as many people started following their activities just for the opportunity of standing face-to-face with their corporate landlords. The first meeting was somewhat frustrating. The landlord's representatives smoothly turned the issues away from the questions raised by the tenants. At the second meeting, an incident occurred which turned this attitude and practice around.

Fred, the newly elected chairman of the council, presented a question to the chief negotiator for the landlord, who then began rambling on about something that happened to him in St. Louis ten years ago. Fred cut him off and repeated his question. The chief agent for the landlord went into a big speech about keeping a friendly atmosphere and about how insulting it was to have been cut off by Fred. A priest, who was attending the meeting with the council, apologized profusely for Fred's actions on behalf of the tenants council. At this point we all anticipated that Fred, a Catholic, a conservative, and the elected representative of a Catholic-Italian constituency, would also apologize. Instead, he told the priest to mind his own business and told the chief negotiator to answer his questions or get out. The tone of every meeting to follow was drastically changed, and the tenants association began to gain significant support from the tenants as a result of taking a hard line against the landlord.

The community leaders offered the tenants council a position on the community negotiating team that was to negotiate a new plan for the proposed high-rise. The team then insisted the construction could not go forward without a commitment by First Realty to institute a fair lease and grievance procedures for that development.

While First Realty and the union went through a number of negotiations and delays, internal divisions in the council began to appear between Fred, an effective but conservative leader, and tenants who were more radical. Nevertheless, working together, they achieved some successes.

The tenants council union was able to get local rent control to cover the development, by getting City Councillors and the Mayor to put through an amendment to the City Rent Control Ordinance to cover this kind of housing.

Thus, when in the summer of 1970 the annual rent increase came, the tenants were prepared to fight it anyway. And they found they were not alone. Two other developments owned by the Kargmans and located in Boston got rent increases as well —larger ones. High Point Village, with 550 tenants, and

Camelot Court, with 160 tenants, established independent councils, and each group put different forms of pressure on the city for hearings held in their local communities before the rent board. It was just before a mayoral election and these hearings became quite extravagant events. The Mayor and City Councilmen attended. The rent board cooperated with the tenants' efforts to get massive amounts of information about their landlord.

The tenants council of Brandywyne found that one tenant had been refusing for years to pay any rent increases. He spoke at their rent board hearing about his extralegal action and its success. The following week he received an eviction notice and his cause became a rallying point for the more activist union members. They got over thirty tenants to go down to City Hall and demand that the rent board deny an eviction certificate in his case. The board refused to see the tenants, so the tenants stormed the Mayor's office. They were told the Mayor was out of town, but they burst into his office anyway and found him there. After an hour's discussion, the board was called for and the tenant was not evicted.

However, the council itself was getting more and more divided. City officials convinced Fred and his allies to take a moderate stand until after the election and that in return they would promise a fair examination of First Realty's situation. The activists didn't trust the city and split off from the council in order to keep the pressure on the Mayor.

The hearings before the rent board resulted in total victories for each of the tenant groups. All the increases were denied and First Realty's economic schemes and bad faith were continually exposed before large audiences of tenants and public officials. The news media gave good coverage to the groups and their success.

Following the rent board's decisions, First Realty took a case to federal court and got a preliminary injunction against the enforcement of the rent board's orders. The tenants adopted a policy of refusing to pay the rent increases anyway and formed a coalition of the three groups in January of 1972, pooling their resources and ideas. The publicity brought two more groups in developments run by the Kargmans into the coalition—Tammybrook Village in Weymouth (fifteen miles south of Boston), and Mountain Village in Worcester (forty miles west of Boston). These groups had no rent control in their localities and had no protective city body to shield them from eviction. However, they had the benefit of the Brandywyne activists' support and information, and decided to fight their increases anyway. They quickly emerged as the most organized unions. While the Boston unions commanded support of only 25 to 35 percent of the residents there, these unions had over 50 percent support from smaller, tighter constituencies.

Each group made decisions democratically. Each section of each development sent representatives to a council, but except in emergencies the representatives' job was to solicit the votes of the rank-and-file members after an issue had been raised at one meeting and return to vote on it at the next. Each tenant supported the union by paying fifty cents or one dollar per month as dues. Easier methods of dues collection were rejected in favor of door to door monthly collections which kept the representatives in constant contact with the rank and file. The coalition met about once a month to formulate general strategy, again by soliciting rank and file opinions, and to exchange information.

The coalition agreed on a few basic principles: 1) don't pay unnegotiated rent increases, 2) force improvements of conditions in the development, 3) take whatever action is necessary to protect union power and policies, 4) organize other Kargman unions, more tenants, and other FHA unions, 5) support other organizing efforts, and 6) *educate*.

As more developments organized, each with local leadership, these leaders got to know each other better and began to take more control of the coalition. Fred withdrew what little there was left of the Brandywyne union from the coalition. The withdrawal of the Brandywyne Union did not create a crisis in the coalition. Rather it opened up the possibilities for action which Brandywyne had restrained in the past.

Soon after Brandywyne pulled out, Jim Skoens, leader of the Worcester development, moved out, leaving its union leaderless. First Realty, thinking the coalition had been weakened, began eviction proceedings against selected individuals in Weymouth and Worcester—who were refusing to pay the increases. They hired one of Boston's most expensive and politically powerful trial law firms to handle the eviction cases. They also brought a libel action for $200,000 against Linda Garcia, a vigorous leader of the Weymouth union.

The Weymouth group met to discuss what they should do. At a meeting of more than half the membership, a number of choices were presented. The most radical one was a rent strike, and it was chosen overwhelmingly by a vote of 38 to 0, with two abstentions. The rent strike was begun to force First Realty to proceed against all the tenants rather than isolating a select few. Fifty-six tenants went on strike and the union collected over eight thousand dollars in rents each month. As expected and planned for, over forty eviction notices followed soon after the strike began, but First Realty had some difficulty delivering them. Constables were chased away by hordes of small children and the notices finally had to be taped to the people's doors on a rainy day.

At the same time, some of the union members at Mountain Village, Camelot, and High Point began paying their rents fifteen days late in support of the Tammybrook tenants.

The strike fund, consisting of the withheld rents, was brought to a bank for deposit, but the bank refused to have anything to do with a tenants' strike. So, it was brought to another bank and deposited in the name of a bowling club.

The coalition planned demonstrations against the evictions.

The first was held at First Realty's offices during the week and the second was on a Sunday at Kargman's mansion in Belmont. Tenants also appeared on radio talk shows and sought other press coverage with limited success.

The trial of the Weymouth-selection evictees began a few weeks later and the attorneys for the landlord promised to have the tenants out by the weekend. They failed. The eviction case—which normally would have taken fifteen minutes —dragged on over a three-week period. The cost to the landlord was considerable and the trial was all the more expensive because Max Kargman and his chief staff people were forced to sit out each day in court under subpoena as defense witnesses. The trial was never completed. After four days, the landlord agreed to negotiate a settlement with no preconditions.

Linda Garcia, the Weymouth leader; the lawyers; and a few other tenants on various occasions met for eight negotiating sessions and forty hours. The first settlement agreement that was reached was on the advice of Linda, but was rejected by the tenants. Finally, after three more months of meetings, a settlement was reached. It provided for a lower rent increase with no more increases for eighteen months, and a three-year period of no increases without negotiations. Eight months of the increases and all the landlord's legal costs were to be paid by the landlord. Twenty-five thousand dollars in repairs selected by the tenants or spelled out in the agreement were to be made prior to the next rent-increase negotiations.

After the settlement talks began, three more Kargman-owned developments either joined the coalition or adopted its policies for their unions. The coalition thus grew to include seven unions representing over seventeen hundred families, and more, they had developed within their membership a number of persons with considerable expertise.

They initiated two federal lawsuits against a coalition of landlords, but their main energy has been devoted to organizing and publicizing their work and recruiting more tenants. One of the union leaders, Sandy Rollo, has been appointed to the Boston Rent Control Board (for FHA housing) and others have joined with a Boston and a statewide coalition of tenant groups. Three community courses have been taught in Boston to other tenants about their work and tenants' rights. And the circulation of their joint newsletters reaches about two thousand families. They have even created a videotape show for presentation over cable TV to membership of the Worcester union.

The coalition's goals have expanded. Where once an elimination of the garbage fine would have satisfied everyone, now the tenants plan to unionize all twelve of Kargman's developments, to join with tenants across the state, and to *stop* increases, not just reduce them.

What once was an idealized desire for justice has become an economic necessity. How far the coalition will go, how many tenants will join together to resist their common antagonist, how strong the tenants' movement will grow, etc. are unforeseeable right now. But the housing crisis is intensifying, and with it the conflict between profit and decent homes deepens. What is clear is that at least some tenants have begun to resist.

Winning Back Jobs at Boston State

by Henry Allen with Charles Shively

On May 26, 1970, after four years of teaching history at Boston State College, I received a "terminal" contract (the language of academia never admits to *firing* anyone; that would make of a college what it is, a workplace). With it was a kindly statement from the acting president assuring me that the college would "be glad to provide assistance to you in your efforts to make arrangements for the future."

The firing came as a surprise. I knew the department chairman wanted me out. I had been involved in political agitation of a liberal and increasingly radical bent. But I was generally considered by students and faculty to be an excellent teacher, and the department evaluation committee had recommended that I be granted tenure. So I thought the college administration would not side with the chairman against the weight of approval by students, faculty, and committee.

My naiveté would gradually vanish as, in the next year, I came to see how logical it was for the college to fire me and others. Considering what we were trying to do at Boston State and the threat we represented to the status quo, the administration and trustees could be expected to follow the pattern of other colleges and universities, indeed all other institutions: get rid of the troublemakers.

I had not always been a troublemaker. When I began teach-

345

ing at Boston State in September, 1966, I more or less fit into the mold. I had gone to school in Boston, graduated from Boston State, and after a year at NYU returned to teach at my alma mater. I taught the way everyone else taught, with lectures, textbooks, and authority. But I soon came to question both the content and method of my teaching. I moved away from a false objectivity toward an increasingly critical history, sympathetic toward socialism. In the American history survey, for instance, I began teaching the history of blacks, women, labor movements, Indians, imperialism, and other subjects that were not considered "objective."

As my course content changed, my ideas about grading were also transformed. More and more, I saw grades as weapons used by teachers to punish or reward students with no relation to creative learning. I forgot the bell-shaped curve and sought new ways of responding to the learning of students. And to the dismay of many at the school I stopped flunking the desired quota.

During the fall of 1969, a number of the faculty at Boston State organized a chapter of the New University Conference. NUC was "a national organization of radicals who work in, around, and in spite of institutions of higher education. We are committed to struggle politically to create a new, American form of socialism and to replace an educational and social system that is an instrument of class, sexual, and racial oppression with one that belongs to the people."

We were thus trying to go beyond the isolated classroom and the isolated radical teacher. Instead, a group of radicals at Boston State were committing themselves to work with one another to fight for certain basic changes at our workplace, to take collective action. All those who were fired shortly after this were either members of, or affiliated with the New University Conference.

We had already worked together—faculty and students— against the firing of a physics teacher who was active against the war in Vietnam and was a member of the Progressive Labor party. He had been hired because he had a Ph.D. from Columbia University, but when the president heard of his political activity, he was fired. We failed to stop this, but we learned something about organization.

We had also worked together to try to get the college to recruit and admit forty-two black students in the summer of 1968. Boston State, while located at the edge of the Roxbury ghetto, had less than one-tenth of 1 percent of black students in 1967. The new black students formed a Black Students Association, and in the spring of 1969 they occupied part of the Administration building and made demands for more black students and faculty and administrators, and a Black Studies Department.

I became more and more active in the New University Conference. We helped to organize a rather loosely structured amalgam of students and faculty called "the Community," which published an underground-type newspaper. The Community agitated and propagandized around issues relating to faculty and students controlling their own lives, in an institution which systematically denied them that right. For two years, the Community acted as the primary force in mobilizing discontent on campus and transforming that discontent into energy which continually challenged the manipulation and control we all lived under at Boston state.

We worked hard against the war in Vietnam. In the spring of 1970, with the invasion of Cambodia and the killings at Kent State and Jackson State, we mobilized quickly to close down the college as part of the nationwide strike. We set up workshops, and made demands to stop military recruitment on the Boston State campus and to end the racist pay differential in the school cafeteria. We won a spectacular victory on military recruiting, which still has not resumed at Boston State. It was later that month—May, 1970—that I received my terminal contract.

When we returned to school in the fall of 1970 we began immediately to organize against my firing. We knew that appeals to reason would not work, that only massive pressure from below, that is, from the students, could possibly succeed. That December, in the midst of our organizing, the administration moved against us in a decisive way. Four other radical faculty members received terminal contracts: Nancy Hafkin, instructor in African history; Nancy White, in psychology; Chris Nteta, an African sociologist; and Richard Kagan, instructor in Asian history.

All these people had been a part of the New University Conference; all were active in promoting Third World studies in the college; all were innovative and popular teachers; all had participated in the Cambodian strike. All had or were soon to have their Ph.D. and were far better qualified than most instructors at Boston State.

We set up a faculty-student Steering Committee Against Arbitrary Faculty Dismissal, which worked out a set of demands. The demands were then ratified at a mass meeting attended by nearly four hundred students. We mimeographed and distributed the minority evaluations of Charles Shively, who was a member of the faculty evaluations committee and who objected to the firings. Our demands called for the retention of those teachers being fired, but went much further, urging that Third World studies be expanded, that the college be governed by democratic procedures, and that a joint faculty-student committee implement the carrying out of these actions, with the entire faculty and students voting on them.

The petition incorporating these demands was made part of a unique campaign, in which students approached other students in the cafeteria, in the library, in classrooms, in the corridors, and not only got them to sign the petition, but to discuss the issues involved and to join the effort themselves. The petition drive was spearheaded by the Radical Action Union, a student group. They published a pamphlet showing how the tracking system worked in education, so that IQ, success, and jobs were not merely a matter of accident. They pointed out that Boston State was being run by a small group of businessmen on the board of trustees, who "are responsive not to the needs of students, but to their own corporate needs and the maintenance of the status quo."

The fired teachers fought back. Nancy Hafkin and Nancy White were considered marginal by their male colleagues, who responded more sympathetically to fired men who "had families to support." Nancy Hafkin attacked the reasoning of the history department that African history was not a part of world history. Its ignorance, she said, would encourage "myopia, ethnocentrism, and racism." Chris Nteta argued that the school was squeezing him out dishonestly, pretending not to have a position available. Richard Kagan refuted the charge that Asian studies were of no interest or concern to Boston State students. These arguments helped convince wavering students, faculty, and trustees.

Eventually, over two thousand students signed the petitions with our demands. But we knew much more would be necessary to get the decisions reversed.

We sent telegrams to the department chairman and the acting president, asking them to attend an open meeting to discuss the firings. Copies of the telegram were widely distributed on campus, and to the television stations in Boston. On the day of the meeting, five hundred students crowded into the room. Up in front, we had empty seats with the names of the two invited administrators on them, and the TV cameras were able to focus on the empty chairs while students asked where the two men were. The meeting then moved to the acting president's office, and then, with hundreds of students looking on, he said that students should not be involved in decisions on faculty firings, and proceeded to lock himself in his office.

Our next step was to plan for a confrontation at the board

of trustees meeting. By state law, such meetings of the board (which administers all the state colleges) must be open to the public. Each time, they met at a different state college, and this time, as luck would have it, their January meeting was just a few blocks from Boston State (at the Massachusetts College of Art), and their February meeting was to be at Boston State. At their January meeting we presented our demands, and asked for a response at the February meeting.

At that February meeting of the trustees, the scene was a dramatic one. We had held a mass rally just before the meeting, and from this rally, five hundred students marched into the trustees meeting in the student lounge. The students faced the trustees, who were seated like a row of judges, flanked by secretaries, recording equipment, cameras, microphones, and other paraphernalia. Press and television crews were there.

At this point, the faculty was together. The chapters of the American Association of University Professors, the American Federation of Teachers, and the New University Conference, ordinarily at odds, presented a united front before the board. The students also, from student government leaders to the Black Students Association, to the SDS, were also united in support of the fired faculty members.

In this setting, the trustees started off by announcing that I would not be fired; they had devised a very complicated set of rules to work this out. I had been concerned about this— that they would try to separate my case from the others to divide us. We were working for much more than our individual jobs, and in our presentation that day, we made that clear.

One of the more colorful moments in the hearing came when a music professor, expressing the views of faculty members who had joined the school in its early years and wanted no changes, took the floor. She said: "I believe school should teach two things. First, how to take orders." The audience responded with shouts of *"Sieg Heil! Sieg Heil!"* The president of the Black Students Association shouted, "Bullshit." The music professor went on to say that the second lesson we all needed to learn was "good manners."

Everyone spoke that day with remarkable eloquence, communicating his deepest feelings about what he believed had gone wrong, his deepest desires for what education should be. The college administration acquitted itself poorly in trying to answer these statements. In one direct confrontation, the head of the Black Students Association shouted to the acting president of the college: "Tell me you're not a liar. You've made promises; you've said things, and now you deny them. Deny what I say if you can." The president's response was feeble, stuttering, and ineffective.

The speeches went on for several hours. Tempers were high. Patience was fraying. We called for an end to the meeting and insisted that the board either grant our demands or promise to meet with us within the next week at the school. The trustees said they could not respond to pressure, and asked for a "three-minute" executive session in an adjoining room. Clearly, there were divisions among the trustees.

After thirty minutes, the trustees returned to the assembly and announced a "moratorium" on all firings at the college. This meant that all jobs were saved—radical, liberal, conservative—for another year. They also granted the demand for a committee to study ways to democratize the school.

Ours was an extraordinary victory. Not only were all of us retained, but under the ruling, some members of the New University Conference would receive tenure. And a committee had been established to move the college toward democracy.

We knew the limits of the victory. We were not surprised when the committee met interminably and failed to come up with any reforms. And the Boston *Herald* headline was not inaccurate: "FACULTY FIRINGS PUT OFF." Firings were only being delayed. As this is written (June, 1973), I have received another terminal one-year contract for next year. So, we will have another battle, and who knows how many more.

But we did fight together, faculty and students. It *is* possible to win.

Conclusion:
Fighting Back

Where are we in this book? We have just illustrated what we believe is the most serious injustice in American society—the injustice of everyday life, where we work, study, and live, deep-rooted in the institutions, and human relations, and ways of thinking right around us. And we have just given a few modest examples of people fighting back against such injustice: the tenants of Boston against greedy landlords, the residents of Dorchester against a corrupt judge, the students and faculty of Boston State College against the unfair firing of teachers.

But more needs to be said about fighting back. It is not enough to have Judge Troy replaced by a better judge if the system of justice remains basically the same: stacked against certain kinds of people from the start, controlled by other kinds of people from the start, based on codes of law which are devised to keep things as they are and to punish those who defy these codes. It is not enough to win back the jobs of a few teachers if the control of our educational institutions still remains with administrators and trustees. It is not enough to stop a particular rise in rents if we still have private profit determining whether houses get built, and who can live in them at what price.

All through American history people have fought back

353

when they felt aggrieved: farmers, workingmen, black people. And the system responded to their anger with reforms. But these reforms—subsidies for farmers, union recognition for laboring men, civil rights laws for blacks—took the edge off the discontent, helped a little to make life better, yet left the basic structure of injustice intact. Indeed, this country has been the most effective in the world in granting reforms in the face of protest—liberal court decisions, new statutes, changes in leadership, educational progress, endless investigations and reports and recommendations by commissions appointed when a crisis erupts.

Through all these reforms, the arrangements of who owns what, who keeps what, who works for whom, and who has power over whom in the society—all this has remained the same. On the only level where reform can be truly evaluated —in our day-to-day lives, we see, in one of the best of American cities, that it has failed to bring about a just society.

We thus face the question: how can reforms be more than superficial? How can they be part of a process of fundamental change in institutions, in human relations, in ways of thinking?

One possible answer is: ignore reforms, spurn small gains, bring about a revolution that will make the basic changes we need. But there is a problem with that: it still leaves unanswered the question of how you make that revolution without organizing large numbers of people all over the country on behalf of the revolution's goals? And how can they be organized except in a process they recognize as aiming at their needs, one which *shows* them, right at hand, at least a bit of the revolution, a sample of what the future will bring? And that means fighting for reforms.

Still, those who say, don't get entangled in reform movements, you will never get beyond them, have a point. Once reformers "win," that is, by some concession from above, they get the idea that change does come from above, and that a paternal government, now "reformed," will take care of their needs. Or that once a good law is passed the work is done, and they can relax. Or that if some organization has helped them win these things, the rank and file can retire and let the organization continue to take care of the problem.

It is just barely possible that we in the United States have reached the point where our accumulated experience with reform is enough to show people that they must do much more than they ever did. We now know—or at least the evidence is there for people to be shown—that all the accumulated Supreme Court decisions on the Bill of Rights have done virtually nothing to diminish the power policemen have to stop us from speaking or from distributing literature, or to invade our homes, or to beat us on the street or in the police station; that all the judicial reforms of the past century have left poor people and minority groups helpless in the local courts before the overwhelming authority of the judge; that all the accumulated wisdom on penal reform has still left the jails as monstrous relics of slavery in a civilization that thinks it eliminated slavery; that all the economic reforms from Woodrow Wilson to Franklin Roosevelt to Lyndon Johnson have not changed the facts of a class structure in America, with the rich living extremely well, the poor inhabitating the rural and urban slums, and the middle class scrambling for its portion of the wealth in a dehumanizing rat race, in which, as someone remarked, even if you win, you're still a rat. And all the civil rights laws have not changed the fact that most blacks, on the job, in school, where they live, grow up knowing that they once were slaves, that whites know it too, and both show the signs of this knowledge.

Perhaps the time has come in America when people can fight for reforms in a different way. What would this mean?

It would mean not stopping the fight when concessions are granted by government, or employers, or landlords, but continuing the struggle with the understanding that even a wiser, more "liberal" Establishment is limited in what it cares to do, that people who want to change their lives must stay organized, stay active and struggling.

It would mean not stopping when some organization representing the victims' interests, whether a labor union or a tenants union or a reform political party, seems to have gained power, because organizations need continuous monitoring by their membership, and need to be kept in permanent combat so as not to develop contented bureaucracies. The labor movement is good evidence of that.

A black community leader once said to me: if people in the ghetto could carry the fight against rats all the way through to its end, they would have to make a revolution.

What might spur people to fight against rats (and against high rents, and tyranny on the job, in school, in the courts) "all the way through to its end"? It would take a vision of a different way of living, a vision clear enough, powerful enough, appealing enough, to keep them going.

That vision would be most clear if it were a vision not of some overall utopia, but of how everyday life would be different. A vision of a life in which we all woke up in clean, healthful surroundings, went to a job in which we had a voice in what was produced and how and what we would do in that process, studied in a situation jointly worked out by students and teachers without absentee administrators, and came home to be among friends and family and neighbors who were free from any notion that one race or one sex or people of one age group or profession or physical appearance or educational attainment were superior to anyone else.

But to be a believable vision, it would have to start coming into effect at once. There would have to be immediate signs of it, even small hints of it. We would have to at least see motion in the direction of deep changes, even if such changes were to take much time and energy. We would have to see changes right away in ways of thinking, in human relations, in control of institutions.

We could see immediate change only if we concentrated on small places we already occupy. Students already occupy their classrooms, working people already occupy their offices and factories, tenants already occupy their houses, even though all these places belong, by law and fact of power, to others.

The law only has meaning because it rests on that power; once the power changes, the law will follow. And that power of control can change once the people occupying the important positions of society—the workplaces, living places, study places—*decide* that they should take control of these places, of their own lives, in cooperation with fellow employees, neighbors, fellow students—against absentee owners, absentee landlords, absentee trustees.

In order for people in any situation to decide that, a certain way of thinking would have to spread among them. They would have to come to discard the notion bred in all of us as we grow up, that the present system of control is legitimate and right, that those who are in power belong there because they are wiser or better—that our political leaders, employers, school administrators, police, judges, or elders belong in positions of command over us. They would have to develop also the idea that they have the power, in spite of all appearances, to change the situation. And they would have to stop blaming themselves, or others who are also powerless, in order to develop the unity which is essential for people to create a new force formidable enough to alter their lives.

We have enough examples in history to know that when people who occupy a ghetto *decide* to make life there uninhabitable for outside police, they can do so; that when working people decide they will take over a factory, or at least stop it from operating they can do so; that when tenants decide a landlord cannot evict one of them, they can do so; that when students want to stop a university from functioning in its accustomed way they can do so; that even prisoners, the most powerless of all, can stop the usual prison routine if they choose to. That is, they can do so *for a while*. Until either concessions end their struggle or overwhelming force from the outside comes in.

Whether this can be done for longer than "a while," beyond concessions, beyond the point where it can be stopped by force, is something we have no experience with in the United States. No one can say for sure yes or no. And if the question is open, we can at least imagine a possibility: that while local and scattered takeovers can be either chastened by reforms or subdued by force—as they have been in the American historical experience—the time could come when, after a long period in which localized actions were stopped (but the forces behind them did not disintegrate) there would be too many local shifts of control to handle from the outside, or from the center.

We learned in Indochina that while a powerful air force could destroy any one target it chose, it could not, even by dropping more bombs than had ever been dropped in the history of the world, destroy a revolutionary movement which had roots in thousands of hamlets and villages. That is true of military combat, but it might also be true of political-economic-cultural combat.

This is only a possibility. In order for people to carry on local struggles for control of their own lives, beyond the point of reform, beyond the point of suppression, they would have to believe in that possibility, and to sustain one another in their belief.

The obstacles are great. Local groups do not face merely local power when they seek change. In a place like Boston, it is not merely individual employers, landlords, police forces, or school administrators who must be overcome. While there is not a conscious and organized conspiracy of wealth and power in Boston, there is, as elsewhere in our country, a semi-conscious, semiorganized linkage of wealth and politics, among various Establishment individuals and organizations in the city, and also with similar interests in the rest of the country.

The fact that most people's lives are directed in some way in Boston by some outside and unreachable force is not a deliberate, planned conspiracy. But neither is it an accident. It is, in some very complicated way, a result of a certain system of wealth and power that has developed over a long period of time. In that system, large organizations—industrial conglomerates, banks, insurance companies, universities—with interlocking leadership, manage large numbers of people. The requirement of corporate profit, and the requirement of American military power in the world both in Boston and in the nation, help determine what will be produced in Boston, who will work at what, and for what wages.

Over 300,000 people in the Boston area—probably half the labor force—work for organizations with over 1,000 employees, which means they are subject to the power of great bureaucracies with connections with one another, which go far beyond Boston. For instance, the largest employer in the Boston area is Raytheon Corporation, which in 1969 employed 31,000 people in the greater Boston area, and was the eleventh largest military producer in the United States, with half a billion dollars in war contracts. And the second largest employer in Massachusetts is the General Electric Corporation, which in 1969 was the Number Two defense contractor in the United States.

There are connections between industries, banks, insurance companies, and even universities. Six of Raytheon's eleven directors hold one or more directorships in six leading institutions in Massachusetts: the First National Bank of Boston, the Boston Edison Company, the Liberty Mutual Insurance Company, the National Shawmut Bank, the John Hancock

Mutual Life Insurance Company, and Northeastern University. For instance, Charles F. Avila, a director of Raytheon, is also a director of John Hancock, Boston Edison, Liberty Mutual, National Shawmut, and Northeastern University.

Among the major employers in Greater Boston are not only Raytheon and General Electric, but other corporations with big war contracts: Honeywell, Incorporated, General Motors, General Dynamics, Polaroid. This means that many people who work in the Boston area, in order to make a living, must work for war-related industries, whatever their individual feelings are about such industries and what they produce.

Five large Boston banks (the largest by far is First National) owned $9,000,000,000 in assets in 1969. Three large insurance companies (John Hancock by far the largest), controlled $14,000,000,000 in assets that year, and eight mutual funds controlled $8,000,000,000. All of these exerted a powerful influence on who got what loans in Boston, and what was built with those loans. And by their wealth, they could have an effect on the political decisions made in Boston. For instance, Prudential Life Insurance received the special tax consideration that would enable it to sink an enormous amount of concrete, steel, and labor into a skyscraper office building, rather than into housing for people who needed it.

On the boards of trustees of Harvard, MIT, Northeastern University, Boston University, and the other large educational institutions in the Boston area, sit many of the wealthy men and important political figures of Massachusetts. MIT's military contracts determine where much of its research energy will be placed. Boston University's desire for Defense Department contracts determined its policies on ROTC and campus military recruiting. All of this took place over the heads of faculty and students.

This is only a brief illustration of how the intersection of wealth and power in education determines production patterns, work, and educational policies—beyond the will of those involved day to day in those institutions. Thus, any attempt to gain control runs up against huge combined power.

We know that determined people, who work hard together, can force even giant constellations of power to give in. We have seen blacks do this, students, employees, and tenants. The question that has not been answered by our experience, is whether such unity can be sustained and strengthened beyond the point of small reform, to bring deep changes.

We will not know until we try.

In the meantime, we can point to very small beginnings, and try to imagine far beyond that.

The Honeywell Corporation is a multinational corporation, specializing in computers and in weapons of war, with facilities in over forty countries, with two billion dollars' worth of sales in 1972, and 96,000 employees. It worked on many of the deadly bombs and other weapons used in the Vietnam War. It has over twenty plants and sales offices in the Boston area, employing several thousand people.

A small group of Bostonians, associated with Clergy and Laity Concerned Against the War in Vietnam, began a campaign to stop Honeywell from making antipersonnel weapons for use in Indochina. It did not stop Honeywell, but it had an effect, immeasurable at this point, on the people who worked for Honeywell. For over a year, protesters visited the Honeywell buildings, making 125 visits, distributing leaflets, handing out lemonade and coffee at lunchtime and having discussions, offering slide shows after work, organizing theater presentations on the street picketing.

In August, 1972, they handed out 600 ballots at Honeywell's Waltham headquarters, asking: "Should Honeywell stop research, development and production of antipersonnel bombs?" Two hundred people returned the ballots; 135 said yes, stop, and 88 said no. Along with the ballots came many comments, for and against. Some of them were strong condemnations of Honeywell's activity in producing bomb parts that killed people in the Vietnam War. One said: "I don't like working for a corporation that profits from killing. There should be a 100 percent tax on war profits."

There was another development in the course of the Honeywell campaign. In December, 1972, William Kohlbrenner, a computer engineer who had won awards for his work, resigned from his job "in protest to the immorality of the corporation as expressed through its management." He wrote later that one day during lunch "a line of silent, placard-bearing people stood in the cold rain, clearly visible from the glass-enclosed cafeteria" and he went down to the lobby and watched, thought of walking outside the door and inviting the pickets in, but didn't do it, went upstairs, and decided to leave his job.

How much would it take for workers, technicians, administrators, and scientists working for Honeywell to decide that its resources should be used for improving people's living conditions rather than for war? A staggering amount of work, time, effort, dedication. What those few people did in Boston was only the faintest hint of what might be possible if enough William Kohlbrenners decided not to quit but to take over, and if enough of those who voted that Honeywell should change its activities would decide they had the power to make it change.

Even that, given Honeywell's connections with other institutions in Boston and in the country, would be just the beginning of a long struggle. It could be successful only when coordinated with similar actions for other corporations in enough places. But it would be a beginning.

Similarly, the tenant campaign to stop rent increases described in this book by Mark Stern is only a small example of what might be possible if tenants organized on a large scale. Tenant unions, even if successful, would not be enough. The whole system of private profit in housing would have to be dismantled and replaced by some system of cooperative ownership and management in order to end the bad effects of the profit motive, on the housing situation in Boston and elsewhere. Robert Ross, in a book called *Tenants and the Urban Housing Crisis,* edited by Stephen Burghardt, writes of the limits of planning and reform efforts for housing. Such efforts, he says, result in nothing but "symbols and slogans" and careers for some in the new bureaucracies resulting from liberal housing reforms. The better path, he says, is "based on popular organization and struggle by the people affected," which results in minor changes but "trains people for the use of their own power."

The campaign against Judge Troy by TPF, in the essay by Shamus Glynn, only begins to touch the problem of justice in the local courts. That problem is deep-rooted in the exaltation of property rights in the larger society. That view of property determines what is called a crime, who is brought before the court, and how much protection someone has when in court.

Still, while spreading the word that changes must take place in these property relations and in our ideas about them, can't we do something immediately about injustice in the local courts, to build up the power and confidence of people? Local judges are accustomed to hold trials and dispense punishment out of sight of the public. We have noted that judges become a bit more sensitive and aware when people sit in their courts and take notes, and there is a possibility the public will learn what goes on. Troy himself, in the brief period when he was returned to the bench after the TPF charges against him, was more cautious in his decisions. Perhaps a citizens corps of court watchers might be organized in every community, to sit in every court, on every case, taking notes and passing on their findings to the public, with the community ready to call for the immediate removal of any judge who begins to act like a tyrant.

Another reform in the judicial process, with revolutionary implications, is to begin removing the lawyer as an intermediary who controls his client. People should participate more and more in the legal settlement of their own problems. In Boston, the formation of several law communes was a step in this direction. Three law communes in Cambridge, including one commune of women lawyers, worked to involve clients closely in their own defense, and did not let fees determine which cases they decided to handle. Members lived on subsistence incomes and met weekly to make decisions about what cases to take and how to handle them.

Police abuses are also deep-rooted, not in the personalities of individual policemen, but in the nature of modern society. Police forces are used to protect the present distribution of property against criminals who want to change that distribution individually in the short run and radicals who want to change it, collectively, in the long run. They will tend to be oppressive and what do we do about this now, while we look toward the larger change in society?

In late 1972, the working-class community of an East Cambridge housing project rose up in anger when a seventeen-year-old boy named Larry Largey died in his cell after being beaten by policemen inside a paddy wagon. He had been arrested for drunkenness, put into the wagon, followed inside by several policemen, and then witnesses had described how they heard cries and saw the wagon shake from the commotion going on inside, before the policemen came out. For four days there were riots and commotion in East Cambridge in protest against the beating and death of Larry Largey.

The results were small: an investigation from the city which concluded that unnecessary force was used in the arrest, but which left open the question of what caused Largey's death. Some said the police were more reluctant to use their clubs after the Larry Largey incident and the community reaction, but that was hard to prove. The fundamental power of the police over people in Cambridge did not seem to change.

But is there a hint in the case of Larry Largey that an aroused community, if it could go beyond spontaneous rioting to organize itself as a permanent observer of the police, might change police behavior? Couldn't a community maintain a continual, forceful presence, on the street, in police stations, even in patrol cars, to keep watch over what the police do, report to the community, and stand between the police and citizens who might otherwise be victims? Couldn't a community gain more and more control—if it worked at it—until the police force became directly responsible to the neighborhood?

As for prisons: while we work for their abolition and for a society in which their abolition will seem natural, we need to do something immediately about men and women caged like animals. Here too, not "reforms" from the top, but counterforces on the spot are necessary. That means prisoners' organizations, and citizen-prisoner groups. The citizen observers who stayed in Walpole Prison for twenty-four hours a day, for months on end, were just the beginning of what could become a national phenomenon: a continuous community presence (including friends and family of prisoners) in prison, to change the way people are treated there and to help ease prisoners out of jail and back to their friends and families.

The rise of prisoners' organizations is the most welcome development of recent years. And prisoners lately have shown an interest in more than their own personal fate. Their view of society is a broad one. More of them see the need for radical change. In Boston, one of the leaders of the prison-reform and prison-abolition movement is an ex-convict named Charley Crafts, who has spent many years of his life in prison for various kinds of thievery, coming out of a wretched background in the working-class life of Everett, just north of Boston. Sometime in the last years of his imprisonment, around the time of the Attica uprising and other dramatic prisoners' actions, Charley became a political thinker and revolutionary, determined not only to do away with prisons, but to change the whole society.

In Walpole, Jimmy Barrett went through another kind of transformation, not becoming as clearly a political radical as Charley Crafts, but certainly developing a larger view of the world and its problems than one might expect from someone serving a life sentence. Jimmy helped organize the Walpole prisoners, and in early 1973 the Walpole inmates adopted en masse a statement on the Vietnam War. It was an act unprecedented in this country's penal history. The "Walpole Prisoners Pledge of Solidarity with the Revolutionary Peoples of Indochina" expressed "solidarity with the revolutionary peoples of Indochina in their continuing struggle for self-determination" and asked inmates at all prisons in Massachusetts to join in this. It asked for release of the hundreds of thousands of political prisoners kept in South Vietnam prisons. It urged prisoners to contribute their tiny pay to help rebuild a civilian hospital that was demolished during an American bombing attack on Hanoi at Christmastime, and added: "As a gesture of our love and solidarity with our brothers and sisters who fell victim to the iron heel of American B-52 bombers, we wish to start blood donations."

What seems central in all this is that people must organize themselves to change their own lives. In Boston, as in other American cities, there have been a number of examples recently of people doing this, with immediate effects. Women have gotten together to make themselves and others more conscious of the special problems of women in a male-dominated society. Homosexuals in Boston organized to support one another in stopping discrimination against them in the courts and in other aspects of their everyday lives. Former inmates of mental institutions have formed a Mental Patients Liberation Front to work toward changing the ways of dealing with mental illness.

Whether these efforts will move beyond traditional reform to deep changes, at first locally, and then in the society at large, no one knows yet. And we will not know unless we begin.

H.Z.

Books by Howard Zinn available from Haymarket Books

Disobedience and Democracy
Nine Fallacies on Law and Order

Failure to Quit
Reflections of an Optimistic Historian

Vietnam
The Logic of Withdrawal

SNCC
The New Abolitionists

The Southern Mystique

Justice in Everyday Life
The Way It Really Works

Postwar America
1945–1971

Emma
A Play in Two Acts About Emma Goldman, American Anarchist

Marx in Soho
A Play on History

order online from HaymarketBooks.org

CPSIA information can be obtained
at www.ICGtesting.com
Printed in the USA
LVHW010451280121
677485LV00001B/1

9 781608 463022